The Mission-Driven Venture

The Mission-Driven Venture

Business Solutions to the World's Most Vexing Social Problems

Marc J. Lane

WILEY

Cover image: Wiley
Cover design: Sunset © iStock.com/PaulGrecaud

For general information on our other products and services or for technical support, please contact our Customer Care Department within the United States at (800) 762-2974, outside the United States at (317) 572-3993 or fax (317) 572-4002.

Wiley publishes in a variety of print and electronic formats and by print-on-demand. Some material included with standard print versions of this book may not be included in e-books or in print-on-demand. If this book refers to media such as a CD or DVD that is not included in the version you purchased, you may download this material at http://booksupport.wiley.com. For more information about Wiley products, visit www.wiley.com.

Library of Congress Cataloging-in-Publication Data:

Lane, Marc J.
  The mission-driven venture : business solutions and earned revenue strategies for nonprofits / Marc J. Lane.
    1 online resource. — (Wiley nonprofit authority)
  Includes index.
    Description based on print version record and CIP data provided by publisher; resource not viewed.
  ISBN 978-1-118-41991-5 (pdf) — ISBN 978-1-118-41679-2 (epub) — ISBN 978-1-118-33605-2 (hardback) 1. Nonprofit organizations. 2. Social entrepreneurship. 3. Social change. 4. Strategic planning. I. Title.
  HD2769.15
  658.4'012–dc23
                                                                                2014030299

Printed in the United States of America

10 9 8 7 6 5 4 3 2

For Rochelle, with love

Contents

Preface   xi

Acknowledgments   xv

About the Author   xvii

About the Website   xix

1 Nothing Stops a Bullet Like a Job   **1**
"Father G" and Homeboy   5
Vanessa Bartram and WorkSquare, LLC   6
The Origin of Mission-Driven Ventures   7
Businesses Drive Social Change   9
Profits and Purpose   13
Our Agenda   17

2 Where to Begin? Constructing the Mission-Driven Venture   **19**
Maximizing the Prospects of Financial Success
    and Meaningful Social Impact   22
Tracking Input, Output, and Outcome Indicators   27
Entity Design Choices   28
Moving from Ideation to Realization   30
Preparing for Launch   35
Zeroing in on Size and Scale   38

3 Communities of Interest: Benefit Corporations and Certified B Corps   **40**
Delaware Rejects Stakeholderism   43
The Benefit Corporation's Impact   46
Delaware, the Outlier   49
Patagonia's Values and Vision   50
Public Good Software Supports Civil Society   52
Ensuring Accountability to Stakeholders   53

Contents

4 PRIs and L3Cs   **55**
The Low-Profit Limited Liability Company (L3C)   59
The "Sustainability Mayor" Leverages His Impact   62
Counseling Data, L3C: A Case Study in Collective Impact   64

5 The Poor and Their Banker Lead the Way   **67**
Professor Yunus' Journey   68
The Visit to Jobra   70
The Banking System's Failure   71
Yunus' Ingenious Solution   72
The Advent of the "Social Business"   74
Grameen Bank and Its Strategy   75

6 Leveraging Grameen   **79**
The Power of Cause-Related Marketing   81
The Grameen Family Expands   84
Social Venture Franchising   86
Grameen Empowers Entrepreneurs   88

7 The Mondragón Miracle: Scaling the Peaks Beyond the Pyrenees   **91**
Italy's "Social Co-Operatives"   97
France's "SCOPs"   99
Why Worker-Owned Co-Ops Succeed   99
The Evergreen Cooperatives Build on Mondragón's Success   100

8 Social Impact Bonds: Aligning Financial and Social Returns   **105**
Funding Targeted Intervention Strategies   106
"Pay for Success"   112
The Massachusetts Initiative   113
New York City Leads the Way   115
Pay for Success Gains Traction   117
Where Social Impact Bonds Work   118
The Social Impact Bond's Progeny   119
Empowering the Social Sector   120

9 Building and Rebuilding Communities   **121**
Donor-Advised Funds   126
The Role Foundations Play   126
Lessons Learned   130

Contents

10 Investing for Impact   **132**
The Origin of Impact Investing   137
Impact Investing Takes Root   142

11 How Impact Investing Works—and Why   **147**
The Form of the Investment   150
Managing Risk   152
Judging Investment Performance   156
Quantifying Social Returns   157
Cashing Out   159
The Challenges of an Impact Investing Market   161

12 Impact Investing: Pursuing Its Destiny   **163**
The Importance of Public Policy   165
The Institutional Investors Weigh In   170
The Growth Trajectory Is Clear   174

13 Keeping Score: What Success Looks Like   **178**
A Safe Haven's Social Impact   179
Crediting the Causes of Positive Social Change   182
REDF and Social Return on Investment   186
Root Capital and Its "Social and Environmental Scorecard"   189
Acumen Fund and Its "Best Alternative Charitable Option"   190

14 Answering the Call: The Demand for Social Metrics   **192**
Scaling Success   194
Shared-Outcomes Networks   198

15 Toward a Universal Metrics Language   **210**
Creating More Social Good   214
The Industry Steps Up   215
Impact Reporting and Investment Standards (IRIS)   216
The Global Impact Investing Rating System (GIIRS)   218
B Analytics   219
Other "Universal" Standards   219
The World Takes Note   220

16 What the Future May Hold: The Triumph of the Mission-Driven Venture   **222**
The Poorest of the Poor Have Reason for Hope   222
The Growing Role of Business   223

Contents

Social Enterprise Gains Influence in the Developing World   224
Business Raises the Bar   225
Governments Reach Out to Mission-Driven Ventures   227
Measurement of Social Performance Becomes
    More Sophisticated   228
Stakeholders Look to Substance Over Form   228
Social Capital Takes Center Stage   230
The Stakes Go Higher   231
Collaboration Becomes the Watchword   233

Index   **235**

Preface

Governments and nonprofit organizations everywhere have compassionately invested billions in social services, yet, wherever we look, we still face stubborn challenges in education, health care, poverty, unemployment, and the environment. Those challenges are tougher than ever: the world has not yet recovered from unprecedented economic shocks, government spending is unsustainable, and charitable resources are inadequate to fund the deepening problems too many face. While public- and social-sector programming has improved the lives of countless people, so, increasingly, have market-based business initiatives.

Alone and in combination with government and philanthropic efforts, business strategies are effectively addressing the most intractable of social problems. For-profit, social-purpose businesses are defining success in terms of both financial and social returns. Nonprofits are becoming entrepreneurial, supplementing charitable donations and government grants with revenue earned by the businesses they own and run, instrumentalities of mission in their own right. Progressive nonprofits are partnering with each other, and even with for-profits, breaking down cultural barriers, leveraging their competencies, and gaining economies of scale.

A growing number of passionate social entrepreneurs are deploying invested capital to test and develop business opportunities intended to drive positive social change. They are the "restless people," as journalist David Bornstein describes them, "so relentless in the pursuit of their visions that they will not give up until they have spread their ideas *everywhere*."

Many social entrepreneurs train and employ the disadvantaged and disabled. Others are disruptive innovators helping those populations access products and services previously unavailable to them.

While traditional businesses remain committed to their commercial imperative, more than ever, they, too, are intent on generating a demonstrable social or environmental impact. Together, mission-driven ventures and traditional business concerns are learning how to reach and sustain scaled social solutions.

Newly validated business models and entity forms that invite collaboration are emerging, including the low-profit limited liability company (L3C), which, by law, places mission above profits and facilitates foundation funding of charitable and educational businesses, and the benefit corporation, which requires its managers to make decisions not only to enrich its shareholders, but also for the good of society as a whole. Social impact bonds—futures contracts on social impact—provide long-term funds for promising social interventions, transfer risk to private capital markets, and tap into public coffers only when specific social benefits are achieved. Microfinance and microcredit are helping the poorest of the poor become self-sufficient business owners. And worker-owned co-operatives are converting the disenfranchised into self-reliant entrepreneurs.

Mission-driven ventures across the globe prize transparency and accountability. They lead by example. They fill a humanitarian vacuum left by government and charity, and they do so sustainably as only the private sector can.

Still, ventures seeking "impact investment" haven't fully persuaded the institutional investment community of the merits of their case. And their measurement of social performance continues to be inexact, inconsistent, and costly.

Against that dynamic backdrop, *The Mission-Driven Venture* was written for those who, like me, are in the empowerment business— nascent and seasoned social entrepreneurs; CSR (Corporate Social Responsibility), sustainability, and supply chain managers of companies committed to partnering with mission-driven ventures; nonprofit and foundation leaders; socially conscious consumers, investors, and donors; institutional funders and financial intermediaries; and professionals and consultants. It provides a roadmap of how a mission-driven venture is designed, built, and scaled—and how each of its stakeholders can best contribute to its financial success and operational effectiveness.

Along the way, *The Mission-Driven Venture* also recounts the life stories of modern-day heroes, people who, for very personal reasons, took on a social challenge as their own and vowed to overcome it through the prudent application of sound business principles. The lessons they learned and the successes they won translate into models worth replicating and adapting. My hope is that their thought leadership will help inform your decisions and inspire your actions.

Marc J. Lane
October 2014

Acknowledgments

I gratefully acknowledge the hard work and extraordinary contributions of Thomas Day, Alexander Konetzki, Mohammad Khaleelulah, Elizabeth Prendergast, and Joshua Kreitzer, without whose thorough research and careful scholarship this work would be a far less useful resource for those who will rely on it.

Of course, any errors or omissions are mine and mine alone.

About the Author

Marc J. Lane, a business and tax attorney and financial advisor, practices law at The Law Offices of Marc J. Lane, P.C. (www. MarcJLane.com). He is an expert on entrepreneurship and entrepreneurial finance and an influential advocate of best corporate governance practices. Twice a recipient of the Illinois State Bar Association's Lincoln Award, Marc, a "Leading Illinois Attorney" and "Illinois Super Lawyer," has consistently earned an "AV® Preeminent™" rating in the *Martindale-Hubbell Law Directory*, the highest ranking awarded. Martindale-Hubbell also includes him in its *Bar Register of Preeminent Attorneys*.

An innovator in helping social enterprises, impact investors, foundations, and philanthropists leverage capital to maximize financial results while driving positive social change, he is the pioneer behind the Advocacy Investing® approach to socially responsible and mission-related investing (www.AdvocacyInvesting.com).

Marc spearheaded the launch of Social Enterprise Alliance's Chicago chapter, which he serves as president and a board chair. He also chairs Illinois Governor Pat Quinn's Task Force on Social Innovation, Entrepreneurship, and Enterprise.

Marc is an in-demand keynote speaker for philanthropic, non-profit, impact investing, and corporate audiences. For more on speaking, and to access some of the resources Marc has featured in The Mission-Driven Venture, visit www.MarcJLane.com.

This is Marc's thirty-fifth book.

About the Website

Marc Lane has made a treasure trove of useful information about mission-driven ventures available to readers. He invites you to visit www.MarcJLane.com, where you will find a growing number of articles he's written for business, investment, legal, and tax publications on all aspects of the mission-driven venture.

The social entrepreneur's entity choice (as discussed in Chapter 2 of *The Mission-Driven Venture*), the features of the Benefit Corporation (Chapter 3) and the Low-Profit Limited Liability Company (Chapter 4), and the power of the Social Impact Bond (Chapter 8), among many other topics, are presented in detail.

In addition, you'll find audios and videos of recent talks he's given all over the United States, including his friendly debate with Nobel Laureate Muhammad Yunus (featured in Chapters 5 and 6). Professor Yunus insists that "social businesses" ought not afford their investors any opportunity to profit from their investment, a position at odds with the author's view that mission-driven ventures are well advised to offer their financial investors commercially reasonable value propositions.

CHAPTER ONE

Nothing Stops a Bullet
Like a Job

In the aftermath of the Great Recession, too many of us are living on the outskirts of hope. As public companies boast about record profits and the Dow sets all-time highs, the U.S. Census Bureau reports that more than one out of seven Americans lives in poverty. More than seventeen million American children—23.5 percent of all the nation's children—live in families with incomes below the federal poverty line, $23,550 a year for a family of four. The National Center for Children in Poverty reports that, on average, families need an income of about twice that amount just to cover the necessities of life.

No less alarming, a survey commissioned by the Associated Press in 2013 found that four out of five American adults struggle with joblessness, near-poverty, or reliance on welfare for at least some of their lives. They are collateral damage in any increasingly global economy that rewards the rich at the expense of the poor and no longer supports a robust manufacturing sector.

The tragedy of impoverished "sacrifice zones"—the post-industrial cities of Detroit, Michigan, and Camden, New Jersey, southern West Virginia's coal fields, and those native American reservations where the twin evils of unfettered expansion and unchecked exploitation keep old wounds unhealed—is spreading at an alarming pace throughout the nation.

But those who are born poor or fall into poverty needn't stay poor.

Breaking the cycle of poverty was once the exclusive domain of governments and charities. But, in recent years, "mission-driven ventures," those organized specifically to do good work, have taken it upon themselves to rescue the poor, the sick, and the undereducated. Occupying the intersection of money and meaning, they use the power of the marketplace to advance their agendas without forcing their managers to make decisions solely to maximize profits, opting instead to be transparently accountable to all the ventures' stakeholders, society first among them. On an ever-greater scale, mission-driven ventures are helping to restore our fraying social fabric and to repair the world.

Take Juma Ventures, a model for entrepreneurial non-profits everywhere, whose visionary CEO, Dr. Marc Spencer, was selected in 2012 by the *San Francisco Business Times* as the Bay Area's most admired non-profit chief executive.

Juma's approach is elegant in its simplicity. The organization provides life-changing employment and educational opportunities to local youth who might otherwise remain forever disadvantaged. They grew up in the inner city, surrounded by violence, drugs, and dysfunction, and they see little reason for optimism. Eighteen percent of Juma's students have been arrested, 30 percent have a family member in jail, 20 percent are foster youth, and 61 percent are from single-parent households. The deck is heavily stacked against them in a society in which competition is everything and birthright too often dictates destiny.

Juma runs for-profit enterprises, not only to help fund its activities but also to improve the lives of the young people it serves. They are on the front lines of Juma's businesses. They work concessions selling hot dogs and ice cream at major sports arenas and ball parks in San Francisco, Oakland, San Diego, New Orleans, and Seattle. And, along the way, they gain a work ethic and see that all things are possible.

Juma's mission is to empower those they serve and to encourage their pursuit of a college education and the ticket it represents. In 2013, according to Juma, 685 young people who participated in Juma's programs worked shifts at 464 events, collectively earning $1,000,000 in wages and saving $238,000 for college, while learning money management, sales techniques, and communications skills. Through its Individual Development Account program, the first of its kind in the nation, Juma multiplies every dollar its beneficiaries save for college by a factor of two, three, or four, using funds from government grants and private donations. Those funds can be used only for college-related costs and are usually paid directly to colleges. Since the program was established in 1999, its participants have saved more than $783,000 in their Individual Development Accounts and earned nearly $960,000 in matching funds. What's more, Juma gives them critical financial literacy training, including budgeting and credit building. Without this knowledge, knowledge they might never have gained without Juma, they might never escape the cycle of poverty into which they were born.

Beyond helping young people earn money, learn how to manage it, and save for college, Juma helps them get into college and succeed once they're enrolled. The organization leads campus tours and helps its beneficiaries define their career paths, study for college entrance exams like the ACT and SAT, and complete applications for financial aid to cover expenses beyond the funds they receive from scholarships and their Individual Development Accounts. Juma also continues to support its students throughout the first two years of their college education by helping them navigate the student financial-aid system, meet their budgeting goals for college expenses, secure the academic advice they need, and, perhaps most important, know they have gained the support of an entire community of people who want nothing more than for them to succeed.

As Juma grad Cruz Ramirez, class of 2008, recounts, "Not only did I get into the university of my dreams, but I was also able to get it all together financially and emotionally and finally go. Juma staff was with me every step of the way." Cruz's story is not unique, or even unusual. In 2011, every one of Juma's young people in the Bay Area graduated from high school. Ninety percent of those high school graduates went on to enroll in college, almost twice the national average of low-income high school graduates who move on to college. As this book goes to press, 83 percent of Juma graduates who started college three years ago are on track to graduate in four years. These numbers are a cause for celebration and a reason for emulation.

We begin with the story of Juma Ventures, not just because it is a mission-driven venture that has achieved enviable—and measurable—success, but also because Juma is a striking example for anyone who sees a problem—whether in his or her own community or in a community across the globe—and wants to take action to help solve it by attacking the problem at its source.

Since it began in 1993 by opening a single Ben and Jerry's Scoop Shop in San Francisco and hiring low-income young people to run it, Juma Ventures has been gnawing away at the root of poverty in America by helping young people from low-income families get a financial and college education and develop transferable job skills by running a profitable small business. All of these things will help them make better life decisions, keep them employed in good-paying jobs, and prevent them from slipping back into poverty. If they don't slip back into poverty, they won't depend for survival on government subsidy or private philanthropy.

This is not to suggest that traditional non-profit organizations—or social enterprises—should attack the source of the world's most challenging social problems, but ignore their symptoms. One million American children go to bed hungry, and fifty million Americans are unable to buy the food they need to stay healthy. So, clearly, traditional non-profits that focus on alleviating the symptoms of social problems (for example, by running soup kitchens or pay-what-you-can restaurants) are more important than ever.

What's so exciting about mission-driven ventures is that their potential is transformational. Organizations like Juma Ventures are game-changers. They do not make the condition of the disadvantaged more tolerable, but innovate and disrupt in ways that governments, philanthropies, and traditional non-profits simply cannot, given the challenges of public budget austerity and declining charitable giving. Juma's approach to combat the scourge of poverty is irresistible: give young people the tools they need to succeed in life and, when they do, encourage them to support Juma's programs by paying forward the life-changing kindness Juma showed them at a critical juncture in their development.

Now, for the first time, a Juma graduate sits on the organization's board of directors, and several other graduates help run Juma.

The organization's goal is to have a graduate serve as its CEO within the next twenty years. If Juma and mission-driven ventures like it are able to continue to grow and replicate their tremendous success, they will significantly contribute to solving the world's most intractable social problems.

Juma's experience is a reflection of social and commercial enterprises' growing commitment to social accountability, environmental stewardship, and financial performance, the elusive new social compact that has been dubbed the "triple bottom line."

"FATHER G" AND HOMEBOY

Drive 350 miles south of Juma's headquarters, and you'll find Father Greg Boyle—"Father G" to some of the high-risk former gang members his Homeboy Industries employs, "G-Dog" to others—a charismatic visionary tackling the pain of poverty and unemployment in the mean streets of East Los Angeles with tactics Marc Spencer would likely endorse. Father Boyle's journey began in 1988 with the "Jobs For A Future" campaign he launched with Dolores Mission, where he served as a Jesuit pastor. Homeboy Bakery, a 1992 response to civil unrest in Los Angeles, came next, followed by non-profit economic development enterprises, including Homeboy Silkscreen, Homeboy/Homegirl Merchandise, Homeboy Diner, Homeboy Farmers Markets, Homeboy Plumbing, and Homegirl Café. The Homeboy strategy, providing training and work experience to rival gang members, brings them together in a common cause. Father Greg's mantra—"Nothing stops a bullet like a job"—is the slogan emblazoned on some of the T-shirts Homeboy Industries sells, and it's also the message he sells to everyone who will listen. G-Dog, a man of faith who believes in second chances and the power of redemption, delivers on his promise: his social conglomerate proudly claims to be the largest gang intervention, rehabilitation, and re-entry program in the nation.

Hector Verdrigo knows that the Homeboy approach works; it worked for him. As he tells it, "Gang lifestyle was in our family—all my aunts and uncles were involved. It was easy to get into the violent lifestyle of being a gang member and looking forward to going to juvenile hall to prove yourself. When you got out, you had to go to state prison." But now Hector, a product of Homeboy, is Father Boyle's right-hand man. Just as Marc Spencer expects Juma grads to take over its operations one day, Father G expects someone like Hector—and not a priest—to succeed him.

VANESSA BARTRAM AND WORKSQUARE, LLC

Across the continent, Harvard M.B.A. Vanessa Bartram found herself inspired by University of Michigan economist C.K. Prahalad's argument that for-profit businesses can successfully fight poverty while delivering goods and services to the poor. Bartram's Miami-based WorkSquare, LLC, South Florida's first certified "B Corp," profitably connects employers with reliable, low-wage temporary or temp-to-perm hospitality workers. WorkSquare keeps its fees low, rejecting the waiting periods and buy-out fees customary in the temp agency world. It even allows employers to hire temp workers permanently at no fee at all. Employers gain a risk-free and economical way to recruit new hires whom they can evaluate on the job before they offer them permanent employment. Low-wage job seekers, often lacking education and English language skills, are put firmly on the path out of poverty and toward permanent employment. What's more, partnering with United Way of Miami, WorkSquare trains its employees for work readiness as well as financial literacy to ensure their long-term financial stability and, ultimately, their financial independence.

Vanessa Bartram's achievements were recognized by the Hitachi Foundation, which in 2012 named her one of the top young entrepreneurs intent on building sustainable businesses in the United States. The workers she's empowered earn more, spend smarter, and build wealth.

Take Hortense, who did a good job when she was a short-term hotel housekeeper, thanks to a WorkSquare opportunity. The organization was able to shift her to another hotel that offered her a permanent opening paying $10.25 per hour. Leveraging her temporary assignment to secure full-time employment positioned Hortense for a brighter, more self-sufficient future.

Social enterprises like Juma Ventures, Homeboy Industries, and WorkSquare, all shining examples of thought leadership, have become mainstream. They disrupt through innovation. They join forces as a community of change-makers. They scale through collaboration. They blur the lines between for-profit and non-profit. They embrace sound business principles. They create business models wherein measurement is integral to the normal course of meeting a challenge. And they abandon the systems that no longer work.

THE ORIGIN OF MISSION-DRIVEN VENTURES

But how did we get here? The origin of mission-driven ventures in the United States can be traced back to pre-Revolutionary New England when for-profit enterprises and organizations that promoted the social welfare were seen as necessarily separate and distinct, such that the latter's missions could only be funded with private donations. This conceptual distinction was preserved throughout the 19th century, with the establishment of charitable trusts and foundations by wealthy industrialists like Andrew Carnegie, and even through most of the 20th century. Adopted as federal law in 1954, Section 501(c)(3) of the U.S. Internal Revenue Code perfected the non-profit organization as we know it today—an organization with the sole purpose of engaging in charitable, educational, or other benevolent activities. Because non-profit organizations engage in only these kinds of activities—and, by definition, do not seek profit—they generally pay no taxes to federal, state, or local governments.

Traditionally, non-profits were funded almost entirely through government grants and private donations. But over the last thirty years or so, non-profits have come to rely more heavily on "earned" revenue generated from businesses that are substantially related to the charitable, educational, or other activities they are organized to carry out for the public good.

Just as non-profit organizations started to embrace for-profit business opportunities to diversify their sources of revenue while pursuing their missions, for-profit businesses began to engage in activities traditionally left to the nonprofit sector. The turning point may have been in 1967 when William C. Norris, then the CEO of supercomputer manufacturer Control Data Corporation, opened production plants in several impoverished cities and rural areas to create jobs that provided stable incomes and high-tech training for people who otherwise would have been left behind, like so many of the youth Juma Ventures serves. Norris was inspired by legendary Urban League president Whitney Young, who rallied against the social and economic injustice young African-Americans had long suffered. Norris also witnessed firsthand the 1967 Minneapolis race riot, painful evidence of that very injustice. Many contemporary corporations have followed Control Data's lead, adopting socially responsible practices either in the form of corporate philanthropy (dedicating a portion of their profits to fund activities that are socially beneficial) or as part of their business models (sourcing fair-trade agricultural products for which buyers pay more so that farmers in the developing world can earn more).

They have many reasons to do so. For one thing, it's good for their bottom lines. According to B Lab, over sixty million Americans today say that it's not just the cost, convenience, and quality of the products they buy that matter to them; it's also their social and environmental impact. Moreover, according to Raj Sisodia of Babson College, publicly traded corporations that compensate their employees generously, invest in their communities, and make a conscious effort to reduce their adverse impact on the environment outperformed the S&P 500 Index by a factor of 10.5 over the years 1996 to 2011.

These companies treat their stakeholders well, so their suppliers are happier to do business with them. Their employees are more engaged, productive, and likely to stay with them for the long haul. They are welcome in the communities in which they do business. And their customers are among the most loyal, according to Sisodia.

But it's not only profitability that motivates these corporations to adopt socially responsible practices. It's also the belief that for-profit businesses can be a force for economic and social good, more so perhaps than any other economic sector.

BUSINESSES DRIVE SOCIAL CHANGE

Consider, for example, the TATA Group, India's largest private employer, whose more than eighty companies employ 200,000 people in steel, automobile, software, consumer goods, and telecommunications ventures. About two-thirds of the equity capital of the company's parent firm, Tata Sons Ltd., is held by philanthropic trusts established in the 1860s. The TATA Group's founder, Jamsetji Nusserwanji, noted long ago that "in a free enterprise, the community is not just another stakeholder in business but is in fact the very purpose of its existence." Decades later, Manoj Chakravati, another corporate officer, framed the company's mission this way: "Corporate Social Responsibility should be in the DNA of every organization. Our processes should be aligned so as to benefit the society. If society prospers, so shall the organization...."

To Ratan Tata, a former chairman of the TATA Group, writing with Stuart L. Hart, Aarti Sharma, and Christian Sarkar in the June 18, 2013, issue of *MIT Sloan Management Review*, "the maximization of profit is not a purpose; instead it is an outcome." Their thesis is: "Profits are like happiness in that they are a byproduct of other things. Those who focus obsessively on their own happiness are usually narcissists—and end up miserable. Similarly, companies need a purpose that transcends money; they need sustainability strategies that recognize that you can make money by doing good things rather than the other way around."

The strategy has worked well over the long term: Tata Chemicals first introduced iodized salt to address iodine deficiency, then fortified iron in Tata Salt to combat anemia. The company has also invented an affordable, nanotechnology-driven water purifier that has transformed the barren village of Mithapur in Gnjarat into a thriving community. The company went on to create an "Innovation Centre," built exclusively around social issues and sustainable value. The initiative has been a leading driver of revenue, profits, and jobs.

A duty to contribute to the social good has recently been incorporated into Indian corporate law. The Indian Companies Act of 2013, which took effect on April 1, 2014, mandates large firms in India (including many American multi-national enterprises) to follow the TATA Group's lead and exhibit greater social responsibility. Firms with a net worth of Rs 5 billion (about US $82 million) or more, annual turnover of Rs 10 billion (about US $164 million) or more, or net annual profits of Rs 50 million (about US $820,000) would be required to invest at least 2 percent of their annual profits on CSR initiatives. Jamsetji Nuserwanji's legacy continues.

•••

Or look at the Bosch Group, a leading global manufacturer of automotive, building, and industrial technology as well as consumer goods. Following a tradition established by its founder, the company sees social and environmental issues inextricably linked to its future: "If Bosch is to remain a stable company, [it must] come to terms with the instability of the world at present. Accelerating globalization, the need for environmental protection and impending energy supply shortages mean that Bosch's corporate strategy must take into account social and environmental concerns." And, indeed, it does: the company has embraced the core labor standards of the International Labour Organization, acknowledging human rights, equality of opportunity, the rights of children, and fair employment conditions.

•••

And then there's Mozilla Corporation, a wholly owned, taxable subsidiary of the Mozilla Foundation, which manages Internet-related applications such as the Firefox and SeaMonkey web browsers. The corporation, which handles the revenue-related operations of the foundation, invests most of its profits back into Mozilla projects to "promote choice and innovation on the Internet." Mozilla is a sustainable, transparent community, which demonstrates that commercial companies can benefit by collaborating in open source projects. Market mechanisms support Mozilla's public-benefit mission.

•••

To cite still another example, Raytheon, the international aerospace and defense contractor, is committed to energy conservation, safety, and diversity. MathMovesU, the STEM education initiative to which the company has contributed more than $100 million since 2005, helps build the U.S. talent pipeline to encourage the next wave of innovators and technologists. Pam Erickson, Raytheon's vice president of community relations, sees that, "Good corporate citizenship is good business."

•••

Garrett Hasenstab, the director of sustainability at the Verdigris Group, the real estate development group, seems to agree. He notes that the company's CSR policy is at the core of its daily operations. Verdigris' clients value its environmentally conscious work because they seek a healthier, more productive, energy-efficient world. No doubt he's right: customers and employees alike are demanding that corporations everywhere operate sustainability and ethically, thereby contributing meaningfully to the global community we share.

•••

Perhaps most notably, TOMS Shoes has built its brand around a buy-one-give-one charity model ever since the company's founder Blake Mycoskie's heart was touched by the enormously disadvantaged barefoot children of Argentina. At first, the well-intentioned Mr. Mycoskie didn't see that a free pair of shoes doesn't bring education, public health services, or economic development to the poor and might, in fact, foster an aid-based local economy. Rather than helping solve a social problem, in-kind charitable donations might actually sabotage local businesses and distort local markets. To its credit, TOMS Shoes is rethinking its business model, for example, committing to manufacture some of its shoes in Haiti, employing Haitians and helping build a sustainable shoe industry there. TOMS understands that merely giving goods to the impoverished, although making its consumers feel good, won't itself ameliorate poverty.

•••

The truth is that Corporate Social Responsibility (CSR) should not be uncritically accepted as a legitimate reflection of a company's commitment to deliver a positive social impact. Some skeptics see CSR as a public relations counter-offensive to offset the ill will that results from a company's perceived social or environmental underperformance or, as in the case of TOMS Shoes, a misdirected, albeit compassionate, branding strategy. Others, following the lead of hawkish economist Milton Friedman, who provocatively insisted that "the social responsibility of business is to increase its profits," continue to dismiss any suggestion that corporations owe a moral duty to society.

Yet, Friedman's take may not radically diverge from the view of Adam Smith, the father of modern economics, who, in his iconic 1776 work, *The Wealth of Nations*, famously declared, "What improves the circumstances of the greater part can never be regarded as an inconvenience to the whole. No society can surely be flourishing and happy of which the far greater part of the members are poor and miserable."

Milton Friedman could foresee a place in our economy for the mission-driven venture. In 1970, when defending profit as the ultimate goal of business, he allowed for the possibility that "a group of persons might establish a corporation for an eleemosynary purpose—for example, a hospital or school. The manager of such a corporation will not have money as his objective, but the rendering of certain services." Although Friedman wouldn't have endorsed a manufacturer's dedication of its profits to launch a soup kitchen, neither would he have objected to a business whose mission is to run soup kitchens successfully within the free-market system. Nor would he have quarreled with a profitable business's pursuit of a market opportunity that provides a direct societal benefit. To him, selling fresh produce in a food desert might make perfect sense; giving away that produce undoubtedly would not.

Although Milton Friedman and other free-market capitalists might support the notion that some private enterprises could legitimately serve a public good, they generally draw a bright line between corporate good—the pursuit of profit—and social good. The opposite view, espoused by noted Harvard Business School professor Michael E. Porter, who popularized the notion of "shared value," invites companies to "take the lead in bringing business and society back together." To function, capitalism needs both a brain and a soul. Without accepting, even embracing, their social and civic responsibilities, most enterprises today simply would not survive.

PROFITS AND PURPOSE

No matter how good companies' intentions are or how deep their commitment to social responsibility, corporate law in the United States and elsewhere is often understood to require them, first and foremost, to maximize shareholder value. While Professor Porter argues that all businesses should reinvent themselves as social enterprises, the shareholder primacy rule continues to collide with concerns about the ends to which profits are pursued, how they are gained, and where their impact is felt. However socially responsible businesses might want to be, whether by ensuring that their employees are well paid or shrinking their environmental footprint, the results of corporations' socially responsible practices just aren't great enough, at least yet, to solve the formidable social problems we face in America and throughout the world.

Sadly, the same applies to government and traditional non-profits. The work they do is critically important, but the hard truth is that their resources are not up to the challenge: some 842 million people in the world go hungry every night according to the Food and Agriculture Organization of the UN, at least 80 percent of the world's population lives on less than $10 per day according to the World Bank, and 783 million people in the world lack access to clean water according to UNESCO. There's much more work to be done, and mission-driven ventures are doing much of the heavy lifting.

Mission-driven ventures in the United States have joined forces in the Social Enterprise Alliance ("SEA"), an organization with sixteen chapters in major American cities that connect mission-driven entrepreneurs, promote their ventures, and advocate for public policy that will help them drive positive social change on a scale as large as the problems they work to solve. Since 2010, SEA has partnered with its sister organizations in other countries to put on the annual Social Enterprise World Forum, which allows mission-driven entrepreneurs from around the world to network and collaborate as they advance social enterprise development internationally.

In academia, centers or programs for the study of mission-driven ventures have been established at some of the world's leading business schools, including Harvard, Yale, Stanford, Northwestern, Duke, and Berkeley. Oxford's Skoll Centre for Social Entrepreneurship has for several years played host to the annual Skoll World Forum, the world's premier conference for international social enterprise collaboration. More and more MBA students are forgoing high-paying, status-conferring jobs and instead are pursuing careers with mission-driven ventures in order to make a positive difference. Business schools have responded to this shift. According to the Bridgespan Group, the number of social enterprise courses offered by the nation's top MBA programs has more than doubled over the last decade. And members of America's most educated and tech-savvy generation, the Millennials, are founding startup companies that make money by solving social and environmental problems through the use of such tech innovations as crowd-funding and computer application software.

The Association to Advance Collegiate Schools of Business (AACSB) International, numbering 670 accredited institutions in nearly fifty countries and territories, recently revised the core principles underlying the business curricula it sanctions to encourage an academic commitment to environmental sustainability and corporate social responsibility. According to Linda Livingstone, AACSB's vice chair and the dean of the Graziadio School of Business at Pepperdine University, "Early on, this movement was probably very much driven by individuals who had a personal passion. Some of them created their own companies around that passion, whereas others brought it into the companies they were part of. But I think, as it has developed and become more widespread, companies began to realize it can also be good for business and it can be profitable."

At the same time, many of the most influential members of the private sector have called for the reinvention of capitalism as a force for social good in the 21st century—a *sustainable* capitalism in which long-term success is inextricably linked with serving a higher social purpose. Jay Coen Gilbert, a co-founder of the successful basketball shoe and apparel company AND1, believes we have reached a turning point in the evolution of capitalism where the 20th century model of maximizing the value of shareholders' investments without regard to the social and environmental impact of companies' business activities is giving way to a 21st century model of companies doing business in a way that creates value for their shareholders, their workers, the communities in which they do business, and the environment. Gilbert and his partners, Andrew Kassoy and Bart Houlihan, are using B Lab, the non-profit organization they founded, to build a nationwide community of certified "B Corps" to make it easier for people "to tell the difference between good companies and good marketing." Certified B Corps (like Vanessa Bartram's WorkSquare, LLC) are sustainable businesses and for-profit social enterprises that meet B Lab's rigorous standards of social and environmental performance and legal accountability. The chairman and CEO of the British retailer Marks & Spencer, boasting over 1,000 stores in forty countries, issued a warning to companies everywhere that B Lab might echo: if companies fail to adopt sustainable business models, they will become casualties of the combined forces of population growth, diminishing resources, and global climate change.

Governments, both in the United States and abroad, have also begun to see the power of the mission-driven venture. In the United States, the Obama Administration created a White House Office of Social Innovation and Civic Participation within the President's Domestic Policy Council in May of 2009. The Office is tasked with engaging individuals, non-profit organizations, for-profit companies, and government entities to develop community-based solutions to America's social problems. Most notably, it established the Social Innovation Fund (SIF), administered by the Corporation for National and Community Services, which mobilizes public and private resources to find and grow community-based nonprofits with evidence of strong results. SIF makes annual grants ranging between $1 million and $10 million for up to five years to intermediaries that provide technical assistance and funding to innovative social programs in local communities. SIF has already raised more than $350 million in private capital to support more than 200 nonprofit organizations, many of them social enterprises, and it has led the way for similar programs within the U.S. Department of Education, the U.S. Department of Commerce, and the National Aeronautics and Space Administration.

Reflecting the growing national commitment to social enterprise, Rhode Island Congressman David N. Cicilline, joined by eleven co-sponsors from eleven states, introduced a bill in the U.S. House of Representative on May 17, 2013, that would create a Social Enterprise Ecosystem and Economic Development Commission. The Commission would identify opportunities for the federal government to engage social enterprises more effectively in creating jobs and strengthening local economies.

In the United States, government has been most encouraging of mission-driven ventures at the state and local levels. A growing number of states, laboratories of innovation, have adopted legislation that authorizes the creation of "Benefit Corporations"—business corporations pursuing a material, positive impact on society and the environment, as measured by a third-party standard. Eight states and two tribal nations have adopted legislation that authorizes the creation of low-profit, limited liability companies ("L3Cs"). The L3C combines the financial advantages and governance flexibility of the traditional limited liability company with the social advantages of a non-profit entity.

Illinois has even created a Task Force on Social Innovation, Entrepreneurship, and Enterprise (which the author chairs), whose purpose is to make recommendations to the governor and legislature on how the state can create, scale, and sustain innovative social programs; build the capacity of non-profit organizations and government to pursue entrepreneurial ventures; and attract funding to the state to support these ventures.

New York City stands out among municipalities in its steadfast determination to fund innovation. The NYC Center for Economic

Opportunity (CEO), the 2011 winner of the Innovations in American Government Award, collaborates with twenty-eight city agencies to launch and scale up more than fifty programs and policy initiatives. CEO, the brainchild of then-Mayor Michael Bloomberg, not only designs, implements, and measures unique programs intended to combat poverty. It also spurs private-sector investment and fosters a culture of invention and evidence-based decision making throughout city government.

Innovative, private-sector efforts are also grabbing the attention of governments outside the United States. In the United Kingdom, 131 elected officials, including Prime Minister David Cameron and Liberal Democratic Party Leader Nick Clegg, pledged their support for the social enterprise movement by signing a charter published by the Social Enterprise Coalition, a sister organization of the Social Enterprise Alliance in the United States. In addition, the European Commission has established a Social Business Initiative to create an environment favorable to the development of mission-driven ventures in Europe.

The Pay for Success model, piloted in the United Kingdom and Australia as Social Impact Bonds and Social Benefit Bonds, respectively, is a new way of financing social services to help governments target limited funds to achieve a positive, measurable outcome. The approach has been adopted by the U.S. government in separate efforts to reduce recidivism rates and homelessness. A number of U.S. cities, counties, and states are following suit.

This surge of enthusiasm for mission-driven ventures is itself empowering. More and more non-profit organizations, businesses, universities, and governments in the United States and abroad have become believers and dedicate the talent, capital, knowledge, and spirit it takes to help mission-driven ventures realize the enormous potential each of them clearly sees.

OUR AGENDA

This book was written for those who, like Juma Ventures', Homeboy Industries', and WorkSquares' champions, have enthusiastically signed on to the new social compact—entrepreneurs; socially conscious individuals; thought leaders; impact investors; and non-profit, social enterprise, and foundation managers who are passionately committed to social innovation and positive social change. It will offer actionable guidance about business models and entity choices available to the social entrepreneur, governance issues that can arise when mission and profit objectives clash, funding challenges and solutions, tax advantages and traps, entrepreneurial linkages between non-profits and for-profits, certification opportunities, and the measurement of social outcomes. We hope that the real-life case studies we report will inspire you to become the agent of change you were destined to become, to face down the most daunting of social problems that plague society, and to empower the disenfranchised whose lives you never imagined you'd change forever.

CHAPTER TWO

Where to Begin?

Constructing the Mission-Driven Venture

The mission-driven entrepreneur—whether a socially conscious individual, a member of a startup team, or a nonprofit's social enterprise champion—is likely to agree with management guru Jim Collins, the author of the groundbreaking bestseller *Good to Great*, who once observed that "When [what you are deeply passionate about, what you can be best in the world at and what drives your economic engine] come together, not only does your work move toward greatness, but so does your life." But how does the mission-driven venture take shape?

A growing number of professionals are encouraging their entrepreneurial clients to forego formal business planning in favor of a "lean startup," an alternative the mission-driven entrepreneur should seriously consider. After all, the conventional process—drafting a comprehensive business plan, pitching it to likely investors, recruiting talent, bringing a product or service to market, and lining up customers—hasn't worked very well. According to Harvard Business School's Shikhar Ghosh, as quoted in *The Wall Street Journal*, three-quarters of all startups fail. The odds are probably even worse for the mission-driven startup, balancing objectives including positive social change and its own financial sustainability.

To mitigate risk, proponents of the lean startup argue in favor of iterative business design rather than systematic business planning. Customer input is invited at an early stage so that the entrepreneur need not guess about whether or not a product or service would be well-received in the marketplace. Trial-and-error, which eventually reveals a marketable value proposition, takes the place of granular planning.

Lean startups reject the notion that an entrepreneur can realistically develop operating assumptions and financial forecasts—and divine the needs and wants of customers—before money has been raised or while the embryonic business idea has yet to be executed. Rather than guessing, the founder identifies the elements of his proposed business model as well as the hypotheses he'll need to test. Both are charted in Table 2.1.

Once the hypotheses have been identified, the founder then goes out and determines empirically whether or not he can build a sustainable business around the product or service he envisions. Fully consistent with the mission-driven entrepreneur's unwavering commitment to both transparency and accountability, would-be customers and partners are canvassed about every aspect of the business model. Their reactions help inform the founder's course corrections, or "pivots," to assumptions that will then be revised accordingly and presented in their new form for customers and partners to consider. While never forsaking research and analysis, the founder repeats the cycle as necessary—building, measuring, and learning—until consensus is reached. The idea is to validate customer interest in a "minimum viable product" (MVP) with just enough features to see whether it will work in the real world without the expense of building a "finished" product from scratch. The MVP is the right-sized product for the entrepreneur and his customer, big enough to invite customer adoption, satisfaction, and sales, but not so big as to be bloated and risky.

While traditional startups implement systematic business plans, lean startups are hypothesis-driven quests for the optimal business model. While traditional startups introduce products into the marketplace only after a step-by-step product development process is concluded, the lean startup—through the very process of testing hypotheses—is designing its product. Lean startups enlist early adopters, add employees as hypotheses are refined, and already have customers in place by the time their product is ready for wide distribution. This "hit the ground running" approach is

TABLE 2.1 The Business Model's Elements and Hypotheses

Key Partners	Key Activities	Value Propositions	Customer Relationships	Customer Segments
Who are our key partners? Who are our key suppliers? Which key resources are we acquiring from our partners? Which key activities do our partners perform?	What key activities do our value propositions require? Our distribution channels? Customer relationships? Revenue streams?	What value do we deliver to our customers? Which one of our customers' problems are we helping to solve? What bundles of products and services are we offering to each market segment? What customer needs are we satisfying? What is our minimum viable product?	How do we get, keep, and grow customers? Which customer relationships have we established? How are they integrated with the rest of our business model? How costly are they?	For whom are we creating value? Who are our most important customers? What are the customer archetypes?
	Key Resources		**Channels**	
	What key resources do our value propositions require? Our distribution channels? Customer relationships? Revenue streams?		Through which channels do our customer segments want to be reached? How do other companies reach them now? Which ones work best? Which ones are most cost-efficient? How are we integrating them with customer routines?	

Cost Structures

What are the most significant costs inherent to our business model?
Which key resources are most expensive?
Which key activities are most expensive?

Revenue Streams

For what value are our customers really willing to pay?
For what do they currently pay?
What is the revenue model?
What are the pricing tactics?

Adapted from www.businessmodelgeneration.com/canvas. Canvas concept developed by Alexander Osterwalder and Yves Pigneur.

likely to help the mission-driven entrepreneur innovate rapidly and eventually to transform business as we know it.

MAXIMIZING THE PROSPECTS OF FINANCIAL SUCCESS AND MEANINGFUL SOCIAL IMPACT

Still, those who contemplate launching a mission-driven venture face unique challenges and must take extra care to avoid a misstep, or even a calamity, and maximize the prospects of both financial success and meaningful social impact.

Step One: Reality Check

The prospective mission-driven entrepreneur—an individual, a team or, in the case of a nonprofit considering the launch of a social enterprise, a champion within the organization's leadership who commands the respect of its board—must look within and ensure a willingness and ability to take on the inevitable challenges ahead. Nonprofits shouldn't see mission-driven ventures as a quick fix to plug a funding gap. They are tough to set up, slow to get going, and expensive to run, especially if their mission includes employing and supporting people facing barriers to employment, the mission most commonly pursued by social entrepreneurs. There's no way around the fact that workforce development initiatives come with the extra costs of reduced productivity and on-the-job support.

Researching and developing a mission-driven venture could take as long as a year, and it might be another three or four years before the venture is financially self-sustaining. Some ventures, structured as subsidiaries of nonprofits, never reach that point, defining success as making a measurable social impact while contributing to their nonprofit parents' revenue.

It never gets easier. Even the most successful mission-driven venture cannot responsibly count on continuing success. As with any business, consumer appetites can change, ties with suppliers can break, key employees can move on, costs can rise, and competition can stiffen. So the need for talented, consistent, and proactive management will never go away.

If the entrepreneur is truly committed to launching and operating a mission-driven venture and is prepared to give it all it takes, he needs to be realistic about its prospects for financial and social success. Before it makes sense even to start developing an embryonic business idea, the founder should be able to satisfy himself that it's realistic to move ahead.

- Is it likely that enough people would pay enough for the product or service he wants to sell to cover his costs?
- Is he confident that his venture would drive positive social change?
- Is the venture one that might be scaled up?
- Does he know enough about the industry he would be entering, or would he need to recruit expensive talent?
- Does he have relationships with partners or networks that might give him a "natural advantage"?
- Does he have the interest and ability to run such a business?
- Is he excited to take the challenge on, stay focused, and motivate others, even when success eludes him?
- And, if he's part of a team, does each member understand his role, demonstrate the competency and commitment to meet his responsibilities, and work well with other team members?

Step Two: Testing the Feasibility of the Mission-Driven Venture

Once the founder is convinced that it's realistic for him to consider launching a mission-driven venture, it's time to drill down and test his assumptions about his potential customers and the way his business would actually operate.

Defining the mission-driven venture's market involves the same process any entrepreneur follows. Identify and categorize the likely customers for the venture's products or services—whether they be individuals, traditional businesses, and/or other mission-driven ventures. That's called "segmentation." Then, based on the venture's strengths and social aims, select one or more grouping as most opportune. That's called "targeting." Finally, make the case for the value proposition: Why should the targeted customers purchase goods or services from the venture rather than from a competitor? That's called "positioning."

For example, if a mission-driven venture were to employ people outside the economic mainstream to plant flowers during the spring and shovel snow during the winter, the entrepreneur might identify homeowners, businesses, and municipalities as market segments. He might go on to target municipalities because he can negotiate relatively few contracts to generate significant revenue; he can more efficiently concentrate his employees in relatively small public areas; and he can put a relatively large number of employees to work on each job. The municipalities might favor the venture over other service providers if it would create jobs for the disadvantaged and provide quality services at competitive rates.

The mission-driven venture's assumptions about its market should be based on primary market research—talking to prospective customers, testing its product with actual purchases of similar products or services, and observing competitors—and "secondary" research, including trade journals, competitors' literature and price lists, government and industry reports, and the Internet. The goal is to gain a clear understanding of his potential customers' relevant buying habits, the prices they pay for similar products or services, and what it takes to earn both their business and their loyalty.

As the entrepreneur evaluates his market research, he should always be mindful of the broader market forces that will favor or disfavor the venture. Professor Michael Porter in his 2008 *Harvard Business Review* article, "The Five Competitive Forces That Shape Strategy," identified five variables that can affect every business and should inform every business's market strategy. Here they are, along with some key questions they suggest:

1. Competitive rivalry
   - Is there already an abundance of competitors selling the same or similar products or services in the proposed venture's market?

- Are customers' buying decisions primarily based on price?
- Is there room to increase profits by offering better products or services than the competition does?

2. Supplier power

- Are there only a few key suppliers in the market?
- Does the entrepreneur's ability to deliver products or services critically depend on the materials or services provided by those suppliers?

3. Customer power

- Are there only a few key customers in the proposed venture's market?

4. Threat of new entrants

- Do incumbents in the market have significant advantages over new entrants?
- Does it take significant capital to enter the market?
- Is it difficult to get in front of prospective customers and suppliers?
- Must regulations or licensing requirements be met before the business can operate?
- Are newcomers to the market likely to face retaliation from incumbents?

5. Threat of substitutes

- How inclined are customers to purchase a substitute product or service?

It's not that tough competition or even low profitability effectively disqualifies the venture from succeeding in a given market. What counts is whether the venture can meet the competition—or, better yet, beat it at its own game—or change the market.

The venture's ability to do so turns on its financial model. Although financial forecasts will always be a work in progress, it's important to get an early start on realistically estimating the venture's sales on a weekly, monthly, and annual basis. The entrepreneur will also want to begin estimating capital costs, such as equipment; fixed costs, including rent and office payroll; and variable costs that are tied to sales, such as commissions. If the entrepreneur maintains assumed income-and-expense data on an Excel spreadsheet, he can run "sensitivity analyses" that will tell him which variables would have the most positive or negative impact on the venture's profit and loss statement. Building a line-by-line financial model in this fashion will serve the entrepreneur well; as his assumptions are revised, he'll more easily be able to see the implications on the venture as a whole.

But financial viability is only one of the mission-driven venture's objectives. The entrepreneur also must plan for social success. After all, the very purpose of the venture is to harness the power of business to drive positive social change. So thinking about how his proposed venture's theory of social change—its view of the results it must achieve to be successful in meeting its mission and how it will achieve them—and how the venture will measure its social impact are just as crucial as testing and confirming its financial assumptions. Engaging the venture's stakeholders—its investors, donors, board members, employees, partners, suppliers, customers, the populations it serves, and even its competitors—will help ensure that the venture makes good decisions based on a collaborative and thoughtful theory of change:

- Who will the venture seek to influence or benefit?
- What results will it seek to achieve?
- Over what time frame will the venture achieve those results?
- What activities and strategies will drive those results?
- In what context will the venture do its work?
- Why does the venture think its theory of change will actually work?

A theory of change isn't a mission statement. It doesn't recite lofty aspirations, but aims for measurable outcomes to which the venture will hold itself accountable.

TRACKING INPUT, OUTPUT, AND OUTCOME INDICATORS

The entrepreneur must be specific and identify the input, output, and outcome indicators the theory of change itself suggests must be tracked. This is often described as creating a "logic model." Only by tracking those indicators often enough will the entrepreneur know what's working, what's not working, and where to deploy resources. Once the venture is up and running, he'll make the most of his theory of change by continuing to refine it, creating a "learning agenda," a list of assumptions and hypotheses the venture's management can test at regular intervals.

The mission-driven entrepreneur should always frame his social objectives in terms of outcomes, whether directly addressing social needs by providing products or services to mentally, physically, economically, or educationally disadvantaged people as customers; by providing job and career training services to disadvantaged people as employees; or both. So the mission-driven venture—as distinguished from a traditional venture that exercises good corporate citizenship by the giving of money, or facilitating the giving of money, to accomplish a social mission—will place mission first.

The venture will see each of its business activities, while generating earned revenue, as purpose-driven, leading inexorably to a desired social outcome. If on-the-job training, mentoring, and job placement services are to be offered, they are single-mindedly calculated to help the "customer" secure permanent employment and gain financial self-sufficiency. The venture's activities, then, are means to those ends and nothing more. To ensure that every activity is goal-oriented, the venture may rely on both the "logical framework" approach (the "log frame"), which helps managers execute projects without losing sight of their objectives, and impact mapping that links stakeholder objectives to activities and ultimate outcomes. Methods and tools for impact mapping are discussed in detail in Chapters 14 and 15.

If the mission-driven venture doesn't measure its social performance, it won't be valued by the venture's stakeholders. So even while assessing the venture's feasibility, the entrepreneur should consider how the venture will develop and maintain data to demonstrate how successful it is at achieving the outcomes it's pursuing. The method that's selected to collect data need not be onerous or even comprehensive to start, but it should be easy to implement, reliable, and consistent. Over time, the venture may track its social performance in increasingly sophisticated ways; the important goal for now is to commit to a data-collection and impact-measurement plan from the very beginning.

ENTITY DESIGN CHOICES

The mission-driven venture can be organized in several different forms, each within its own governance, tax, funding, and signaling attributes. As a general rule, a nonprofit is funded by tax-deductible charitable donations and grants, and its earnings are free of income tax. But the entity has no owners, so it has no equity to sell, and its principals are bound by strict rules prohibiting self-dealing and private inurement or benefit and limiting compensation to a reasonable amount for the services they actually render. A for-profit entity is taxed on its earnings, even if it has a social purpose, but its owners have a free hand to invite equity investments, manage the venture as they see fit, and eventually even negotiate a sale of the business for their own gain.

A nonprofit may wish to pursue an earned-income strategy and thereby become less dependent on philanthropic support or government grants and contracts. The nonprofit can establish a venture, in furtherance of its tax-exempt purpose, as a project or activity without its own separate legal identity. But for asset protection reasons, many nonprofits decide instead to set up a for-profit subsidiary or affiliate to own and operate mission-driven ventures, thereby generally isolating the nonprofit from the debts and obligations of the social venture and from the reputational damage it might suffer should the venture fail or inadvertently create ill will.

A hybrid, nonprofit/for-profit business model may create an opportunity to simultaneously accept tax-deductible donations, invested capital, and loans. However, such a structure should be carefully designed to avoid conflicts of interest. For example, the nonprofit and for-profit entities operating in tandem should be legally independent of each other, with separate and largely independent boards. Their respective rights and obligations should be negotiated at arm's length and be commercially reasonable and fully documented, and no "insider" of the nonprofit should gain any personal benefit from the for-profit venture.

Although a for-profit mission-driven venture can be organized as a corporation, a limited liability company, an association, a partnership, or even a sole proprietorship, a growing number of entity designs are specifically intended for nonprofits that organize affiliated enterprises and for entrepreneurs who organize free-standing social enterprises.

Two emerging entity forms are gaining prominence in the United States: the Benefit Corporation and the low-profit limited liability company or "L3C." A Benefit Corporation is one that, by enabling state statute, imposes upon its directors a fiduciary duty to make a material positive impact on society and the environment and to publish an annual benefit report on its social and environmental performance. (Some states have enacted laws authorizing similar entities with other names, including California's Flexible Purpose Corporation; Hawaii's Sustainable Business Corporation; and Oregon's, Texas', and Washington's Social Purpose Corporation. In addition, Delaware recognizes its own version of the Benefit Corporation (more on that in Chapter 3). By taking on these duties, directors are no longer bound by the "shareholder primacy" rule, which otherwise would require them to maximize financial rewards for shareholders. The Benefit Corporation might be a natural choice for ventures whose mission is central to their existence.

The L3C is a specialized form of limited liability company whose purposes by law must be primarily charitable or educational, with the generation of income only a secondary concern; with those constraints, the entity is designed to facilitate "program-related investments" from foundations. But the L3C also has governance advantages: when owned by a nonprofit, an L3C needn't justify or defend the commercial purposes for which LLCs are traditionally organized. Instead, avoiding tension between otherwise conflicting goals, the L3C tackles the mission of its nonprofit parent and furthers its exempt purpose. Similarly, when investors become L3C owners, the venture's overarching charitable or educational purpose galvanizes them around shared social interests, trumping their concerns about power and money. Both the Benefit Corporation and the L3C also offer signaling advantages, inviting consumers and other counter-parties to favor them over their competition because of their primary social objectives.

Social enterprise entity forms are authorized by law beyond the United States and throughout the world. The United Kingdom's Community Interest Company (CIC) is a business that can be of virtually any form so long as it primarily pursues social objectives and surpluses are reinvested, to the extent required by law, either in the business or the community at large. In Canada, British Columbia's Community Contribution Company, or C3, is incorporated with a defined social goal and the commitment that at least 60 percent of its profits will be dedicated to the corporation's social purpose. Specialized social enterprise forms are also sanctioned by law in South Korea, India, Malaysia, the Philippines, Thailand, the Czech Republic, Finland, and elsewhere. The mission-driven entrepreneur will be well-advised to seek professional assistance in selecting and designing the optimal legal structure for his venture. The features of the most popular entity choices for U.S. social enterprises are shown in Table 2.2.

MOVING FROM IDEATION TO REALIZATION

The entrepreneur will now have gained confidence, through soul-searching and hands-on research, that the mission-driven venture he envisions can be both financially viable and socially impactful. But the acid test of feasibility will be his confirmation of objective facts about the venture's potential and the founder's (or his team's or organization's) capacity to realize it. His answers to the following questions should encourage him to move ahead from idea to reality.

The Market

- What is the business idea?
- Is the founder satisfied with the depth and quality of his market research?
- Who will be the venture's customers?
- From whom do they purchase the same or similar products or services now?
- What will motivate them to purchase from the venture instead?
- What elements will the venture's marketing strategy include?

The Venture

- Why does the founder want to launch and operate the venture?
- What is the venture's social purpose?
- How will social impact be measured?
- Is the founder wholly committed to achieve the venture's objectives?
- Does the founder have the requisite expertise and experience?
- Are other mission-driven ventures doing substantially the same thing and, if so, are they successful?
- Are the relevant stakeholders supportive of the venture and its mission?
- Does the founder (or his team) have the capacity to deliver on his financial and social promises?

TABLE 2.2 Popular U.S. Social Enterprise Entities

Popular U.S. Social Enterprise Entities

	Tax-Exempt Nonprofit Corporation	Traditional Corporation	Benefit Corporation	Flexible Purpose, Social Purpose, or Sustainable Business Corporation	Limited Liability Company (LLC)	Low-Profit Limited Liability Company (L3C)
Purpose	Charitable purposes as defined in the Internal Revenue Code	Any lawful business purpose	Generally, any lawful "general public benefit," meaning "a material positive impact on society and the environment, taken as a whole, assessed against a third-party standard, from the business and operations of the Benefit Corporation"	Any lawful purpose, but tailored to advance environmental, employment, or more specified purposes. Any purpose that promotes positive effects or minimizes negative effects on employees, suppliers, customer, community, or environment	Any lawful purpose	Charitable or educational purpose
Federal Income Tax Treatment	Generally, tax-exempt	Corporation taxation: 15 to 35 percent corporate-level tax and generally 20 percent + shareholder-level tax, unless elect Subchapter S status, in which case flow-through taxation applies	C corporation taxation: 15 to 35 percent corporate-level tax and generally 20 percent + shareholder-level tax, unless elect Subchapter S status, in which case flow-through taxation applies	C corporation taxation: 15 to 35 percent corporate-level tax and generally 20 percent + shareholder-level tax, unless elect Subchapter S status, in which case flow-through taxation applies	Flow-through tax treatment (assuming no election of corporate tax treatment)	NOT tax-exempt. Flow-through tax treatment (assuming not election of corporate tax treatment).

Federal Income Tax Treatment of Distributions to Owners	No owners. If entity does not obtain federal tax-exempt status, then same treatment as a traditional corporation.	Subject to Subchapter S election, dividends taxed at 20%+.	Subject to Subchapter S election, dividends taxed at 20%=.	Generally, distributable share of income or loss taxable to members based upon the character of income.	Generally, distributable share of income or loss taxable to members based upon the character of income
Federal Income Tax Benefits	Contributions received tax-deductible, earnings related to charitable purpose exempt from income tax	None	None	None	None

Expenses

- Have all the likely operating costs been conservatively identified and tallied?

- Is cost information reliable?

- Are the costs of sales known or reasonably predictable?

Profits

- How long will it take before the venture becomes profitable? Cash flow positive?

- When will the venture break even?

- What milestones will be established along the way?

- What will the venture's profit margin be?

- How much of the profits will be returned to the owner or owners and how much reinvested in future growth?

Capital

- How much cash will be required pre-launch?

- How much additional cash will be required until the venture breaks even?

- When is that expected to happen?

- Will the venture always require supplemental funding to defray the extra costs required by its mission and, if so, how will those costs be funded?

Property

- Will the venture immediately need to lease or purchase real estate, or can it occupy its founder's premises, at least initially?

- Is the location available to the venture optimal?

- What equipment, furniture, fixtures, tools, and vehicles will the venture need, and when?

Personnel

- What staff must be recruited and when?
- What skills and experience will they need?
- Will they require further training or certification?

Suppliers

- Who will be the venture's key suppliers?
- What payment terms can the venture negotiate?

Controls

- Which bookkeeping system should the venture use?
- What cash controls should the venture introduce?
- What credit control system will the venture need?
- How will the venture monitor business performance?
- How will the venture monitor social performance?
- Which security precautions will the venture need to protect its systems?
- What back-up system will the venture have?
- What will the venture's disaster recovery plan be?

PREPARING FOR LAUNCH

Through research, analysis, collaboration, and serious thought, the founder will arrive at a "go" or "no-go" decision. Assuming he's ready to proceed, he and those who support the initiative may prepare a formal "feasibility study," which answers all the questions he's now considered; identifies the proposed venture's strengths, weaknesses, opportunities, and threats (a SWOT analysis); analyzes the political, economic, social, and technological environment in which the venture will operate (a PEST analysis); and reveals any critical gaps in planning that will require his attention. From there, he and his advisors may go on to draft a formal business plan or perhaps various versions of a business plan for management, funders, staff, and other stakeholders. A typical business plan is a comprehensive roadmap describing in detail the proposed venture's organization, theory of change, capital and financing needs, marketing plan, and operations, including three years' classified budgets (assuming varying levels of financial performance), and more. The plan will be a living and breathing document, its underlying assumptions updated as the mission-driven venture rolls out.

Or, just as likely, a formal business plan may be bypassed, the founder opting instead for a lean startup. Either way, the rigorous discovery process the entrepreneur will have followed will serve him well as the mission-driven venture proceeds to launch.

Finally, It's Time for the Mission-Driven Entrepreneur to Give Life to His Vision

All that he's learned will be put to good use.

He now knows that significant expense will be incurred before any revenue is generated. Not only will occupancy, staffing, and supply costs precede sales, but the venture will likely incur higher costs than other startups because of its mission. If, for example, the venture aims to create jobs for the disadvantaged, it will probably hire more employees and trainees, whose productivity may fluctuate, than most similarly sized enterprises.

The funding gap, including the venture's capital needs and cash flow deficits, can be filled in many different ways. If the venture is organized as a nonprofit tax-exempt organization or one of its projects, it can invite tax-deductible charitable donations from individuals and corporations; grants, program-related and mission-related debt investments from foundations; grants from governments; and loans from banks, socially conscious individuals, and institutional impact investors, among others. But each such source of funding is limited, often the object of fierce competition and frequently subject to restrictive terms and conditions. If the venture is organized as a for-profit entity, it won't be eligible for tax-deductible donations, but may be a candidate for grants, loans, program-related and mission-related investments, as well as equity investments, which may be more desirable for mission-driven ventures seeking capital from patient investors willing to forego periodic interest and principal payments.

Since revenue will now be a top priority, the mission-driven entrepreneur will also need to front-burner his marketing efforts, applying his research to the recruitment of actual customers. His marketing campaign may generate "buzz" through "earned media"—public relations exploit the many opportunities of social media—or invest in trade shows, networking experts, paid advertising, cold calling, the development and maintenance of a sales force, or any combination of these tactics.

The right strategy will be the one that most cost-effectively engages and educates the venture's target customer about its products or services. Investing in customer service will reap its own rewards. By treating customers well, the venture will become the beneficiary of "word of mouth"—positive comments as referrals by existing customers, the truest test of any business's commitment to its market. Coherent marketing efforts, always focused on the customer, should never stop.

Once the venture secures startup funding and begins to sell its product or service in the marketplace, it must track its financial performance, capturing the specific data of greatest interest to its stakeholders, to whom management will be accountable and must report. Selection of a suitable accounting package should be an early step. If the venture is a project or activity of a nonprofit, it will likely need its own software; nonprofit budgeting and financial reporting are very different from the way a for-profit business monitors income and expenses.

While tracking financial performance, the venture will also need to monitor its social performance, regularly collecting reliable data, inputs, outputs, and outcomes, and periodic reporting to the venture's stakeholders on its social impact. Social measurement is likely to remain an ever-evolving work in progress. Sooner or later, the venture may bring in an outside expert to evaluate and confirm the extent of its social impact, ensuring the seriousness of its dedication to mission and the credibility of its claims as an agent of change.

All these operational requirements won't be met without astute management capable of leading the charge, inspiring the staff, and ensuring that plans are executed and policies honored every step of the way. Management, working in concert with key personnel, will develop and oversee implementation of the action plans and timelines to drive marketing, finance, human resources, business developments, and other initiatives. It will be management's charge to make sure the right people are in place to identify opportunities and problems as they arise and address them quickly, responsibly, and effectively. But, most of all, management's function is to nurture a culture, providing leadership from the top down, respectful of prudent business practices but always mindful of the paramount values the venture embraces as it passionately seeks to help those it serves, day in and day out.

ZEROING IN ON SIZE AND SCALE

As the mission-driven venture gains its footing, its leadership may wrestle with twin questions of organizational size and scale. Skeptics may, for good reasons, insist that the organization remain small. There's no point in taking on risk, new funding, new personnel, or new locations if, for example, the venture's evidence of social impact is only tentative or its relationship with beneficiaries might become more bureaucratic and less individualized.

Still, growth can be a positive and healthy goal for the mission-driven venture. The venture might expand its social reach, diversify its sources of revenue, leverage relationships and platforms, offer donors or investors greater financial and social returns, and achieve more sustainable profit margins. In short, the venture moves beyond the transactional to the transformational.

In evaluating a plan for growth, expanding management might consider its current product's or service's market share; cross-selling new products or services to the venture's current or prospective customers; replicating the venture's business model in one or more new locations, either on its own or in strategic alliance with one or more like-minded ventures; or even franchising, licensing to others the rights to use the venture's business strategies and trademarks.

But before embarking on a deliberate growth strategy, the venture's leadership has to ensure that it is sustainable; growth is not a strategy to repair a broken venture. Indeed, growth will demand new investment and may cut into cash flow, at least for the short term. Scale comes at a cost, and that cost should only be borne by ventures that are strong enough.

While funding may be easier for a venture with a strong positive track record, the new activities must justify themselves. If they aren't likely to have strong financial and social returns on investments, they will be an unwarranted, and ultimately unwise, distraction from the venture's management challenges and mission. Growth will also present an opportunity cost, the cost the venture incurs by not deploying its limited resources in some other fashion.

Positive change is to be valued within the venture, as it is within society at large. So when the time is right for the venture to make a bigger social impact, a "new" and even more successful mission-driven venture will emerge and the social entrepreneur's vision will be fully realized.

CHAPTER THREE

Communities of Interest

Benefit Corporations and Certified B Corps

"Why," wondered Unilever's chief executive Paul Polman, in a recent interview with *Guardian Sustainable Business*, "would you invest in a company which is out of synch with the needs of society, that does not take its social compliance in its supply chain seriously, that does not think about the costs of externalities, or of its negative impacts on society?" The short answer is that the classical model of corporate law, as it has been interpreted by the state of Delaware's influential courts and elsewhere, emphasizes shareholder benefit. In turn, shareholders, it has been assumed, uniformly demand that their companies maximize profits notwithstanding the competing interests of employees, suppliers, customers, creditors, and communities. After all, it is the shareholders whose capital is at risk, and management should have no choice but to place their interests above all others' interests.

But the doctrine of shareholder primacy and its preoccupation with financial returns to shareholders is giving way to realistic demands for long-term sustainability. Under the "business judgment rule," courts will generally show deference to any board decision made with the interests of the corporation and its shareholders in mind, even if those interests are long-term and tangential or attenuated, so long as the decision wasn't uninformed or made in bad faith. Today, in forty-one U.S. states, Delaware (where most public companies are domiciled) remaining the most notable exception, corporate decision-makers have also been given statutory permission to consider the interests of non-shareholder stakeholders when making decisions.

"Stakeholder" or "constituency" statutes, which have modified a board's fiduciary duty to maximize shareholder wealth, vary in four different ways:

- Only Connecticut's law is mandatory, requiring its officers and directors to consider the interests of stakeholders who don't own company shares when making corporate decisions. Everywhere else that stakeholder laws have been enacted, officers and directors are free to exercise discretion in whether or not to take non-shareholders' concerns into account when making business decisions.

- Most constituency statutes apply only to directors, and not to officers. Wyoming, for example, is in the majority. Illinois, however, is in the minority of states that also allow company executives to consider stakeholder interests.

- Most constituency statutes allow corporate management to consider both the short-term and long-term interests of stakeholders, but some statutes don't permit a consideration of their "interests" at all, permitting only a consideration of the "effects" of management decisions on stakeholders.

- Finally, nearly half of the states' constituency statutes allow stakeholders' interests to be considered only in corporate takeover or change-of-control situations. After all, such corporate events have historically hit non-shareholder stakeholders the hardest, often denying local communities the social and economic benefits on which local residents and businesses heavily depend. But only a slim majority of constituency statutes go further, authorizing corporate directors to consider the interests of non-shareholder stakeholders in any actions that might affect them.

Some constituency statutes are prototypes, others unique unto themselves. For example, Alabama's constituency statute, which states "the board of directors may condition its submission of the proposed merger or share exchange on any basis," is the standard formula for those constituency statutes that are limited in applicability to takeovers or mergers and permit decisions to be made on any basis at all.

Iowa's constituency statute is typical of "limited applicability" statutes that specify factors a director may take into account:

> A director, in determining what is in the best interest of the corporation when considering a tender offer or proposal of acquisition, merger, consolidation, or similar proposal, may consider any or all of the following community interest factors, in addition to consideration of the effects of any action on shareholders:
>
> 1. The effects of the action on the corporation's employees, suppliers, creditors, and customers.
> 2. The effects of the action on the communities in which the corporation operates.
> 3. The long-term as well as short-term interests of the corporation and its shareholders, including the possibility that these interests may be best served by the continued independence of the corporation.

The Louisiana and Missouri laws are atypical among limited applicability constituency statutes in that they provide in-depth guidance as to what factors directors may consider in the face of a takeover or merger. Both statutes permit them to take into account the financial health of both the corporation and its acquirer; political factors affecting financial conditions; and the competence, integrity, and experience of the acquiring party.

The most typical example of "broad applicability" constituency statutes is New Jersey's law:

> In discharging his duties to the corporation and in determining what he reasonably believes to be in the best interest of the corporation, a director may, in addition to considering the effects of any action on shareholders, consider any of the following: (a) the effects of the action on the corporation's employees, suppliers, creditors, and customers; (b) the effects of the action on the community in which the corporation operates; and (c) the long-term as well as the short-term interests of the corporation and its shareholders.

Illinois' constituency statute is perhaps the most far-reaching law, extending the ability to consider stakeholder interests to officers of the corporation, allowing both directors and officers to consider impacts even on a subsidiary's stakeholders, and permitting directors and officers to condition their decisions on any factor they choose:

> In discharging the duties of their respective positions, the board of directors, committees of the board, individual directors, and individual officers may, in considering the best long-term and short-term interests of the corporation, consider the effects of any action ... upon employees, suppliers, and customers of the corporation or its subsidiaries, communities in which officers or other establishments of the corporation or its subsidiaries are located, and all other pertinent factors.

With the exception of Connecticut, not a single state obligates a corporate officer or director even to consider the interests of non-shareholder stakeholders, let alone act on their behalf.

DELAWARE REJECTS STAKEHOLDERISM

Delaware proudly remains first among guarantors of shareholder primacy. In the 2010 case of *eBay v. Newmark*, for example, the Delaware Court of Chancery drew a bright and unambiguous line. In the court's judgment, the two majority shareholders of Craigslist, Inc., a small, privately held Delaware corporation, breached their fiduciary duties to the company's sole minority shareholder in devising a defensive "poison pill" plan because the plan's purpose did not relate to shareholder profit maximization. The two majority shareholders of Craigslist—founder Craig Newmark and CEO and president Jim Buckmaster—viewed the corporation as more of a public, community service than a commercial, for-profit corporation. By contrast, Craigslist's third, minority shareholder was eBay—a global enterprise focused on profit maximization.

Under Craigslist's stockholders' agreement, eBay could compete with Craigslist in online classified advertisements. However, the agreement also provided that, if eBay took advantage of this ability, "eBay lost certain contractual consent rights that gave eBay the right to approve or disapprove of a variety of corporate actions at Craigslist."

Upon eBay's launching of its own competing online classified service, Craigslist's two majority shareholders asked eBay to sell its shares back to Craigslist or to a third party that would preserve the unique Craigslist corporate culture of community service over profit maximization. When eBay refused to do so, Craigslist's majority shareholders took advantage of the shareholder agreement provision by adopting a shareholder rights plan that restricted eBay from purchasing additional shares or transferring shares to third parties, implementing a staggered board that effectively prohibited eBay from unilaterally electing a board member, and establishing a right of first refusal for the sale or transfer of eBay's shares. The majority shareholders stated that the purpose of the plan was to ensure neither eBay nor its transferees would ever control Craigslist, thereby protecting Craigslist's corporate values, culture, and business model from future monetization and a focus on profits rather than community service. In response, eBay filed suit against Newmark and Buckmaster, arguing the plan breached the fiduciary duties they each owed to eBay as a minority stockholder.

Despite Craigslist's unique anti-monetization and pro–community service culture and business model, the court noted that Craigslist chose to organize itself as a for-profit Delaware corporation, and was therefore bound by the fiduciary duties of Delaware corporations, including the duty to promote stockholder value. Because the majority shareholders could not prove that the plan supported a legitimate corporate interest, the court held that Newmark and Buckmaster had violated their fiduciary duties to eBay, and both the rights plan and the right of first refusal were rescinded. The decision was based on the conclusion that the majority shareholders "failed to prove that Craigslist possesses a palpable, distinctive, and advantageous culture that sufficiently promotes stockholder value to support the indefinite implementation of a poison pill." So, because the stated goal of the plan was to preserve the corporation's culture and values rather than maximizing shareholder profits, the plan was not justified under Delaware corporate law.

The Court of Chancery's ruling in *eBay v. Newmark* drew criticism from academics and practicing lawyers alike, primarily because the court emphasized the traditional obligation of shareholder value maximization at the expense of non-shareholder considerations such as corporate values and ideology. This criticism was magnified because of Craigslist's unique culture which, unlike most for-profit corporations, eschewed monetization and cold-blooded profit maximization in favor of providing a community service with a small-scale corporate organization. The decision undermined corporate leaders and shareholders whose goal was not profit maximization, but whose ambitions reflected their values or even their mission.

It also put corporate directors on notice that sustainable business practices were not to be tolerated in Delaware should stockholders cry foul:

> Delaware courts have guarded against . . . the less visible, yet more pernicious risk that [directors] acting in subjective good faith might nevertheless deprive stockholders of value-maximizing opportunities.

The case highlights the fact that, under Delaware law, corporations have an absolute obligation to promote shareholder profit maximization, even if corporate leaders and shareholders seek a different end-goal.

So constituency statutes are imperfect instrumentalities available for director and sometimes officer use only at their option and only under specified circumstances. Delaware, the most important corporate domicile in the nation, continues to eschew stakeholderism. No wonder legal scholar Jonathan D. Springer observed fifteen years ago in his "Corporate Law Corporate Constituency Statutes: Hollow Hopes and False Fears": "Perhaps the greatest value of [stakeholder] statute is aspirational—that they point toward a change in corporate law that will account actively for [stakeholder] interests." His words were to become prescient. The marketplace of ideas would need to deliver a new voluntary form of corporation, one unquestionably accountable to its stakeholders—the benefit corporation.

THE BENEFIT CORPORATION'S IMPACT

Although benefit corporation laws vary from state to state, each law requires qualifying corporations to meet specific standards with respect to their purposes, their accountability, and their transparency. A benefit corporation's purpose is to create a material, positive impact on society and the environment. That purpose must include creating a "general public benefit" and may include one or more "specific public benefit" purposes. Compare that with the nation's traditional for-profit corporate laws, which permit business corporations to be organized for any lawful purpose, including a public benefit, but don't otherwise specify that their purposes be identified in their charters.

The benefit corporation's "general public benefit" mandate is informed by the enabling statutes' requirement that directors, when considering the best interests of the corporation, are obligated to take into account the effects of their decisions on shareholders, employees, customers, suppliers, the community, and the local and global environment. The mandate also ensures that, while pursuing a specific mission, the benefit corporation's director won't lose sight of his overarching obligation to pursue a general public benefit, in part so that the specific mission won't inadvertently do harm on other social fronts. For example, a company seeking to reduce waste won't cavalierly increase carbon emissions or, for that matter, turn a blind eye to the poor or underserved communities.

Still, the benefit corporation is permitted, but not obligated, to declare one or more specific public benefits it intends to pursue. Without limiting the mission a company's founders may define, the California Benefit Corporation law does a good job of suggesting specific public benefits they might identify in the company's charter:

1. Providing low-income or underserved individuals or communities with beneficial products or services;
2. Promoting economic opportunity for individuals or communities beyond the creation of jobs in the ordinary course of business;
3. Preserving the environment;
4. Improving human health;
5. Promoting the arts, sciences, or advancement of knowledge;
6. Increasing the flow of capital to entities with a public benefit purpose; or
7. The accomplishment of any other particular benefit for society of the environment.

Whether the benefit corporation sticks with the general public benefit for its watchword or opts also to include a specific public benefit, it's critical—and required by law—that the company's social and environmental performance be periodically measured against a third-party standard and reported to shareholders, usually on an annual benefit report posted on the company's website and thus also made available to all the company's stakeholders, including the public at large. The company may select any third-party standard, but certain statutes, California's and New York's among them, require that the company also report on the process and rationale it used in selecting the third-party standard.

The California law requires that the third-party standard be "a standard for defining, reporting, and assessing overall corporate social and environmental performances" which is:

1. ...a comprehensive assessment of the impact of the business and the business's operations...

2. ... developed by an entity that has no material financial relationship with the benefit corporation ...

3. The standard is developed by an entity that does both of the following:

   a. Accesses necessary and appropriate expertise to assess overall corporate social and environmental performance.

   b. Uses a balanced multi-stakeholder approach, including a public comment period of at least thirty days to develop the standard ...

Although the benefit corporation is not required to have its benefit report certified or audited by a third party, the legitimate and robust assessment of the company's social and environmental performance will become among the key differentiators by which the company distinguishes itself in the competitive marketplace. For that reason, along with others, the third-party standard must be independent and credible. Among the third-party standards organizations that meet the statutory criteria are the Global Reporting Initiative (GRI), Ceres Roadmap to Sustainability, Greenseal, Underwriters Laboratories (UL), ISO2600, Green America Business Network, and B Lab, the nonprofit engine driving the benefit corporation movement and promoting a model benefit corporation statute. In addition, more than 100 "raters" of corporate sustainability practices are listed in the free "Rate the Raters" report published by the research and consulting firm Sustainability.

Directors of benefit corporations are themselves beneficiaries of certain legal protections for making decisions some shareholders might otherwise challenge as breaching their "shareholder primacy" obligation. For one thing, the benefit corporation laws uniformly provide that considering the interests of non-shareholder stakeholders doesn't itself violate the directors' duties to exercise good faith, to take the care of an ordinarily prudent person, or to consider the best interests of the corporation. Directors are also protected from lawsuits by beneficiaries of a benefit corporation's general public purpose; third parties simply have no private right of action. But shareholders do enjoy the right to sue directors who fail to pursue the general public purpose or a stated specific public purpose, who fail to consider the interests of protected stakeholders, or who do not meet the transparency requirements of the law.

DELAWARE, THE OUTLIER

Then there's the special case of Delaware, which in 2013 did, in fact, authorize the organization of benefit corporations. Delaware's law is different from the rest and, for many commentators, troubling. Accountability measures are included in B Lab's model law: "Benefit Corporations are required to produce an 'Annual Benefit Report' which will include an assessment of how they performed in achieving their social and environmental goals, tested against an independent, third-party standard." Yet, in Delaware, benefit corporations need report only every other year, and their reports need not be made available to the public or measured against a third-party standard. Moreover, while B Lab's model law requires benefit corporation directors to consider the interests of stakeholders affected by corporate acts, "including shareholders, employees, the community and the environments," the Delaware law merely imposes on directors a duty "to consider the interests of those materially affected by the operation of the corporation, in addition to the pecuniary interests of the stockholders," never categorically identifying those non-stockholder stakeholders.

Along with the low-profit limited liability company (discussed in Chapter 4), the benefit corporation represents a real opportunity to address the needs—and growing demands—of social entrepreneurs and impact investors for a for-profit entity whose social business purpose is central to its existence. For now, despite Delaware's undisputed leadership in corporate law, the state's legislation, with its loose reporting standards and limited accountability, is an unfortunate outlier, inviting greenwashing by corporations that seek competitive advantage by hiding behind benefit corporation status, but with no intent to honor its noble purpose.

PATAGONIA'S VALUES AND VISION

When in 2012 Ventura-based Patagonia, Inc., the environmentally conscious outdoor apparel clothing and gear company, became California's first benefit corporation, Yvon Chouinard, the company's founder, declared that "Patagonia is trying to build a company that could last 100 years. Benefit corporation legislation centers the legal framework to enable mission-driven companies like Patagonia to stay mission-driven through succession, capital raises, and even changes in ownership, by institutionalizing the values, culture, and processes, and high standards put in place by founding entrepreneurs."

Patagonia was a values-led business from the very start. Chouinard, a pioneering rock climber, has been an environmentalist at least since the 1950s when he started making equipment to replace pitons, metal spikes that permanently damaged rock walls. He quickly gained a loyal following among fellow rock climbers who agreed with him that their sport ought not damage the environment, and Patagonia was born, dedicated to finding and implementing business solutions to the environmental crisis.

Chouinard wrote an essay, appearing in his company's October 1974 catalogue, that recalled the company's "clean climbing" origin, proudly proclaimed its then-unorthodox mission, and telegraphed his enduring legacy:

> It was both surprising and revolutionary. Here was a company that made climbing hardware advocating a more pure, equipment-light approach to the sport. Why? Because popular climbing areas were being defaced by the constant pounding of pitons, and the overuse of gear only detracted from the real challenge—the climb. Such an argument could have hurt sales, but it didn't, because climbers saw that it was the right thing to do. Since then, Patagonia has taken many such stands in favor of the environment and the purity of sport. And we continue to grow.

Alpinism remains at the heart of Chouinard's company, which still makes clothes for climbing, but has expanded into simple and utilitarian apparel for skiers, snowboarders, surfers, fly fishermen, paddlers, and trail runners, all sportsmen who cherish their connection with nature. Patagonia and its principals are leading protagonists in the never-ending fight to protect the wild and beautiful venues "silent sportsmen" share and call their own.

Patagonia is a clear reflection of Yvon Chouinard's values and vision. Although the company remains privately held, its board includes independent members who represent the community, and more than 40 percent of its managers are women or ethnic minorities. Patagonia shares its financial reports with its employees. It generously covers 80 percent of its full-time employees' health insurance premiums and extends health benefits to its part-time, retail, and warehouse staff. Half of its full-time employees participate in external professional development programs.

But it's Patagonia's environmental performance, its specific public purpose, that sets it apart from its peers. It was Patagonia that in 1994 discovered the environmental hazards cotton presented, accepting only pesticide-free cotton in its products and creating California's organic cotton industry. Seventy-five percent of the materials the company uses are organic, recycled, or otherwise environmentally preferred, according to B Lab. Staying true to its mountaineering roots, the company uses sustainable manufacturing processes and works within its industry to develop social and environmental standards.

Since 1986 the company has "tithed" for environmental activism, committing 1 percent of its sales or 10 percent of its profits, whichever is greater, to grassroots environmental organizations, even paying employees to work on local environmental projects so they could commit their full-time efforts to them. In 2011, Patagonia launched the "Common Threads Initiative" to encourage the repair, recycling, and resale of garments via eBay, urging the public in a full-page *New York Times* ad: "Don't buy this jacket unless you really need it."

Yvon Chouinard is not only a daring mountain climber, but a maverick entrepreneur. His world view fosters creativity and provides a sense of purpose, producing the highest quality products while doing the least possible harm to the environment. Patagonia's metamorphosis into a benefit corporation was inevitable.

PUBLIC GOOD SOFTWARE SUPPORTS CIVIL SOCIETY

So, too, was Dan Ratner and Jason Kunesh's decision to organize Public Good Software, Inc., as an Illinois benefit corporation. Ratner and Kunesh, among the tech wizards behind Obama for America 2012, are committed to creating the world's best software to build capacity among nonprofits.

Kunesh and Ratner—the social entrepreneur whose successes include Snapdragon, an early provider of DSL high-speed Internet access, and Sittercity, the nation's largest service dedicated to helping parents find quality childcare online—have vowed to apply the lessons they learned from their work in re-electing the President to putting together, along with a team of world-class engineers, a site that uses crowdsourcing to rate nonprofits, build online communities, and serve as a hub for charitable donations. Think travel website Orbitz, where Kunesh was once a lead information architect.

For both men, each a disrupter by any measure, Obama for America 2012 proved to be an education in how best to convert passion into cash. Kunesh, the campaign's director of user experience, tells it this way: "We added a quote from the president [on the webpage] that said, in essence, 'We need to finish what we started' . . . and that single quote raised conversation [rates] almost 11 percent. We actually had to re-test it because we thought it was an error . . . that quote is probably worth $35 million."

Ratner, who served as the campaign's director of development, emphasizes that its donation page couldn't have made the one-click process any easier or more user-friendly. Reflecting on the power of the click, he also sees that the tools and tactics the campaign successfully employed can be harnessed to address the social sector's fundraising, volunteering, and data interoperability challenges. Through the company's online marketplace, Publicgood.me, donors find and connect with public-benefit organizations they can support by giving money, volunteering, and building awareness.

Launched in 2013, Public Good Software, Inc., secured early financial support from Matt Mullenweg, a founder of WordPress, and is already helping build the capacity of nonprofits, including foster care provider UCAN, Open Books, and the American Red Cross of Greater Chicago. According to Jason Kunesh, "Civil society is changing. The relationships between people, their communities, and organizations that serve the public good are being reconsidered." He's right, of course, and Messrs. Kunesh and Ratner and their software startup, Public Good Software, Inc., are helping re-tool civil society to make the most of those relationships.

ENSURING ACCOUNTABILITY TO STAKEHOLDERS

As a benefit corporation, Public Good Software, Inc., seeks to create a "general public benefit," but also seeks to increase the flow of capital to entities with their own public benefit purposes (its "specific public benefit"). In selecting the third-party standard against which its performance is to be judged, the company considered the Ceres Roadmap to Sustainability, the Global Reporting Initiative, and Good Guide Company ratings before settling on B Lab's Impact Assessment. In addition, the company will track the number of donated dollars flowing through its system, an easy-to-measure and objective indication of its progress in achieving its specific public benefit.

The B Corp Impact Assessment is a comprehensive survey of business practices, intended to measure a company's impact on all its stakeholders. The assessment considers the company's performance in its governance, its community relations, its environmental practices, and the extent to which its business model is beneficial. It thus informs the Annual Benefit Report required of benefit corporations. But the B Corp Impact Assessment is also useful for an entirely different reason—as part of the process by which any for-profit business, whether a corporation or not, can become a "Certified B Corp" or "B Corporation," a company B Lab recognizes as having satisfied a high standard of social and environmental performance.

The B Corp is a B Lab–sanctioned certification, not a legally recognized status. It is earned primarily by achieving a verified minimum score of 80 or more out of 200 points on B Lab's rigorous Impact Assessment.

The more than 1,000 Certified B Corps enjoy the benefits of a triple-bottom-line community. The mission-driven entrepreneurs in that community share and respect accountability to all they touch. They are likely to donate to charity regularly, to use on-site renewable energy, and to favor suppliers from low-income communities. They are among the prime movers to be credited for helping build our evolving ecosystem in which stakeholder interests are institutionalized and each of us is empowered as never before.

CHAPTER FOUR

PRIs and L3Cs

In exchange for the tax benefits they enjoy, private foundations are required by U.S. law to distribute 5 percent or more of their assets for charitable purposes every year. This obligation has historically been met primarily by making grants to charities that are too often in feverish competition with one another to win them. But, increasingly, foundations are discovering another, arguably better way to meet their distribution requirements—"program-related investments," or PRIs, that support charitable projects or activities that further foundations' own missions.

PRIs can take the form of loans, loan guarantees, lines of credit, linked deposits, or other investments—even including equity investments in for-profit businesses. (Since nonprofits have no owners, they have no equity to sell.) Therein lies an accounting advantage the plain-old grant could never match. Whereas a grant is an expense, once paid never to be recouped, a PRI is an asset carried on the foundation's balance sheet until it is recovered one day, together with interest or gain, and then redeployed as a charitable grant, program-related investment, or a combination of the two. Unlike a grant, which is calculated to do some good, but only once, the PRI offers foundation managers, stewards of the resources entrusted to them, a financial multiplier benefit and, with it, a seemingly irresistible social multiplier benefit.

A program-related investment is one that meets three definitional tests:

1. Its primary purpose is to accomplish one or more of the foundation's tax-exempt purposes. The investment simply would not have been made if not for its tax-exempt purpose.

2. The production of income or the appreciation of property is not a significant purpose. So if investors seeking profit—but not social impact—would have likely made the same investment on the same terms, the investment is not a PRI. But if the investment happens to produce significant income or capital appreciation, that fact, on its own, doesn't disqualify the investment as a PRI.

3. The investment can't be made to influence legislation or take part in political campaigns on behalf of candidates.

To meet the IRS' "expenditure responsibility" requirements in making a program-related investment, a private foundation must require that each investment be the subject of a written commitment signed by an appropriate officer, director, or trustee of the recipient organization. The commitment should specify the purpose of the investment and should contain an agreement by the organization:

1. To use all amounts received from the private foundation only for the purposes of the investment and to repay any amount not used for those purposes;

2. To submit, at least once a year, a full and complete financial report of the type ordinarily required by commercial investors under similar circumstances and a statement that it has complied with the terms of the investment;

3. To keep adequate books and records and to make them available to the private foundation at reasonable times; and

4. Not to use any of the funds to carry on propaganda, influence legislation, influence the outcomes of any public elections, carry on voter registration drives, or, when the recipient is itself a private foundation, to make grants that do not comply with the requirements regarding individual grants or expenditure responsibility.

Meeting those requirements, the program-related investment will not only help the foundation discharge its annual distribution requirement, but will do so without risk that the IRS will impose an excise tax on the foundation or its managers for jeopardizing the exempt purpose of the foundation, a tax that might otherwise be assessed when the foundation's assets are put at risk in speculative investments. Moreover, investments in PRIs do not subject foundations to the "excess business holdings" tax, which otherwise applies to foundations that own more than 20 percent of a business enterprise.

But PRIs have long been disfavored, presumed by many foundations to be risky, tricky, and more trouble than they're worth. Although supply, for those reasons, has been limited, so has demand: relatively few operating charities or mission-driven ventures have sought debt or equity funding. Those that exist are mostly in the fields of housing and economic development.

All that is changing. While the competition for grants intensifies and nonprofit managers become more sophisticated, the economic downturn has taught foundation managers that a distribution strategy relying exclusively on grants can deplete capital, but loan repayments or equity investment returns can themselves be put to work in furtherance of their charitable aims.

The Internal Revenue Service has responded to foundations' growing interest in PRIs as a tool to make the most of their limited assets. For the first time since 1972, the IRS has published guidance to foundations that helps them make PRIs more easily, with greater predictability and with lower transaction costs. The IRS has also given comfort to foundations about the ventures they can fund and the way in which their PRIs might be designed. For example, the IRS has now confirmed that the existence of a potentially high rate of return on an investment does not, by itself, prevent the investment from qualifying as a PRI; also, an investment that funds activities in a foreign country may further the accomplishment of charitable purposes and qualify as a PRI. A PRI may accomplish a variety of charitable purposes, such as advancing science, combating environmental deterioration, and promoting the arts.

The IRS offered new examples of program-related investments it would sanction, including:

- An equity investment in a for-profit drug company made for the purpose of developing a vaccine to prevent a disease that predominantly affects poor individuals in developing countries
- An investment in a new recycling business in a developing country that will recycle solid waste currently being disposed of in a manner that contributes significantly to environmental deterioration
- A loan to a business that purchases coffee from poor farmers in a developing country

While the development of affordable housing and community development programs in the United States and microfinance initiatives in the developing world have long attracted PRIs, we now see greater reliance on them in the arts, education, social and health programs, and environmental sustainability.

PRIs are commonly used to fund low-interest or interest-free loans to needy students; high-risk investments in nonprofit, low-income housing projects; low-interest loans to small businesses owned by members of economically disadvantaged groups when commercial loans at reasonable interest rates are not readily available; investments in nonprofit organizations combating community deterioration; and investments in businesses in blighted urban areas under plans to improve the economy of an area by providing employment or training for unemployed residents.

Program-related investments, when carefully and collaboratively developed and implemented by the funder and the operating charity or mission-driven venture, can and should be wins for both parties. The funder can recycle the same dollars to advance program goals, redeploying eventual loan or equity investment proceeds in support of new projects; can pursue capital-intensive initiatives that exceed its typical grant size; can partner with other foundations, corporations, or the government and thereby contribute to the more significant social impact large-scale projects can deliver; and can exercise thought leadership, inspiring and empowering other foundations to see themselves as social venture capitalists. For its part, the charity that invites program-related investment can create a partnership of trust and action with its investor-funder, both parties pursuing the programmatic and financial objectives they share; will press ahead in building its capacity when it becomes accountable to an investor reasonably demanding data-driven results; and can become more bankable as it meets its financial obligations to its investor.

Not surprisingly, some of the nation's most prominent foundations are exercising the thought leadership it takes to inspire smaller foundations, including family foundations, to follow suit. The Kellogg Foundation, for example, recently invested $75 million in mission-driven ventures that provide nutritious food to at-risk children and their families. The Bill and Melinda Gates Foundation used a PRI to purchase a $10 million equity stake in a for-profit biotech company delivering vaccines to the poor, as part of the foundation's 2009 commitment to allocate $400 million to program-related investments taking the form of low-interest loans, loan and bond guarantees, and equity investments.

THE LOW-PROFIT LIMITED LIABILITY COMPANY (L3C)

A growing number of mission-driven ventures—whether free-standing social purpose businesses or subsidiaries or affiliates of nonprofits—are being organized as "low-profit limited liability companies" (L3Cs), a business form designed to access and leverage program-related investments. A for-profit entity, the L3C combines the financial advantages and governance flexibility of the traditional limited liability company—distinguishing the LLC as the nation's most popular form of doing business—with the social advantages of a nonprofit.

The LLC is like a corporation in that the liability of its owners, called "members," is limited to their investments. The form is also like a partnership in that its members are free to enter into an operating agreement that allocates management powers, profits, and losses among themselves in just about any way they see fit. When, for example, a mission-driven venture is to reward for-profit capital investors with a disproportionate share of profits, but vest ultimate decision-making authority in social-benefit, nonprofit actors, the LLC might be an obvious entity choice.

The L3C is a new limited liability company form which, like any other LLC, shields its owners from the debts of their enterprise and affords them flexibility in governance and tax planning, with one striking difference: the L3C's articles of organization are required by law to mirror the standards for program-related investing that the law imposes on foundations. So the business form itself gives the foundation comfort that the target company is specifically organized to accept PRIs, thus satisfying a significant item on any foundation investor's due-diligence checklist.

A foundation seeking social impact over economic rewards can invest in an L3C (whether a subsidiary or an affiliate of a charity, or a stand-alone venture) and forego market-rate returns. The foundation's financial give-up can thus catalyze a potent social-purpose strategy. By taking on higher risk in exchange for lower financial returns, the foundation affords the L3C the opportunity to attract private-sector investment that otherwise might never be tapped to support a social venture. Together, the foundation and the L3C's private-sector funders can help ensure its long-term sustainability. Not only can the foundation's financial commitment to the venture's mission draw urgently needed private investment into the social sector, but the foundation's support may actually reduce the social enterprise's entrepreneurial risk: the talent, expertise, and experience of a foundation's management will often elevate the foundation's role to that of a social venture capitalist, which has a stake in both the viability of the venture and the social impact it delivers.

It is primarily as a capital formation platform that the L3C has captured the imagination of mission-driven entrepreneurs. The base-case strategy involves leveraging private foundations' PRIs to access market-driven capital for ventures with only modest financial prospects, but the real possibility of major social impact. The key is to strategically allocate risks and rewards among private foundations and any other nonprofit or for-profit investors, giving each the benefit of its bargain. This may be accomplished through the design of a tranched, or multilayered, capital structure that promises a unique value proposition for each investor, respectful of its discrete investment objectives and fiduciary obligations.

A simplified example should illustrate the strategy. If a private foundation makes a PRI into a low-profit limited liability company as its first investor, it thus bears a greater financial risk than later investors will. Yet, because it's mostly concerned about its charitable mission, it contents itself with less than market-rate returns. The foundation's investment lowers risk for concurrent or future investors, and its give-up of market-rate returns can subsidize returns for financial investors who might not otherwise see the L3C's risk-reward profile as attractive. Moreover, through the foundation's commitment to the L3C, it implies endorsement of its management and mission and may signal its willingness to provide additional resources should the venture require them, all positive signals to prospective investors who may thereby be encouraged to co-invest. The foundation's investments thus become a catalyst to attract private investments into the social sector, an accomplishment a grant is unlikely to achieve.

As appealing as the L3C is as a vehicle to facilitate program-related investments, the truth is that virtually any business form can be tailored to accommodate PRIs. Moreover, many L3Cs aren't even seeking PRIs, nor do foundations need to have a role in L3Cs.

The L3C is unique in its capability to engage diverse stake-holders around a clear and unambiguous ordering of statutorily imposed fiduciary priorities, priorities that can't be waived or negotiated away:

- The L3C must pursue charitable, tax-exempt purposes above all others.
- Although realizing profit and enhancing value are permitted purposes, the profit motive must be subordinated to the charitable purpose.

Those priorities clearly trump the money-and-power goals most traditional investors and entrepreneurs pursue. They also signal to other counterparties—including customers, employees, strategic alliance partners, funders, and regulators that—although the L3C is intended to be financially self-sustaining—and, in the case of an L3C owned or partly owned by a nonprofit, intended to help diversify its parent's funding sources—the L3C is, above all, a mission-driven enterprise. That branding and positioning advantage, and the fiduciary commitment behind it, may be reason enough for the social entrepreneur to select the L3C as the "right" business form for his or her venture.

THE "SUSTAINABILITY MAYOR" LEVERAGES HIS IMPACT

Former Chicago Mayor Richard M. Daley, the longest serving mayor in the city's history, left an unprecedented legacy. Acknowledging his leadership in greening the city he loves, the U.S. Green Building Council created the Mayor Richard M. Daley Legacy Award for Global Leadership in Creating Sustainable Cities in 2010 and, to no one's surprise, named him as its first recipient at USGBC's annual Greenbuild conference. When awarding Daley the J.C. Nichols Prize for Visionaries in Urban Development, the Urban Land Institute described him as an "Urban Artist" who "transformed this Rustbelt city into a revitalized international metropolis, bringing together the built and natural environments to make the city more sustainable, livable, and lively."

During the former mayor's tenure, Chicago added more than eighty-eight LEED-certified buildings; 1,300 acres of new open space; 600,000 trees; more than eighty-five miles of landscaped medians; and 600 rooftop gardens and green roofs, including, notably, a 20,300-square-foot green roof built atop City Hall. Mayor Daley also oversaw the building of his crowning achievement, Millennium Park, an unparalleled example of successful urban planning. Blair Kamin, the Pulitzer Prize–winning architecture critic for the *Chicago Tribune*, concluded his 2004 review of the park with these words: "[A] park provides a respite from the city, yet it also reflects the city. In that sense, all of Millennium Park mirrors the rebirth of Chicago ... the ambition of its patrons, the creativity of its artists and architects, and the ongoing miracle of its ability to transform a no place into a someplace that's extraordinary."

When Mayor Daley's twenty-one-year tenure came to a close in 2011, his passion for urban sustainability remained with him. So did his deep understanding of municipal government and the daunting challenges it faces in developing a more sustainable, modern infrastructure. Those challenges are even more imposing when fiscal pressures and political realities conspire to deny cities the expertise and resources they need to fairly consider and implement cutting-edge solutions to public-sector needs.

Enter former Mayor Daley's low-profit limited liability company, The Sustainability Exchange, L3C.

Working with Harvard University, the University of Arizona, and other institutions and experts, The Sustainability Exchange partners with American cities in conducting detailed data analyses of their energy use and proposed infrastructure projects to identify likely areas of improvement, all at no up-front cost. After analyzing a city's data and operations and identifying the most promising projects, The Sustainability Exchange effectively cuts through local procurement procedures, even educating vendors about the exact requirements they'll need to meet if they are to win a bid. Competition among technology and service providers—as well as funders—is enhanced, and procurement proceeds faster and more efficiently. Only when a city moves ahead with a project will the L3C share in the savings the city realizes over time.

The L3C focuses on energy efficiency, waste and wastewater treatment, waste management, and public transportation. The goal is to permit city partners to unite and approach their sustainability challenges at scale, reducing both completion times and costs.

When former Mayor Daley announced The Sustainability Exchange L3C's launch at the 2013 U.S. Conference of Mayors' meeting in Las Vegas, the mayors of Phoenix; New Orleans; Newton, Massachusetts; Parma, Ohio; and South Bend, Indiana, all backed the reality that healthy cities require partnerships among their governments, their business communities, and a vibrant nonprofit sector; and they all recognized the importance of developing measurable, data-driven results.

The L3C was the natural platform for The Sustainability Exchange. The structure allows foundations and other socially responsible and impact investors to support the venture's operations through debt and equity investments as well as grants. Moreover, it preserves the financial and governance flexibility of the traditional limited liability company while placing social mission ahead of profits, all values promoted by the visionary Mayor Daley.

COUNSELING DATA, L3C: A CASE STUDY IN COLLECTIVE IMPACT

Illinois' share of the $25 billion national foreclosure settlement that state attorneys general, the U.S. Department of Justice, and the U.S. Department of Housing and Urban Development negotiated in February of 2012 with the five largest lenders amounted to $95 million, of which Illinois Attorney General Lisa Madigan first distributed $25 million to legal aid organizations and to establish foreclosure mediation programs to help struggling homeowners, including those at imminent risk of default. In 2013, she awarded $70 million in grants to groups offering housing counseling to distressed homeowners and tenants and to research and policy groups. "Community revitalization" efforts were favored, to help rebuild communities among the hardest hit by the crisis attributed to the unlawful foreclosure practices employed by mortgage services Bank of America, JPMorgan Chase, Wells Fargo, Citibank, and Ally Bank, formerly known as GMAC.

One of the Attorney General's grantees is Counseling Data L3C, a shared subsidiary of two nonprofits, Housing Action Illinois and Neighborhood Housing Services of Chicago, Inc. Housing Action Illinois is a statewide coalition of housing counseling agencies, homeless service providers, developers of affordable housing, and policymakers united in the cause of protecting and expanding the availability of quality, affordable housing for low- and moderate-income households throughout the state.

Neighborhood Housing Services of Chicago, Inc., is a nonprofit Community Development Financial Institution (CDFI) that works in partnership with businesses, governments, and residents to revitalize neighborhoods and help individuals and families purchase, improve, and prevent the loss of single-family homes.

The two organizations joined forces to manage the launch, distribution, and maintenance of a new client management system for housing agencies, which is expected to fundamentally transform housing counseling in Illinois and, potentially, the nation. The cloud-based system, custom-designed by the Pierce Family Charitable Foundation's IT specialists, will allow cash-strapped agencies to move away from antiquated paper-based systems, easing their administrative and reporting burdens, reducing their costs, and boosting their capacities.

The need is clear: in a recently released study, the U.S. Department of Housing and Urban Development reported that nearly 70 percent of homeowners who defaulted on mortgages and then received housing counseling were able to obtain a mortgage remedy. With an integrated system to more easily track their clients—whether receiving pre-purchase, post-purchase, default, or foreclosure counseling—the affordable housing agencies Counseling Data L3C services will protect homeownership and avert foreclosures, benefiting both consumers and their communities.

The Pierce Family Charitable Foundation's commitment to spearhead the system's development and to undertake its installation and support at housing agencies throughout the state is squarely within its mission's sweet spot. The foundation, founded in 2007 by prominent Chicago attorney and philanthropist Denis Pierce, primarily focuses on nonprofits working in housing and homelessness, helping those nonprofits build the capacity they need to operate effectively. Thus, Counseling Data L3C became a natural object of Denis Pierce's and his foundation's generosity.

It was obvious to the leaders of Housing Action Illinois and Neighborhood Housing Services, Inc., that they would need to form a new legal entity for their mission-driven venture. Had they merely created a joint venture or operated as a general partnership, both co-venturers or partners would have been jointly and severally liable for the debts of the enterprise. So, for asset protection and other reasons, they prudently agreed to form a new legal entity. The L3C was an obvious choice for them: Counseling Data's charter is constrained by law to charitable or educational purposes, fully harmonized with the nonprofit, tax-exempt purposes of its two parents.

When two or more operating charities address a need or an opportunity together, as Housing Action Illinois and Neighborhood Housing Services, Inc., have done, good things happen. Not only do they achieve economies of scale and move past the siloed mindset plaguing too many nonprofit organizations, but they also start to think of each other as collaborators, eager to identify other opportunities they might pursue together in furtherance of their shared objectives. The efficiency, effectiveness, capacity, impact, and thought leadership of each organization all improve.

Along with The Sustainability Exchange L3C, Counseling Data L3C stands for still another proposition: large-scale social change requires broad cross-sector coordination. The elements of what John Kamila, a managing director of the global nonprofit consulting firm FSG (formerly Foundation Strategy Group), and Mark Kramer, FSG's co-founder, call "collective impact" are clearly in evidence at Counseling Data L3C. Kamila and Kramer identified those elements in their seminal article in the *Stanford Social Innovation Review*: "a centralized infrastructure, a dedicated staff, and a structured process that leads to a common agenda, shared measurement, continuous communication, and mutually reinforcing activities among all participants." Counseling Data's participants are themselves important actors from different sectors—government, leading nonprofits, and a private foundation serving as a social venture capitalist—all committed to a common agenda for solving a specific social problem, revitalizing neighborhoods by helping low-income residents keep their homes.

The argument behind collective impact is that organizations must coordinate their efforts around a clearly defined goal if they are to create lasting solutions to social problems on a large scale. The Sustainability Exchange L3C and Counseling Data L3C are two high-profile examples of that very phenomenon at work.

CHAPTER FIVE

The Poor and Their Banker
Lead the Way

Goretti Nyabenda's life in Burundi, Central Africa, was headed in a downward spiral. As a thirty-five-year-old mother of six, Nyabenda was stuck in an abusive relationship with a husband who barely spoke to her, restricted her travel in and out of their home, and spent the family's income on local banana brews, leaving them with little to nothing. He frequently beat her. After connecting with other local women and obtaining a $2 microloan, Nyabenda was able to build a small business, brewing the same banana beer on which her husband frequently wasted the family's income, but now for profit. Her business grew quickly and soon she was able to supplement her family's income, send her daughters to school, and pay her husband's medical bills.

Despite her windowless world, Nyabenda managed to overcome the barriers she faced to become a successful businesswoman, garner respect from her community, and eventually even demand respect from her husband. Her many achievements result from the economic security she gained through microfinance, a strategy that has been copied throughout southern Asia, the United States, and all around the world.

Nyabenda benefited from a community microcredit program modeled after Grameen Bank in Bangladesh. Since the bank's inception in 1976, it has grown to become an international model for microcredit programs designed to alleviate poverty. Grameen Bank was born out of a project undertaken by Dr. Muhammad Yunus, a native of Chittagong (present day Bangladesh). Motivated by a trip to a poor Bangladeshi village with his students in 1974, Professor

Yunus came up with the idea of Grameen Bank, a bank targeted specifically for the poor, a market few other banks would see as opportune.

While at the village, Yunus interviewed a woman who made stools from bamboo materials. She told him that she had to borrow from a middleman creditor in order to obtain raw bamboo for each stool she made. In addition to paying the middleman, a moneylender charged rates that left her with a penny profit margin and no opportunity to raise herself above subsistence level and into economic security. Yunus saw a problem he thought he could help solve and embarked on a remarkable career intended to do just that. Through his work, Yunus has become known as the "Banker to the Poor" and a recipient of the Nobel Peace Prize, the Congressional Gold Medal, and the Presidential Medal of Freedom.

PROFESSOR YUNUS' JOURNEY

Muhammad Yunus was born in Bathua, a small village in Hathazari, Chittagong, the business center of what was then the eastern part of Bengal and later became East Pakistan. Nurtured in a big family, Yunus recalls that, while his father always encouraged him to seek higher education, his mother was his biggest influence. Said to have never turned away a poor person who knocked on the family's door, she was Yunus' first inspiration in seeking to eradicate poverty.

After graduating from Dhaka University, Yunus received a Fulbright scholarship to study at Vanderbilt University in the United States, where he later earned a Ph.D. in developmental economics in 1971.

While in the United States, Yunus witnessed from afar the genocide in Bangladesh when West Pakistan began a military crackdown on the eastern wing of the nation to suppress Bengali calls for self-determination. He knew that his countrymen were trapped in a cycle of poverty, devoid of the happiness and prosperity he believed every human being was due. He also saw that the Bangladeshi ecosystem provided little reason for hope.

Yunus and other Bangladeshi natives in the United States worked together to raise funds and awareness about the tragic conditions back home, to organize demonstrations and meetings with legislators in Washington, and ultimately to lobby members of the U.S. House and Senate to help gain recognition for their nation. Through his efforts and those of other patriots, on December 16, 1971, Bangladesh won its war of independence, but not without a heavy toll on its people and the local economy.

Bangladesh was a battered country; millions now needed support in what would require an overhaul of the economy. Yunus had no choice but to return home and participate in the work that he described without hyperbole as "nation building."

Upon his return to Bangladesh, Yunus obtained a position as head of the economics department at Chittagong University, located in a rural area twenty miles east of the city of Chittagong. He commuted daily between the city and the university, and drove though the village of Jobra, which became a symbolic step in his monumental journey to alleviate poverty. Every day, Yunus passed several barren fields and wondered why they were not cultivated. He later learned that there was simply not enough water for irrigation. Yunus' daily observation of the village led to several other questions that helped shape the principles behind Grameen Bank: Who were the poor? How did these villagers make a living? How did they support themselves? Using what skills? And what barriers were preventing them from taking the steps they need to improve their lives?

Yunus saw that the situation in Bangladesh was especially hard on women, who had fewer opportunities than men to raise themselves out of poverty. If they were able to secure employment, they were paid less than men were paid. And their pursuit of self-employment was, at most, a distant dream.

Women were also rebuked by local banks. Before Grameen entered the market, women made up only 1 percent of the borrowers in Bangladesh. Most banks made business loans in a husband's name, even for a wife's business, allowing the husband to use its proceeds as he saw fit. The few banks that did loan to women required their husbands' permission first—or at least that their husbands accompany them to the bank—causing problems in a couple's marriage, especially for those women who wanted to hold their business interests as their separate property.

Cultural factors placed additional burdens on a woman's ability to obtain credit or access employment opportunities in Bangladesh. Widowed, divorced, and abandoned women were often hit the hardest, left with no one to help support them, but children to feed. Often these women were the poorest of the poor, without land or any other assets. When they did find work, it was usually temporary and only left the employer richer. Yunus remembers one woman telling him: "After a few weeks of threshing, we are out of work, and we have nothing to show for ourselves." Yunus knew she was right; he later realized that these women could earn significantly more by eliminating middlemen, easing access to credit and resources, and by launching their own small businesses.

THE VISIT TO JOBRA

This became all too clear to Yunus during one particular visit to Jobra with his students. At the time, Yunus was visiting some of the poorest households in the village to gain a better understanding of the challenges they faced and to find out whether he could help them in any way. Yunus observed a woman squatted on the dirt floor in front of her home, working diligently on plaiting strands of bamboo cane while building a stool. As he and his colleague approached the woman, she became frightened and started to go inside. However, after they greeted the woman and assured her of their gentle nature, she stated calmly that "There is nobody home."

What she meant was there was no *male* at home. In Bangladesh, as was the case in Goretti Nyabenda's home, women are not allowed to entertain strangers, let alone talk to men who are not close relatives. Of the many cultural burdens these women face, this is especially hard because it limits women entrepreneurs' access to economic opportunities, forcing them to hide behind their husbands' lead or restricting them to working with limited-credit partners. These creditors further take advantage of their power by charging the women high fees, knowing they will likely have nowhere else to go.

During his encounter with the woman, Yunus and his colleague asked her whether she owned the bamboo. She answered that she owned it, having purchased it from a *paikar*, the middlemen in the credit market for the village. The woman purchased the bamboo for five *taka* and, as part of her credit arrangement, she was required to sell it back to the middlemen for five *taka* and fifty *poysha*, earning her the equivalent of a two-cent profit. Yunus asked whether this was the best deal she could find, and she replied that she avoided working directly with money lenders because with them she would have to work at a loss, as some of her friends did. The woman then quickly returned to work because, as it turned out, this trade was her livelihood and any further discussion would set her back.

Yunus was shocked at the circumstances this woman faced— the effort required to make a two-cent profit, not nearly enough to keep herself and her children fed, clothed, and housed. He badly wanted to reach into his pocket and hand the women the five *taka*, or 20 cents, she needed for her next purchase, but held off because he knew it was not the long-term solution she or the village required to break their cycle of poverty. Instead, Yunus focused on a more permanent solution.

THE BANKING SYSTEM'S FAILURE

Examining the credit structure in the Bangladeshi banking system was Yunus' first step in understanding the factors perpetuating the poverty these villagers faced, especially among the women. The problem became clear to Yunus during a visit to a local branch of what was then one of the largest government banks in the country. He spoke to the branch manager about allowing some of the poor people in the village of Jobra to obtain loans. He explained that the loans would be used to purchase materials so that women could break their reliance on middlemen and moneylenders for their small trades and instead depend on a more stable institution like a government bank.

Soon, however, Yunus realized that it was the banking system itself that was largely at fault for constructing and maintaining a failing scheme, one tailored only to the needs of those who could afford to use it and not those who truly needed it. Yunus received one farfetched excuse after another from the branch manager as to why the bank could not extend loans to Jobra's villagers: the cost of processing the loans outweighed the profits the bank would earn; the villagers were illiterate and could not complete the paperwork required for processing loans; the bank could not secure collateral from the villagers because the poor simply did not own anything of value; extending loans to women without their husbands' permission, or worse, without their husbands' knowledge, would not be comfortable for the bank.

YUNUS' INGENIOUS SOLUTION

Yunus sought to help the poorest villagers first. He decided to obtain loans for women to provide the resources they needed to practice their skills in building bamboo stools, weaving baskets, or producing floor mats and then selling them at a profit that would be theirs and theirs alone. Not only could they provide the basic necessities for their families, but eventually invest back into their businesses and grow them. But an even bigger issue soon came to light, an issue of human rights.

Poverty became a women's issue in Yunus' eyes because of the cultural burdens they faced in Bangladesh. The women there were often counted as the first ones out whenever there was little or no food remaining for a meal, both men and children taking precedence. Women also faced abuse at home from their husbands and their husbands' families and were seen as disposable, husbands having little restriction in their right to divorce. When a woman was divorced, it became a cultural shame: she was no longer allowed back into her own parents' home.

Creating access to credit markets was the road to economic security, Yunus believed. Once a woman obtained economic security, her standard of living would rise, and she could began to realize the human rights to which she was entitled.

Before poverty could be alleviated, Yunus had to address the failing banking system. How can an entire banking system be so flawed, Yunus wondered. If loans were only available to those who could afford to pay the costs of processing a loan or were sufficiently creditworthy to secure a loan, then the bank was simply extending loans to those who already had money. Those who could not pull themselves out of poverty without a loan were simply shut out.

Yunus and the bankers were at loggerheads, leaving him no option but to become the "banker to the poor" himself. He offered guaranteed bank loans to the poor, effectively borrowing money from the bank and extending credit to the villagers. The bank agreed to the plan, and the seeds of Grameen Bank were planted.

Yunus went on to distribute the money to the villagers and institute a specific repayment plan, one he felt even the poor could reasonably be expected to honor. The plan avoided large, lump-sum payments that would unduly burden the villagers every time they paid off a portion of their debts, and instead asked for extremely small payments almost daily at rates that even the poor could handle. The results stunned both the bank and Yunus himself: more than 98 percent of the borrowers paid back all of their loans on time and every pay period. The villagers' compliance was significant and, even when compared to traditional banking, was remarkable, proving to deliver a more attractive investment yield than loans secured with assets.

Although Yunus was surprised at his initial success, he knew deep down something the bankers could not comprehend. He realized that the poorest of the poor sometimes worked ten or twelve hours a day just to produce and sell their products. Failing to do so would not leave them enough income to eat. To Yunus, this was the best security the bank could ever have, a villager's life. He believed the villagers had every reason to pay back what they borrowed so that they could seek another loan to eat another day.

Yunus admitted he never planned to pay the bank back should a default occur; the truth is that he never expected a default. He became the first entrepreneur to operate what Yunus has called a "social business," one that eschews profit.

THE ADVENT OF THE "SOCIAL BUSINESS"

Muhammad Yunus' "social business" is just like any other business, with the singular exception that its goal is to promote a social benefit, in one of two ways:

- A company is established by investors to provide a social benefit rather than maximizing profit for its owners, or

- A profit-maximizing business owned by the poor helps them improve their standard of living and that of those around them.

A social business may earn a profit, but its investors may not. At most, they recoup their initial investments while any profits go directly to benefiting the poor or are reinvested in the business. Unlike a charity, the social business remains self-sustaining, without a need for new capital every year. Yet, a social business must be run like any other business, with decisions made in the best interests of the venture.

By remaining self-sustaining, a social business gives the poor something a charity cannot, self-empowerment. That's why Yunus believes that charity is not always the answer: in his view, when people know they can receive things "for free," they lose their initiative and their sense of responsibility. Social businesses, on the other hand, encourage creative energy, self-help, and self-confidence. They promote accountability. They allow people to see the direct results of their work and encourage them to put in the effort that's needed to help the business sustain itself. Only when the social business is self-sustaining can the poor benefit from it, earn from it, and eventually raise themselves out of poverty.

Some may wonder why investors would seek social business opportunities without any possibility of realizing a return on investment. Yunus explains that Americans, as one example, have shown an enormous interest in giving. Nearly $300 billion a year is given to charity, proving there is not only a willingness to give, but a hunger. By fostering self-empowerment of those poor or disadvantaged, Yunus believes donors will see even greater merit in investing than in giving.

So just how did Yunus take this idea of a social business and improve the lives of the villagers of Jobra forever, and then the lives of millions of poor around the world? Yunus remembered just how little it took for the stool-maker in Jobra to practice her trade and realized the world of microfinance was the perfect solution for others in analogous situations.

Microfinance has become the principal financial services vehicle for the poor and the disadvantaged. Primarily using small loans, microcredit institutions reach out to poor borrowers, issuing loans and usually securing them with no collateral at all. Character trumps credit score.

Microfinance has caught the eye of many interested investors, activists, and philanthropists because of its strong social aspect—its use of capital for a greater good. It has proven to be one form of socially responsible investment that produces a direct positive impact on the lives of poor people everywhere.

GRAMEEN BANK AND ITS STRATEGY

Grameen Bank was built on this idea. Although it started very small and, at first, grew very slowly, it set out to remove the institutional barriers to economic security the poor faced. It first targeted borrowers who would never be eligible for a traditional bank loan—poor women. Yunus saw them as the linchpin of economic growth because they not only cared about themselves, but also about their children and families, perhaps even more than their husbands did.

The bank fostered an atmosphere in which those who borrowed were vested both in the bank and in other borrowers. It did so by building close relationships with borrowers and requiring them to join together in small groups in their villages, as part of even larger regional groups. The groups served multiple functions, first among them solidarity: Members of the group provided encouragement, psychological support, protection, and business assistance to one another. Grameen learned that the individual in a group rallies around the group consensus and builds a common group desire not to upset the balance of the relationships within the group. The bank ensured that borrowers knew that no one who borrowed from Grameen Bank stood alone. They were even invited to recruit new members who, like them, were struggling to escape the vicious cycle of poverty.

Groups of four to six women would meet with ten to twelve similar groups every week or two, coaching one another, participating in group business discussions and exercises, and helping the bank itself grow. Grameen functioned as a lender to individuals, but required the groups to take responsibility for one another. In that way, it encouraged each member to pay back her loans and remain faithful to her commitments and relationships with other group members. One Grameen member said she was always motivated to pay back her loans "because [she] would feel terrible to let down the other members of [her] group." Thus, the bank successfully zeroed in on the benefits of groupthink, resulting in financial rewards for its poor members and a high success rate for the bank.

The formula was working and working well for Grameen, so much so that it was encouraged to perfect its banking methods and expand into other areas. When Grameen discovered the group method was crucial to the success of its operations as well as the success of the poor, it required every applicant to join a like-minded group before requesting a loan. After forming a group, the borrowers were required to present themselves to the bank as a group, undergo group training, and learn the policies and expectations of the bank that were focused on their success. Following training, borrowers were tested on the policies, both individually and as a group, before they were able to request and obtain loans.

But the bank did not stop there. It soon began to attract capital from the villagers themselves, leveraging their funds to source financial support for housing loans, insurance, and the like. During its peak, Grameen Bank was opening one and a half branches a day and obtaining deposits that allowed the bank to grow much more quickly than before. A large number of deposits in the new branches came from the very borrowers who previously obtained loans. Using its full complement of financial services, the bank brought the opportunity of economic security into the lives of its borrowers, beyond the security they originally sought as self-employed tradespeople.

By introducing insurance to business owners, Grameen allowed the village to come together in times of disaster or emergency, re-energizing them to continue their progress. This was an entirely new phenomenon. In a small village, hanging on by a thread, a disaster meant a family was only thrown deeper into the cycle of poverty. But thanks to Grameen Bank, a different mindset led to a different reality.

Grameen Bank continues to grow. Today, the bank is owned primarily by the borrowers themselves, who own nearly 95 percent of the bank's equity. It has served more than eight million borrowers, created more than 25,000 jobs, and distributed more than $11.5 billion in loans, which have engaged a 97 percent repayment rate. The microfinance system around the world serves nearly 100 million people in a $25 billion industry. However, there is still plenty of room for growth. A recent study by Deutsche Bank Research estimated that there are one billion people who could directly benefit from micro-borrowing, with a total loan demand of $250 billion.

Grameen Bank has done more than its part in driving global growth. By 1989 Yunus and the bank had founded Grameen Trust, a nonprofit organization to promote microfinance around the world.

Through the trust, the founders of Grameen have provided consulting, evaluation, monitoring, and other forms of assistance to anyone involved in microcredit programs. The trust works with hundreds of microfinance institutions in nearly forty countries. The trust has both directly funded new projects and brought in new partnerships to help new projects grow. Projects have sprung up in some of the world's most impoverished countries, including Myanmar, Turkey, Zambia, Kosovo, Costa Rica, Guatemala, and Indonesia. The trust had expanded on the bank's agenda of achieving a social benefit, staying true to its purpose. Many microfinance institutions around the world owe their start to Grameen Trust, including several in the United States.

In 2008 Yunus, along with several corporate sponsors including large U.S. banking institutions like Citi Foundation and Capital One, launched Grameen America, based in New York City. Although other programs had been influenced by Grameen's system, this was the first of its kind with a direct input from Yunus himself. In its first four years, Grameen America made loans to more than 9,000 borrowers in excess of $35 million and collected at a 99 percent repayment rate. Grameen America reflects the overall potential for social business and microfinance here and around the world.

In Bangladesh, Yunus started the social business movement though Grameen Bank, but his movement continues to expand. After twenty-five years, the Grameen family of companies has grown to include organizations improving agricultural practices, offering access to health care, developing technology services, providing affordable housing, promoting safety, ensuring good nutrition, and offering educational assistance.

Leveraging Muhammad Yunus' thought leadership continues to inspire and empower. The social business has unlocked economic prosperity, reversed environmental degradation, raised life expectancy rates, and restored human rights in surprising ways that will be discussed in Chapter 6.

CHAPTER SIX

Leveraging Grameen

When Nobel laureate Dr. Muhammad Yunus, the founder of Grameen Bank, and Frank Riboud, the CEO of the French food-products conglomerate Group Danone (known as Dannon in the United States), shook hands in October of 2005, a bargain was struck that would forever change the lives of Bangladeshi children and forge a partnership that would take the social business to a new level. Given their bond of trust, that handshake is all the men would need to commit their organizations to a joint venture and a new company called Grameen Danone. To Yunus' surprise, Riboud shook on the deal before many of the details were even discussed. As far as Riboud was concerned, the bargain was struck as soon as Yunus proposed the idea of manufacturing healthy foods aimed at improving the diets of rural Bangladeshi children at a cost their families could afford. Their simple handshake was based on Grameen Bank's own moral imperative, pursuing risk and reward on the basis of a handshake and the integrity behind it, rather than a bevy of legal documents and the rights and obligations they technically memorialized.

Owing to Grameen Danone's efforts, children in rural Bangladesh have seen a direct improvement in their health. The company's yogurt named Shokti Doi—"Yogurt for Power"—provides children with a natural source of nutrients at a price equivalent to about 7 cents—something even the poor in Bangladesh can afford. Today the joint venture puts enough vitamin A, iron, zinc, and iodine into a 60- or 80-gram cup of yogurt to meet a child's daily needs. But Grameen Danone's impact does not end with the children's health; direct benefits can also be seen along the manufacturing chain. The milk for the yogurt is provided by local farmers, who themselves started their business based on the principles of the social business; the production plants are localized; and the sales teams consist primarily of local women, giving as many local people as possible jobs and the self-sufficiency they represent.

The thriving venture did not occur without its challenges, most significant among them the production of the right product and attracting the right attention for it. Yogurt was already popular in Bangladesh, where children grew up eating an especially sweet variety that did not have the nutrients Danone's offered. The company knew it had its work cut out it for it if it was going to compete in the marketplace. The company had to make sure that its product would not only be acceptable to the children, but also to their mothers. After several trials, Danone developed a recipe that mimicked the level of sweetness the rural children expected and desired, while still being nutritious for them and appealing to their mothers.

Only then did Danone work on product concept and packaging. The decision was made to name the product "Shokti Doi," based on the benefits that the nutrients from the yogurt would provide. A friendly cartoon lion on the package served as a good symbol for the nutrition the yogurt delivered.

With a finished product in which Grameen Danone strongly believed, the company needed a strategy to actually sell the yogurt, and relied on a type of marketing that promoted its social benefits—"cause-related marketing." When adopting a cause-related marketing strategy, companies or organizations associate a brand or product with a specific cause that capitalizes on the consumer's hunger for a social return. Cause-related marketing may be tied to a profit-making initiative or, as here, simply a campaign to raise brand awareness and consumer engagement in a social issue. In fact, true to Professor Yunus' principles, Grameen Danone Foods Ltd. invests all its profits into the creation of new opportunities for the welfare and development of people.

Danone, whose product line also includes global brands like Volvic, Evian, and Activia, has done very well by doing good. For one thing, the company has learned valuable lessons in product development and factory design by selling yogurt to the bottom of the pyramid. As Phillipe Pages, Danone's director of nutrition for emerging markets, told the story in 2010: "Two years ago, I was pushing to have people from the Western world interested in what we're doing. Now I'm bombarded with requests."

For another, the Grameen venture has served as a template for how Danone might push deeper into the developing world. The mass-media celebrity endorsement by Muhammad Yunus has also helped boost the commercial effectiveness of its television advertising.

THE POWER OF CAUSE-RELATED MARKETING

Professor Yunus has now founded more than sixty social businesses in Bangladesh alone, some in collaboration with other international companies like Danone, including Veolia, Intel, Unique, and BASE. Other commercial enterprises may be well advised to follow their powerful example when, like those companies, their interests are carefully and authentically aligned with those of a charity, social enterprise, or cause. Cause-related marketing—most typically characterized by a "commercial co-venturer's" contribution of an agreed portion of a product's sale price to a nonprofit with the expectation that consumers will, for that reason, favor the product—can improve a company's financial results, elevate buyer enthusiasm for both its product and its affiliated social cause, and ultimately boost related revenue. In addition, it can be of value to companies in other ways, including:

- *A direct positive effect on employee recruitment, retention, and production.* Many employees look at the overall culture of a company before deciding to apply for a position, let alone before making the decision to accept a job with the company. A company that demonstrates a commitment to an employee's well-being and the well-being of society is more likely to attract and retain diverse talent and increase productivity with more satisfied employees. Cause-related marketing can thus reflect a company's positive culture and improve its overall performance.

- *A stronger bond with the consumer market and loyal customers.* Consumers take more than price into account when purchasing goods and services. Among the factors they consider are reputation and the values behind the company. A consumer is more likely to buy from a company that seeks to drive positive social change. Through cause-related marketing, a company can project its values, associate itself with causes that are significant to them, and gain loyal customers who feel good about purchasing from a company directly connected to a social cause they care about.

- *Growing the company value and improving investor relations.* A 2013 study by Cone Communications showed that nearly two-thirds of people consider a company's dedication to social causes and societal values before investing their money. Cause-related marketing can attract more investors, shore up support from existing stakeholders, and help a company become more valuable, both by raising its brand perception and by demonstrating a commitment to social causes.

- *Providing an image boost and increased positive publicity.* A company's reputation can mean everything. Striving for positive publicity can be very expensive. Cause marketing, on the other hand, can provide an immediate jolt to a company's reputation through a marketing strategy that allows the market, consumers, and society to build positive publicity for the company. Publicity aligning the company with a social cause can get people talking and the media reporting—which can benefit a company's image, especially when that publicity is associated with the well-being of society.

These benefits are proven to deliver results for a company, as shown in a recent Cone Communications Social Impact Study:

- 80 percent of consumers would switch to a brand that supports a cause, when price and quality are equal.

- 41 percent have bought a product because it was associated with a cause or issue.

- 83 percent wish more of the products, services, and retailers they use would support causes.

- 85 percent have a more positive image of a product or company when it supports a cause they care about.

- 79 percent of employees feel a stronger sense of loyalty to their employer at companies with cause marketing programs.

- 69 percent of employees decide where to work based on a company's support of a cause.

Cause-related marketing presents a unique opportunity for nonprofits to align themselves with for-profit businesses in promoting their social-purpose missions. The pattern is, by now, commonplace: a nonprofit organization and a business enter into a contract to raise money to promote a cause they both support. The Better Business Bureau recommends that, in such contracts, the parties "clearly disclose how the charity benefits from the sale of products or services ... that state or imply that a charity will benefit from a consumer sale or transaction. Such promotions should disclose, at the point of solicitation:

a. the actual or anticipated portion of the purchase price that will benefit the charity (e.g., 5 cents will be contributed to ABC charity for every XYZ company product sold),

b. the duration of the campaign (e.g., the month of October),

c. any maximum or guaranteed minimum contribution amount (e.g., up to a maximum of $200,000)."

Nonprofit organizations and for-profit companies have built strong, multi-year campaigns, taking advantage of cause-related marketing, including some that have branded the for-profits as the lead on a social cause. One prominent example is Yoplait and its "Save Lids to Save Lives" campaign. Yoplait's marketing, which has become one of the world's best-known breast cancer awareness initiatives, asks consumers to save and mail in the by-now well-known pink lids from their yogurt brand, to raise 10 cents apiece in support of the Susan G. Komen for the Cure organization. Yoplait revives the campaign every year and supplements it with sponsorships, donations, and media attention. To date the company has raised millions of dollars for research.

Another highly influential cause-related marketing campaign comes from (PRODUCT)^{RED}. Founded by musician Bono and activist Bobby Shriver, (PRODUCT)^{RED} is a privately held company that licenses itself out in the name of raising money for the Global Fund to Fight AIDS, tuberculosis, and malaria. Companies have partnered with (PRODUCT)^{RED}, and sometimes even with Bono himself through his music. The likes of The Gap, Apple, Armani, Nike, and Starbucks have participated through retail promotions and raised tens of millions of dollars for the cause.

THE GRAMEEN FAMILY EXPANDS

Early on, Professor Muhammad Yunus recognized the advantages of such affiliations. Driven both by the circumstances of the poor villages around his hometown and the early success of Grameen Bank, he and his team began experimenting with other new businesses that, over time, have become a family of companies under the Grameen name.

Operating as social businesses or nonprofits, these companies have had a remarkable impact on the lives of Bangladeshi families and villages. Although each company carries a name that differs slightly from the rest, the larger mission of all the companies remains the same—an effort to pull all Bangladeshis out of poverty, into an economic subsistence level and beyond.

Perhaps the most important of these is Grameen Trust, a nonprofit organization whose mission is to harness the global development community's intense curiosity about the strategies employed by Grameen Bank and to promote microcredit around the world. Because of the effort and attention to detail required not just to create a microcredit program, but to structure one that is poised to succeed, Yunus and his team positioned Grameen Trust to focus solely on new organizations' needs.

Grameen Trust provides consulting, training, evaluation, and monitoring to nascent microcredit programs. In some dire cases, the organization's involvement goes even further, bringing its Bangladeshi team to launch a local program, manage it, and operate it until it achieves sustainability—then ceding control to local operators who will have gained the requisite experience to take over its management. Grameen Trust is credited with assisting hundreds of programs get their start through a process Grameen describes as "replication."

Grameen's replications are by no means limited to the developing world. Perhaps the most notable example is Grameen America, a nonprofit microfinance organization Professor Yunus launched in 2008 at the nadir of the largest financial crisis of modern times. Grameen America provides loans, savings programs, financial education, and credit establishment for American women who live in poverty, but are committed to building their own small businesses. As Yunus observed at the time:

> New York City is the world capital of banking. In these skyscrapers that New York built, they control world finance. What I pointed out is that they do the banking with the world but they don't do the banking with their neighbors. We are here to show that there is nothing wrong with doing banking with neighbors. So we hope we will create some confidence in them. If we change the banks' mind, the whole world will change.

Since that time, Grameen America has expanded its presence throughout New York State and California and in cities in Indiana, Massachusetts, Nebraska, New Jersey, North Carolina, and Texas, each branch supporting women who seek to launch or expand their businesses, typically including food carts, flower stands, tailoring, jewelry and crafts, and salon services. As of the second quarter of 2014, Grameen America had distributed over $171 million in microloans to more than 32,000 women living below the U.S. poverty line. Interestingly, Grameen America and other replications are not affiliated with Grameen Foundations. Instead, they may be viewed as social venture franchises.

SOCIAL VENTURE FRANCHISING

Franchising usually brings to mind franchisors propping up new cookie-cutter restaurants dozens at a time. However, the restaurant industry represents only about 16 percent of the franchising industry, which also includes health care and medicine, education, professional services such as tax preparation, and manufacturing.

Social venture franchising is a groundbreaking, but increasingly attractive business model. As with any franchise, a social venture franchise is a license to market a product or service in a standardized way. It is usually granted in exchange for a set fee, an ongoing percentage of the franchisee's profits, and the franchisee's agreement to uphold the standards of the trademark that the franchise, its owner, may impose. It affords the mission-driven franchisor the opportunity to extend the reach of its social impact while diversifying the sources of its revenue.

For the mission-driven franchisee, the model avoids some of the risks of a new business without sacrificing the personal satisfaction of initiating one's own venture. Its appeal to the franchisee is obvious:

- *Existing goodwill.* The franchisee will be dealing in a proven and well-known socially beneficial product or service. It stands to reason that the franchisee should get off to a faster start and significantly reduce the risk of failure.

- *Relatively small capital investment.* The franchisor will have already undertaken substantial steps in research, marketing, and advertising and the franchisee won't be responsible for most of the costs. What's more, the franchise name might help the franchisee attract financing.

- *Good help from the beginning.* The franchisor may help select the franchisee's location, negotiate the franchisee's lease, raise the franchisee's capital, and supply the franchisee with equipment and a time-tested design for the franchisee's physical layout.

- *Continuing managerial expertise.* The franchisee will benefit from all the franchisor's experience. The franchisee may be offered management assistance, on-site employee training, inventory control aids, accounting help, and more.

- *Mass buying power.* A large franchisor can demand volume discounts and pass them along to the franchisee.

- *Wide-area promotion.* The impact of the franchisor's advertising program may do more for a small social entrepreneur than he could ever afford to do for himself.

The National Center for Charitable Statistics reports that 1.4 million nonprofits in the United States generate 70 percent of their revenue from earned income, yet, in most cases, still do not achieve their revenue targets. Of course, each for-profit venture depends exclusively on earned revenue. At the same time the franchise industry continues to explode, representing more than 3,500 franchisors and 900,000 franchised business units in the United States alone. These "businesses in a box" offer the mission-driven venture a proven earned-income opportunity that dodges many of the impediments startups usually face. For them, the odds of success are improved.

The franchise sensibility is in evidence everywhere throughout the Grameen social empire. Grameen Uddog and Grameen Shamogree are both licensees under the Grameen umbrella, creating jobs and improving the local economy through manufacturing. Bangladesh has a long history of creating textiles, but the local industry has suffered from imports from neighboring countries. With the founding of Grameen Uddog and Grameen Shamogree, many small local weavers were given the resources to create beautiful fabrics in a variety of colors and patterns that suited the local culture, and young Bangladeshis took pride in wearing shirts, saris, and other garments produced by the local fashion industry. With the success of these ventures, competitors emerged with their own textile and garment businesses, creating their own jobs, promoting economic growth, and cultivating pride in locally produced goods that all help raise Bangladeshis out of poverty.

GRAMEEN EMPOWERS ENTREPRENEURS

Creating jobs alone won't alleviate poverty. But promoting economic activity among the poorest may be the most significant impact mission-driven ventures can achieve. For that reason, Grameen Fund, the venture capital arm of Grameen Bank, and Grameen Byabosa Bikash (Business Promotions and Services) were founded to focus solely on entrepreneurship, big and small. Among the private ventures Grameen Fund runs are Grameen Capital Management Limited, Grameen CyberNet Limited, Grameen Bitek Limited, Grameen Solutions Limited (previously known as Grameen Software), Grameen IT Park Limited (also known as DataEdge), Grameen Star Education Limited (which started Grameen-Daffodil IT Education Limited), Grameen Knitwear Limited, GlobeKids Digital Limited, and Rafiq Autovan Manufacturing Industries Limited. These Grameen social businesses were created to contribute to the business infrastructure needed for startups and small businesses to succeed and let people grow out of poverty. The Grameen Fund helps self-employed individuals put together the financing and business models needed to launch their small trades, and Byabosa Bikash serves as a loan guarantor for slightly larger enterprises that are seeking to expand and take the next step in their business's life cycle.

Grameen ventured even further when it opened Grameen Fisheries and Livestock, one of the very first ventures to operate outside of microfinance and within the everyday lives of Bangladeshis. Despite Grameen Bank having no experience with managing fish ponds, the government of Bangladesh convinced Grameen Bank to take over underutilized ponds and try to turn them into economic assets for the villages that surrounded them. The few previous attempts at making use of the ponds saw the process tangled in political corruption and red tape.

Gradually, Grameen was able to hire and train local villagers to raise fish and maintain the ponds, while earning a share of the gross income and benefiting from the food supply. The livestock program was additionally secured through the help of local women who were trained to become dairy farmers and who were taught veterinary care and other support services to manage daily operations.

The program went on to become one of the main dairy suppliers of Grameen Danone's joint yogurt venture. Moreover, Grameen Fisheries and Livestock helped validate the social business model by illustrating how a project can employ local workers to produce goods that can be sold at market prices and used by those workers, among others, for their everyday needs.

The Grameen strategy of collaboration extended still further when Grameen ventured into education systems. Supporting education was always considered a big part of the social philosophy of the organization, so Grameen decided to try to do something about it. Some of the educational needs in the Bangladeshi villages were glaringly obvious: for example, many of the women borrowers from the bank were illiterate and could not even sign their own names. Grameen Shikkha, founded to promote education not just for youth but also for adults, started with this very basic goal—teaching villagers to write their own names. Despite how simple it sounds, in a community where education and literacy for women were never emphasized, learning to write one's own name brought a great sense of confidence to borrowers, self-empowerment that seeped into other facets of their lives, including their small businesses.

Grameen Shikkha followed that effort with a focus on other basics like learning the alphabet and counting, before formulating the Scholarship Management Program, specifically designed to assist poor Bangladeshi families to overcome the economic barriers that prevent their children from attending school. In order for the program to work, Grameen needed to convince the families to forego any potential income the children could generate by working instead of attending school. Child labor was an important part of a family's income in Bangladesh. To counter that reality by creating an incentive for children to go to school, the program invested scholarship money in a time deposit with a guaranteed 6 percent annual return to fund the child's upkeep while he or she went to school. This ensured that the child had financial value while remaining in school and discouraged the family from pulling the child out for full-time work instead. Since its inception, Grameen Shikkha has helped thousands of students obtain a basic education and beyond, for as little as a few hundred dollars each.

Grameen understands that education can be the tool to empower the next generation of Bangladeshis to growing the country's economy. It also understands that providing a better living standard starts with a higher quality of health care. The staggering cost of health care in Bangladesh is a common cause of poverty, always leaving the poor a step behind. Grameen saw this as an opportunity to create Grameen Kalyan and Grameen Health Care Services, providing good quality, affordable health care for villagers as well as those involved in the family of Grameen franchises and social businesses.

Grameen set up local health clinics affiliated with Grameen Bank branches that helped finance them. The health clinics aim to be self-sustaining with income generated from franchises. Through Health Care Services, Grameen has also targeted eye and pregnancy care, two topics about which the villagers lack knowledge and training.

These are just some of the Grameen family of companies that are continuing to grow and positively impact the lives of millions. Through its global system, Grameen has been able to attract the funding it has needed without promising anything more than a return of one's initial investment. The Grameen companies embody a near-perfect example of the philosophy behind social venture franchising: support from the top and a shared vision can have a sustainable, long-term positive impact.

Social businesses have empowered Bangladeshi villagers and social business owners everywhere to become more self-sufficient than anyone might have imagined. Starting in 2014, Muhammad Yunus' Yunus Social Business Global Initiatives launched a unique series of global incubator funds. Built on the proposition that "A charity dollar has only one life. A Social Business dollar can be invested over and over again," the funds, supported by impact investors who forego financial returns, provide debt and equity financing and coaching to worthy social businesses in target countries with the singular goal of solving human problems. The credit belongs to Yunus himself, the banker to the poor and thought leader without peer who mastered the art of leverage and the leveraging of inspiration.

CHAPTER SEVEN

The Mondragón Miracle

Scaling the Peaks Beyond the Pyrenees

Spain's Basque country is nestled in the western foothills of the majestic Pyrenees mountains, which straddle the country's border with France. The people of the region, the oldest surviving ethnic group in Europe, are unique. Their language, now in decline, is unrelated to any other, current or extinct. Their traditional music is played on the txalaparta, their own version of a wooden xylophone. Their sports include stone-dragging with oxen and pelota, a bat-and-basket game you're unlikely to see elsewhere. And, as one might expect, their cuisine boasts cod, bream, and hake from the contiguous Bay of Biscay, but also txikiteos, a bar-hopping ritual that involves eating miniature hors d'oeuvres called pintxos while drinking small glasses of wine called txikitos.

The Basque region has always been favored by nature. The area is rich in coal, silver, iron, sugar, and other resources. For centuries, its traders found it easier to sail north to England than ride horses over the 10,000-foot mountains that separate Basque country from the Spanish capital. The Basques' commercial connection to England exposed them to the Industrial Revolution long before it touched other regions of Spain.

So it should come as no surprise that the Basque region is best known by some for its economic and social innovation. But one might never guess that José María Arizmendiarrieta (sometimes called Arizmedi), a young and idealistic Catholic priest who established a polytechnic school in Mondragón more than seventy years ago, would alter the lives of hundreds of thousands of workers throughout the world.

Mondragón was once a thriving manufacturing center, but the Basque people were targeted for especially harsh treatment in the 1930s by Generalissimo Francisco Franco and his fascist party. By the time Don José María arrived there in 1941, the Spanish Civil War had taken its tragic toll on the 7,000 Basques who called the town home, but suffered in unspeakable poverty, hunger, exile, and despair. Arizmendiarrieta's technical college would impart technical knowledge and humanistic values to generations of local managers, engineers, and skilled laborers who honed their skills and learned their trades in harmony with traditional Catholic teachings.

The school took its rightful place in history when, in 1956, it went on to launch a worker-owned co-operative, a stove factory which, thanks to both serendipity and intention, was to become the antecedent of the Mondragón worker co-operatives, the largest employee-owned business in the world, whose industrial, financial, and retail concerns today employ an astonishing total of nearly 100,000 people. Over 260 companies, including more than 120 worker-owned co-operatives in and around the town of Mondragón, have pooled their resources through the Mondragón Cooperative Corporation, creating wealth and achieving the economies of scale that allow the stronger ventures to compete aggressively in the expanding world economy while supporting the weaker ventures, including those that might not otherwise survive economic downturns.

The Mondragón strategy, now a model of thought leadership for hundreds of worker-owned companies outside Spain, is itself based on an earlier European collaboration, the Rochdale Society of Equitable Pioneers, often credited as the first worker-owned co-operative anywhere, at least in modern times. The Rochdale Society, founded in Rochdale, England, in 1844, brought together twenty-eight artisans, each contributing a single pound sterling to capitalize a store that would sell their goods, ironically, goods priced beyond their own financial reach. The store quickly earned a reputation for high-quality merchandise and sparked a co-operative movement, first in England where, by the mid-1850s, 1,000 co-ops had been organized, and then throughout the globe. To this day the Rochdale Society's "Principles," which inform the way in which virtually all co-operatives run their affairs, have morphed into a "Statement on the Co-Operative Identity" adopted by the International Co-Operative Alliance in 1937, and later by the Mondragón co-operatives.

International Co-Operative Alliance's Statement on the Co-Operative Identity

Definition

A co-operative is an autonomous association of persons united voluntarily to meet their common economic, social, and cultural needs and aspirations through a jointly owned and democratically controlled enterprise.

Values

Co-operatives are based on the values of self-help, self-responsibility, democracy, equality, equity, and solidarity. In the tradition of their founders, co-operative members believe in the ethical values of honesty, openness, social responsibility, and caring for others.

Principles

The co-operative principles are guidelines by which co-operatives put their values into practice.

First Principle: Voluntary and Open Membership

Co-operatives are voluntary organizations, open to all persons able to use their services and willing to accept the responsibilities of membership, without gender, social, racial, political, or religious discrimination.

Second Principle: Democratic Member Control

Co-operatives are democratic organizations controlled by their members, who actively participate in setting their policies and making decisions. Men and women serving as elected representatives are accountable to the membership. In primary co-operatives, members have equal voting rights (one member, one vote), and co-operatives at other levels are also organized in a democratic manner.

Third Principle: Member Economic Participation

Members contribute equitably to, and democratically control, the capital of their co-operative. At least part of that capital is usually the common property of the co-operative. Members usually receive limited compensation, if any, on capital subscribed as a condition of membership. Members allocate surpluses for any or all of the following purposes: developing their co-operative, possibly by setting up reserves, part of which at least would be indivisible; benefiting members in proportion to their transactions with the co-operative; and supporting other activities approved by the membership.

Fourth Principle: Autonomy and Independence

Co-operatives are autonomous, self-help organizations controlled by their members. If they enter into agreements with other organizations, including governments, or raise capital from external sources, they do so on terms that ensure democratic control by their members and maintain their co-operative autonomy.

Fifth Principle: Education, Training, and Information

Co-operatives provide education and training for their members, elected representatives, managers, and employees so they can contribute effectively to the development of their co-operatives. They inform the general public—particularly young people and opinion leaders—about the nature and benefits of co-operation.

Sixth Principle: Co-Operation Among Co-Operatives

Co-operatives serve their members most effectively and strengthen the co-operative movement by working together through local, national, regional, and international structures.

Seventh Principle: Concern for Community

Co-operatives work for the sustainable development of their communities through policies approved by their members.

The success that the Mondragón co-ops increasingly enjoy is the product of a fortuitous combination of Don José María's charismatic leadership, socioeconomic imperatives, an unwavering commitment to social justice, and a durable yet flexible governance and financial system that ensures the alignment of stakeholder interests.

Much of the success of the Mondragón co-ops can be attributed to their ability to finance themselves internally. A part of the explanation is that each co-op allocates only a portion of its retained earnings—its "patronage dividend"—to its employee workers. The balance of the co-op's retained earnings goes into a consolidated account owned by all the co-op's employees. The individual accounts become available to each employee at retirement, but the consolidated account remains the co-op's, wealth transferred as a sacred trust from each generation of workers to the next.

But the co-ops can also finance their own activities because they have their own bank, Caja Laboral Popular, which provides financing for both working capital and new investment. Caja Laboral, now one of Spain's largest banks and certainly its most successful credit co-operative, is owned and controlled by its depositors, mostly worker-owned enterprises and their workers. The bank is a friendly and ready source of capital at commercial bank rates. In addition, Mondragón's businesses are linked through second-degree co-operatives, which provide social security, health benefits, and unemployment insurance for their members.

The Mondragón network's capital policies and entrepreneurial spirit effectively guarantee the co-ops' workers lifetime employment. Even if a co-op were to fail, another Mondragón co-op stands ready, willing and able to hire its workers.

The co-ops' use of capital also guarantees that profits aren't diverted to fat cat executives or venture capitalists. Instead, earnings are democratically distributed, reserved as seed corn for new businesses, shared with regional nonprofits, and pooled into shared institutions, including an accredited university and a research center. The members of each co-op thus see benefits from the financial stability and growth of all the co-ops.

The co-operatives' commitment to job security operates within and across its co-ops, in an open and transparent way deliberately calculated to minimize hardship. If one co-op needs more workers and another fewer, democratic rules provide for a shift in manpower. Since other rules require the sourcing of inputs from the best and least costly suppliers, whether a Mondragón-affiliated co-op or not, Mondragón enterprises are held to the highest, most accountable standards at the cutting edge of new technologies, with state-of-the art research and development funded by a portion of every enterprise's net revenue.

Mondragón's workers collectively select, hire, and fire their directors. For that reason, top-paid workers earn only 6.5 times the lowest-paid workers' pay. Compare that with the American and other capitalist systems. U.S. CEOs saw their pay spike 15 percent in 2011, following a 28 percent jump in compensation the year before, according to a GMI report cited by *The Guardian*. The CEOs' pay continues to climb at a seemingly unstoppable pace: according to research conducted for *The New York Times* by Equilar Inc., the executive compensation analysis firm, the 2012 median pay package for the top 200 chief executives at U.S. public companies with at least $1 billion in revenue was $15.1 million, representing a jump of 16 percent over their 2011 compensation. Yet, rank-and-file American workers saw their inflation-adjusted wages decline 2 percent in 2011, according to the U.S. Department of Labor. The trend goes back at least three decades. An Economic Policy Institute study reports that CEO pay grew a whopping 127 times faster than worker pay between 1978 and 2011 while, according to the Federal Reserve Bank of St. Louis, workers nearly doubled their productivity during the same period.

CEOs and their friends in American executive suites continue to pocket increasingly larger shares of company gains: in 2011, U.S. CEOs earned 209.4 times more than American workers, compared to 21.5 times more in 1978. By contrast, Mondragón's co-operatives pay-equity rules contribute to the larger society with far greater income and wealth equality than is found elsewhere in the developed world. Yet the Mondragón network, now operating seventy-seven businesses outside of Spain, effectively competes on equal footing with companies all over the world.

All of Mondragón's co-operative businesses are formed into federations, both geographic and sectoral, to capture economies of scale and collectively pursue the planning and development of the growing opportunities they share. By any measure, the system clearly works: the Mondragón network, both democratic and humanistic, is the fourth largest industrial and seventh largest financial group in Spain, boasting annual sales of €14 billion.

Over time, the Mondragón co-operatives' biggest success may lie in the lessons they continue to teach those who replicate their remarkable business model.

ITALY'S "SOCIAL CO-OPERATIVES"

Italy, like Spain, now enshrines support for co-operatives in its Constitution, which provides that "the Republic recognizes the social function of co-operation with a mutually supportive, non-speculative nature. The law promotes and encourages cooperation through appropriate means and ensures its character and purposes through appropriate checks." Italy's policies give meaning to the mandate. By law, a co-op's profits are exempt from income tax as long as 30 percent or more of its profits are allocated to the co-op's "indivisible" reserve. Regional economic development agencies provide technical assistance to co-ops. The government helps capitalize co-operatives with development funds earmarked to create new co-ops, develop existing ones, and convert private firms into worker-owned co-ops.

Small "social co-operatives," conceived to furnish welfare services to the "economically weaker layers of society," are the largest category of worker-owned co-operative in Italy and are gaining popularity throughout the European Union. Under the 1991 Italian law that defined the form, social co-operatives infuse business operations with social goals, as is the case with all mission-driven ventures. What's unusual is the social co-operative's universe of stakeholders, typically including not only its workers and beneficiaries, but often volunteer members as well.

A social co-operative may provide health, social, or educational services, or may seek to integrate physically and mentally disabled people, drug and alcohol addicts, or ex-offenders into the labor market. Members may include paid employees, beneficiaries, investors, public institutions, and volunteers who can constitute as much as half the membership. At least 30 percent of members of a social co-operative with a workforce development mission must be individuals in the targeted population.

The social co-operative offers its members democracy rights (the one person–one vote rule prevails) and limited liability. No more than 80 percent of profits may be distributed to members (but nothing at all upon dissolution), and interest payments are limited to the prevailing bond rate. They are relieved of social insurance charges, but otherwise gain no government subsidy.

Social co-operatives are believed to have an advantage over many nonprofits, because they have access to the financial markets, roots in the community, and a market orientation as they seek to win the contracts they'll need to survive. They also are seen by some as enjoying benefits unavailable to most other for-profits, given their ability to tap into lower-cost sources of productivity, including voluntary work and donations. The social co-operative offers a promising opportunity to transform public welfare systems while fostering local development for job creation, social capital, and cohesion and the growth of the third sector.

FRANCE'S "SCOPs"

The French worker-owned co-op, or "SCOP" ("Société coopérative et participative"), shares familial characteristics with its Spanish and Italian cousins.

SCOPs, consisting primarily of professionals and skilled tradesmen, mostly construction workers, are required to vest financial and governance control in their members. Workers must own at least 51 percent of the capital and have 65 percent of the votes, flexibility allowing outsiders to invest capital and exercise some external control. It's largely because of the form's financial sophistication that it enjoys the success it does: French law preserves the principle of indivisible reserves, requiring that at least 15 percent of surpluses are permanently owned by the co-op. Moreover, at least 25 percent of surpluses are allocated to all employees, members among them, helping ensure both the equitable distributions of profits and the independence and sustainability of the co-op.

SCOPs are required by law to finance France's worker-owned co-op movement: 0.42 percent of SCOP revenues are shared among federations of worker-owned co-ops that provide financial services and technical assistance to them (a SCOP is said never to be alone) and financial institutions, including SOCODEN (Société coopérative de dévelopement et d'entraide), which offers co-ops equity loans, loan guarantees, and financing for working capital requirements.

Worker-owned co-ops receive tax benefits from the French government. SCOPs are not only exempt from the "professional tax," 1.5 to 2.5 percent of revenues, but income on worker shares is also exempt from income taxes.

WHY WORKER-OWNED CO-OPS SUCCEED

The worker-owned co-ops of Mondragón, Italy, and France share features that help explain their success. Each of them has access to capital and supportive technical assistance. Each is subject to a legally mandated indivisible reserve, with the balance of profits required to be shared with employees. Each has strong federated associations funded in part by member dues. Each is largely organized by industry, affording it ready access to technical expertise along with economies of scale. Each prizes solidarity and cooperation. And each has achieved critical mass sufficient to earn the respect of both governments and the public.

But Mondragón rightly claims first position in thought leadership. As Dr. David Ellerman, an expert on workplace democracy and a founder of the Industrial Co-Operative Association, persuasively made the case (as quoted in Bonnie Richley's doctoral dissertation published by Case Western Reserve University in 2009):

> [Mondragón] basically shows that there is an alternative way to organize the workplace and contribute to society. You always have dreamers and many ideas, and you do not know which one works. Here you have an example of one that works, and it is not just candies and sweets, it is technologically sophisticated products and that's remarkable . . . and part of it is the way they have driven this whole regional development in the Mondragón region . . . and that is a model that other people in the world could learn from . . .
>
> One reason Mondragón is so important is that it shows a real alternative, and they know the question of how to get from here to there . . . it can be done elsewhere.

THE EVERGREEN COOPERATIVES BUILD ON MONDRAGÓN'S SUCCESS

Perhaps the most compelling example is Cleveland's Evergreen Cooperatives, which the leaders of the Mondragón Co-Operative Corporation have themselves described with admiration as the "point of reference for all cooperative development in North America."

The Evergreen Cooperatives, inspired by Mondragón's grand experiment, are enjoying their own success, success still others are replicating. They create wealth and jobs in poverty-stricken, Rustbelt communities by selling sustainable goods and services to "anchor" institutions—local universities and hospitals, "eds and meds" for short—which spend billions of dollars on them every year, little of which has historically remained in Cleveland's poorest neighborhoods to fuel their revitalization. Evergreen is an unprecedented partnership among the Cleveland Foundation, the Democracy Collaborative at the University of Maryland, the Employee Ownership Center at Kent State University, and the place-based institutions of Cleveland's Greater University Circle.

Cleveland, a victim of de-industrialization, was ripe for such innovation. Northeast Ohio was under enormous economic and social pressure. By 2011 the city's population had dropped below 400,000, its lowest population in a century, representing a 17 percent decline since 2000. Policymakers were desperate. Cleveland's mayor, Frank G. Jackson, put it this way: "We need to create economic stability and sustainability in the region and ensure inclusion is a central part of that sustainable process. And it doesn't matter to me who does it."

Anchor institutions proved to be one obvious choice, so the Evergreen Cooperatives tap into the purchasing needs not only of eds and meds, but also of health care facilities such as nursing homes, cultural institutions, and municipal governments.

Moreover, the cooperatives are beneficiaries of Cleveland's "buy local" strategy, which encourages eds and meds to procure and invest in the community. University Hospital's "Vision 2010," for example, successfully captured almost all of a $1.2 billion construction and procurement initiative for the region's economy, still benefiting more than 100 businesses owned by women.

The Evergreen Cooperatives—fifteen or so of them will have been organized by 2015—are owned and operated by Greater University Circle residents who see Cleveland's anchor institutions as a stable and attractive market and recognize the anchors' growing commitment to sustainability. Rejecting trickle-down economics, Evergreen promotes the building of a local economy from the ground up, capturing its fair share of the green economy along the way. It's creating living-wage jobs in six low-income neighborhoods with 43,000 residents, jobs at businesses that workers own.

Cleveland's—and the nation's—universities and hospitals are a potent economic force. According to David Schwartz, campaign director for the Real Food Challenge, U.S. colleges and universities spend at least $5 billion a year just on food. The Center for Medicare and Medical Services reported in 2011 that the combined annual purchasing power of the 6,000 U.S. hospitals exceeded $750 billion. Together, hospitals and universities account for more than $1 trillion of the $15 trillion American economy, employ 8 percent of the nation's workforce, and control more than half a trillion dollars in endorsement investments. The purchasing decisions of universities and hospitals can be leveraged to reduce waste, reward durability, minimize environmental hazards and toxins, increase the use and market for recycled materials, energize distressed communities, and create living-wage jobs. That's exactly what the Evergreen Cooperatives are doing.

Evergreen's maiden venture, its cooperative laundry, opened its Leadership in Energy and Environmental Design (LEED) gold doors in October of 2009. An affordable, green laundry service for local institutions, The Evergreen Cooperatives Laundry was funded in part by a long-term, low-interest federal loan facilitated by the city's Economic Development Department, which also helped structure a $5 million New Market Tax Credit deal.

Evergreen's cooperatives typically seek such public subsidies, readily available to them since they hire from poor communities and locate their businesses there. While the lower cost of capital affords the co-ops a competitive advantage—allowing them to invest in state-of-the-art equipment and to bring in new clients at a fast clip, and with them, new workers—the co-ops strive for self-sufficiency and seek to grow beyond any need for subsidy.

The laundry was followed in quick succession by Ohio Cooperative Solar (OCS) and then by Green City Grocers Cooperative, both ventures providing competitively priced, yet profitable products and services to their anchor institution customers while sustainably building community-based wealth.

OCS maintains photovoltaic arrays on its customers' buildings and sells the power it generates to those customers at a fixed rate over a long term. The customers—including Cleveland Clinic, the city's largest private employer, University Hospitals, Case Western Reserve University, and the nearby city of Euclid—not only save money through the arrangement, but they avoid tying up capital, thereby more easily achieving their own social and environmental missions. A supply chain thus becomes a value chain. For the co-op's part, the guaranteed revenue from creditworthy obligors supports bank loans, obviating any long-term need to rely on philanthropic and government support.

When City Grocers opened its doors, it was the largest hydroponic project in any American city, producing four million heads of lettuce and 300,000 pounds of herbs in a four-acre greenhouse. Its customers—Greater University Circle's hospitals and schools as well as grocery chains and food service companies as far as 150 miles away—had previously imported their produce from California, Hawaii, and even Colombia, but now find Green City Grocers' value proposition irresistible.

The Mondragón model is everywhere in evidence. Both efforts are committed to a culture of solidarity, collective wealth creation, and well-being. In the words of Ted Howard, the Democracy Collaborative's visionary co-founder and a key strategic thinker behind the Evergreen initiative, "What we have learned from Mondragón is a way of relating to capital, a sense of our responsibility as stewards of it." For that reason, Evergreen pursues a long-term, inter-generational mission built on sustainability.

As Mondragón's highest paid employees earn no more than 6.5 times the earnings of its lowest paid workers, the chief executive of an Evergreen co-op can earn no more than five times the lowest-paid entry-level worker's salary. Six months later, he or she will be admitted as a co-op member, automatically receive a $2-per-hour raise, and qualify for fully employer-paid health care.

As the Mondragón Cooperative Corporation ties together and sustainably supports a growing network of cooperatives, the Evergreen Cooperative Corporation (ECC), a §501(c)(3) "holding company," has been established in Cleveland to offer shared services for the Evergreen co-ops, an Evergreen Land Trust, and a revamped Evergreen Cooperative Development Fund. ECC's nine-person board includes executives from anchor initiatives, representatives of each of the co-ops, financial professionals, and leaders of the Cleveland Foundation. In turn, the ECC has a seat on each co-op board and owns 20 percent of all of them, the corporation's veto right ensuring that no co-op will exit the system or jeopardize the viability of the other co-ops. So the nonprofit's "golden share" guarantees that the Evergreen vision won't be undercut by a risky decision, however well-intentioned, by any of the growing roster of Evergreen co-ops.

All the cooperatives are also protected from the failure of any one of them—or the possibility that a co-op might try to "demutualize"—by an ingenious real estate model that separates land ownership from building ownership. The Evergreen Land Trust, a limited liability company, acquires land for each of the Evergreen co-ops, which then enters into a ninety-nine-year land lease with the Trust. While the co-ops own and manage their own buildings, the rents they pay on the land they lease are tied to an economic index or the co-op's profitability. Should a co-op fail, the Trust can step in and stall or avert foreclosure and, as the owner of the underlying land, is in the strongest possible position to cut a new and better deal with the mortgage lender.

Lillian Kuri, the program director for Architecture, Urban Design, and Sustainable Development at the Cleveland Foundation, reports that the Greater University Circle initiative continues to consider innovative ways to share wealth, including micro-enterprises and the purchase of private companies from retiring owners for the purpose of converting them into employee-owned ventures. While she acknowledges that the Evergreen model on its own may not be scalable at a fast enough clip to meaningfully reduce local poverty levels, she sees that the strategy has catalyzed other economic development and remains committed to the Evergreen ambition: "Our goal is equitable wealth creation at scale."

Indeed, The Evergreen Cooperative Development Fund provides seed funding to other green cooperatives in the Cleveland area. Evergreen's mission is clear—to leverage the vast resources that flow through eds and meds to build community wealth through local purchasing, hiring, real estate development, and investment; to capitalize on the federal push for green jobs; to lead by example; and to scale the legacy of a pious innovator who in the middle of the last century precipitated the launch of a workforce-development social enterprise long before those words had ever been uttered.

CHAPTER EIGHT

Social Impact Bonds

Aligning Financial and Social Returns

The residents of Peterborough, a resilient "heritage city" standing on the River Nene 45 miles north of London in the heart of rural East England, proudly trace their roots to a settlement pre-dating the Bronze Age. This is where archaeologists unearthed what they believe to be the oldest wheel in Britain. Peterborough is also the site of the ancient Cathedral Church of Saint Peter, Saint Paul, and Saint Andrew, a Norman church without architectural precedent but distinguished as the burial place of two queens—Mary Queen of Scots, whose remains were later removed by her son James I to Westminster Abbey when he became King of England, and Catherine of Aragon, resting at the Cathedral Church to this day.

The people of Peterborough, numbering fewer than 200,000, glory in their storied history, but they also eagerly anticipate the promise of tomorrow. The city has been designated an "environment city," one of only four in the U.K., and it alone is seen as its inevitable "environment capital," already boasting the largest mix of environmental businesses in the nation. Peterborough's destiny is bolstered by a £1 billion redevelopment initiative that has attracted service-sector companies to the city, replacing manufacturing concerns that have shuttered in Peterborough, as elsewhere, along with a realistic hope for urban regeneration.

Yet Peterborough's reputation has suffered from a singular blot. In 2008 Her Majesty's Prison Peterborough was ranked dead last, 132nd out of 132 prisons and prison clusters in England and Wales, in six performance categories, including re-offending, organizational effectiveness, and "decency." To their credit, British policymakers, unwilling to accept Peterborough Prison's failure, took innovative steps in 2010 to turn the prison around, steps other countries around the world, the United States among them, are closely watching and already following.

FUNDING TARGETED INTERVENTION STRATEGIES

By no means is the problem of recidivism unique to Peterborough Prison. Every year 60,000 prisoners re-enter British society after serving sentences of less than one year; and 60 percent of them re-offend, many losing their freedom again within twelve months. Every short-term prisoner who re-offended after being released in 2007 was convicted, on average, five more times within a year. This tragic cycle has contributed to a ballooning of the U.K.'s prison population, which nearly doubled between 1992 and 2010, at enormous costs to the criminal justice system, British taxpayers, and society at large. But the prisoners themselves suffer the most. Their human potential has been stifled because the public sector lacks the resources to fund their rehabilitation. Dame Anne Owers, a former Chief Inspector of Prisons, put it well: "We know that prisons have revolving doors and the reason is because the problems that people had before they went to prison are the same problems they encounter after they leave prison. If you don't deal with the before and the after, then all you create is a circle."

Nonprofit organizations have empirically demonstrated that investments in targeted intervention strategies work. Forty-eight percent of the ex-offenders who participated in Blue Sky's workforce development initiative found full-time, long-term employment. Seventy-two percent of the graduates of RAPt's intensive drug treatment program were not re-convicted within twelve months of their release. And St. Giles Trust's ex-offenders' mentoring program has been shown to reduce recidivism by 40 percent.

Yet, the public funds that would likely drive down the rate and costs of re-offending are tough for appropriators to justify. For one thing, any cost savings that might be realized are not immediate and, consequently, cannot be shifted to current preventive programming. For another, if such interventions were to prove ineffective, the taxpayer would be doubly burdened—once with the costs of the failed intervention and then with the costs of the second incarceration.

For those reasons, the pilot project at Peterborough Prison didn't depend on government funding. Instead, this grand social experiment relied on the private sector to invest in social innovation not constrained by government regulation. The first "Social Impact Bond" contract was inked by then-Justice Secretary Jack Straw in March of 2010. Between then and September of that year when the initiative was launched, Social Finance, the nonprofit organization managing the initiative, raised £5 million from seventeen social investors in the U.K. and the U.S., including the Rockefeller Foundation, to fund comprehensive supportive programming for 3,000 male prisoners leaving Peterborough Prison after serving short sentences. The programming included support in prison and in the community by St. Giles Trust, support for prisoners' families by Ormiston Trust, and longer-term support by the YMCA.

The investors, looking to generate both social impact and financial returns on their investments, were not funding good intentions, hard work, or lofty promises. The Peterborough Prison pilot was all about genuine outcomes. Rockefeller and its co-investors were to receive a return on their money only if re-convictions dropped 7.5 percent, and investors would earn a "bonus" of no more than 13 percent per year over an eight-year period. The maximum return was only to be paid if recidivism was reduced by at least 10 percent more than at other prisons with similar populations. Returns to investors were to be funded by the U.K.'s Ministry of Justice and its Big Lottery Fund out of the savings the penal system realized. But if re-offending rates did not come down more in Peterborough than in other similar prisons, the government would pay nothing at all and the investors' money would be lost.

The Social Impact Bond wasn't really a bond; it was a futures contract on social outcomes. Although its investment returns to impact investors were capped much as a bond's returns are, those returns were to be tied to performance much the way an equity investment works.

The "Bond" was to finance the multi-year gap from the time a service provider incurs expenses until the government's success payments are eventually made. The Bond also assumed the risk that those payments might never be made.

How the Peterborough Social Impact Bond Worked

1. The government contracts to pay for better social outcomes.

2. Impact investors provide the cash.

3. The investment capital funds innovative intervention strategies.

4. The investors get their money back only if the interventions pay off through improved social outcomes.

5. Financial returns are linked to social returns.

The Social Impact Bond was elegant in its design. By aligning the investors' stake with social returns, the instrument could effectively finance long-term social action to reduce re-offending rates. Inconsistently funded, piecemeal programs were replaced by cohesive strategies. Government contracts that simplistically treat all prisoners alike were replaced by prisoner-specific services and systematic strategies. The focus moved from immediate, but illusory outputs to sustainable rehabilitation. Service providers and offenders were given the time they needed for training, skills, and recovery to be nurtured.

How Cash Flows

1. A bond-issuing organization raises money from private-sector investors.

2. That money is distributed to service providers to cover their operating costs.

3. If measurable social outcomes are achieved as agreed, the government makes payments to the bond-issuing organization.

4. Those payments are used to make investors whole—and to reward them if social outcomes exceed agreed targets.

The most obvious, but often neglected interactions with prisoners before and upon their release—such as supporting them as they exit the prison gates—can positively impact their actions and break the cycle of re-offending. Consider the testimony of John, who had been in and out of prison since age fourteen. He was interviewed by Social Finance Ltd. personnel shortly after his release from Peterborough Prison and quoted in the organization's November 2011 newsletter.

> ... To begin with I stole things because I knew my mum couldn't afford them. Trainers and luxury stuff. If I'm honest I also got a buzz from it. It wasn't like I was in a crowd of people all doing crime, I wasn't.
>
> I've always lived around Peterborough. I've not thought about going anywhere else. The car park is the furthest I've been! I'm still in touch with my mum which is good but I can't live there. When I was 18 I started using drugs and things changed. I began stealing things because I needed the money to feed my habit. I've been in prison on and off for the last ten years.
>
> The council found me a flat a year or two ago. I thought because they got me the flat they'd have done all their own housing benefit forms and that but apparently they didn't. No forms were filled in or anything and I owed £1,600. I couldn't pay it so I gave them the keys back. I was on the gear (drugs). I can't really read or write.
>
> Since then I've been in prison or on the streets or dossing [rooming] with a mate here and there, well not mates really, just other users. It's no good. I shouldn't be hanging about with them. This time I stole from an undercover police car and got a 20 weeks sentence.
>
> Every other time I've left jail I head into town with my discharge money and buy gear. Straight away. It's never been like this, where someone meets me. I know it's only been like a day or two but it's all different already. I'd be sleeping rough right now but instead I've been in temporary accommodation. I'm so grateful, it's all different. I don't know anyone else in the place where I'm staying so that's a really good thing. I'm doing good stuff with these people. This is new for me.

But the Peterborough Prison pilot was abruptly terminated in April of 2014, shifting into a model whereby tailored support to their prisoners one year after their release would continue to be offered on a fee-for-service basis by the St. Giles Trust, Ormiston Families, MIND, YMCA, and John Lang Training—the same service providers that participated in the pilot—but without the outcomes payment that distinguished the experiment. When the experiment was halted, it had already reduced reoffending by 8.4 percent (from an eye-watering 155 reconvictions per 100 prisoners to 142 reconvictions), and Social Finance, Ltd., was confident that even better results would be achieved over time.

Some might see the Ministry of Justice's abandonment of the Peterborough Social Impact Bond as a vote of no confidence in the strategy. Yet the evidence is clearly to the contrary: the very announcement that a different funding arrangement would be pursued acknowledges a steep drop in re-offending by the first cohort of prisoners who benefited from the rehabilitation support the experiment made available to them. It was only because the United Kingdom broadly embraced a new strategic opportunity, "Transforming Rehabilitation," which promotes wider privatization and cost reduction along with rehabilitation, that the Social Impact Bond trial was cut short.

Ironically, the U.K.'s last-in-class prison, an unhappy footnote to Peterborough's otherwise laudable story of self-renewal, has earned acclaim as a beta site for social innovation. Indeed, thanks in part to the Peterborough Social Impact Bond, a new statutory obligation has been enacted in the United Kingdom, requiring that short-sentence offenders gain access to rehabilitation support. Undaunted by the shift in British policy, the Social Impact Bond continues to have enormous potential, even beyond the funding of interventions intended to curb re-offending. The investment model presents an unprecedented opportunity to afford successful nonprofit organizations pursuing a variety of missions a long-term and reliable revenue stream, allowing them to compete in the capital markets based on the social value they create. In doing so, they can develop empirical evidence to support successful techniques and engage the impact investor to scale effective social innovation.

But the Social Impact Bond, as versatile as it is, can't be expected to address every social problem. One couldn't imagine private investment funding multi-million-dollar experiments in public education or Medicaid. And even where an intelligent intervention leads to better social outcomes, challenges in measuring results or attributing impact might rule out such a strategy.

Indeed, incentive-based payment systems can present significant challenges. Service providers may demand outsized budgets to take on the risks of performance, especially when outcomes are determined in part by factors outside their control. Incentives are strong to manipulate outcomes lest funding evaporate. Worse still, service providers that fail to meet performance targets could decide to cut their losses by shutting the program down, stranding the very people the program seeks to benefit. For those reasons, investors and bond-issuing organizations may see it as in their best interest to offer carefully designed, incentive-based contracts to their service providers.

Nonetheless, the Social Impact Bond can deliver significant benefits to governments and impact investors alike when a credible, neutral authority measures outcomes and resolves disputes. Fundamentally, though, only those interventions should be supported:

- That are likely to achieve success in light of historic evidence,
- Whose measurable outcomes are based on reliable data and reasonable evaluation methods,
- That are directed by expert managers willing to adjust their operating assumptions as facts unfold, and
- Where the government would realize significant savings if anticipated social impact is achieved.

These criteria suggest several other prevention approaches that might attract Social Impact Bond financing. In each case, social impact might be replicated and scaled, and government savings realized. Beyond multi-system therapies that reduce recidivism by offenders such as those being tested in Peterborough, such approaches include:

- Early childhood interventions that reduce costly long-term special education placements of children whose mild learning disabilities or behavioral problems could be better treated early on;

- Summer academic programs for disadvantaged students that accelerate and maintain academic gains;
- Elder-care services that reduce the number of elderly who are inappropriately placed in costly nursing homes; and
- Transition services for youth with disabilities that enable young people to enter postsecondary education and obtain employment.

"PAY FOR SUCCESS"

The Social Impact Bond's American cousin, the "Pay for Success" contract, was introduced in President Barack Obama's ill-fated fiscal year 2012 budget message in which he proposed that $100 million be invested in projects in seven pilot areas, including job training, education, juvenile justice, and the care of children with disabilities. Although the President's budget was never passed, the Pay for Success principle nevertheless has been embraced by federal and state policymakers. The concept is the same as the Social Impact Bond, so the terms are used interchangeably in this book.

In January 2012, the White House quietly let it be known that the federal government would fund Pay for Success projects supporting vulnerable populations through the U.S. Departments of Justice and Labor. The Department of Justice was to give funding priority to Second Chance Act grant solicitations from Pay for Success applicants seeking to improve outcomes for people returning to their communities from prisons and jails, and the Department of Labor would make up to $20 million available for Pay for Success programs focusing on employment and training outcomes through the Workforce Innovation Fund. Other federal agencies would soon follow suit. The Administration's intent was to catalyze state and local initiatives by funding pilot projects.

President Obama's 2014 budget accelerated his commitment to Pay for Success, nearly doubling fiscal year 2013's commitment with pilots initiated throughout the federal government, including $185 million to support nine new projects in four federal agencies and the creation of a $300 million Pay for Success Investment Fund calculated to scale the strategy. But by this time, the states had already taken the lead.

THE MASSACHUSETTS INITIATIVE

On May 6, 2011, the Massachusetts Office for Administration and Finance issued "Requests for Information" to learn:

- Which social services are the most promising candidates for pay for success contracts?

- Are there innovative solutions to social problems that have been demonstrated on a relatively small scale that have the potential to be scaled up using Pay for Success contracts in a way that would reduce costs/or improve outcomes?

- Are there areas where targeted investments in preventative services would have a high likelihood of reducing future budgetary costs by more than the cost of the services?

- Are there other areas of government activity where up-front investments and innovative contracting strategies could improve performance and reduce costs?

- How should pay for success contracts and social impact bonds be structured to support these goals?

- What information would be useful to the Executive Office for Administration and Finance in drafting a more detailed procurement solicitation for these contracts?

As Governor Deval L. Patrick put it in his May 9, 2011, announcement at the BCYI Mildred Community Center in Boston: "Working with the legislature and the private sector, we will fund what works and defund what does not, and we will together develop measures for success and progress."

By January 2012, the state was ready to move ahead. The Executive Office for Administration and Finance issued "Requests for Response" seeking partnerships as it cranked up its effort to break the backs of two of the state's most daunting social problems. Gov. Patrick's administration sought to partner with social entrepreneurs to provide stable housing for hundreds of chronically homeless people, both to improve their well-being and to reduce housing and Medicaid costs.

At the same time, the administration reached out to social entrepreneurs to support youth aging out of the juvenile corrections and probation systems and to help them make successful transitions to adulthood. The contract was to be designed with the stated goal of reducing recidivism and improving education and employment outcomes over a six-year period for a significant number of the more than 750 youth who leave the penal systems every year.

But this was only the beginning. Massachusetts, which has authorized $50 million to launch Pay for Success projects, continues to explore social innovation financing options as it pursues solutions to other social problems. The state is developing projects to help the homeless and to provide transitional employment for recently released adult offenders, as is the state of New York. Some financing arrangements may contemplate up-front funding by third-party intermediaries and investors to allow service providers to enter into Pay for Success contracts with the government, as is the case in Peterborough. Other arrangements may allow the state to pay service providers once they demonstrate success under multi-year performance contracts.

The nation's largest Social Impact Bond to date is a seven-year, $27 million Massachusetts Juvenile Justice Pay for Success Initiative launched in January 2014. Significantly, the Massachusetts effort, different from most Social Impact Bond designs, was not guaranteed by any foundation or other nonprofit. "All dollars are at risk, with no backstop. Everyone stands to lose or gain on this," according to John Grossman, a partner general counsel at Third Sector Partners, which secured $18 million in private financing for the program, which also benefited from a first of its kind $11.7 million grant awarded by the U.S. Department of Labor in September of 2013. So this Massachusetts program signals that Social Impact Bonds, when carefully structured, can create a risk-reward profile attractive to investors in their own right. Chelsea, Massachusetts–based nonprofit, Roca, Inc., is using the funds to provide outreach, life skills, and employment training for nearly 1,000 men in more than one dozen Massachusetts cities. The goal: to reduce recidivism and help them pursue successful lives. Gross savings from a reduction in re-offense rates could range between $1 million and $45 million, with corresponding "success payments" as high as $27 million.

NEW YORK CITY LEADS THE WAY

While Massachusetts became the first state in the nation to seek performance-based investments to spur innovative solutions to social problems, to achieve better outcomes and, at a time of unprecedented fiscal pressure, to save public money, New York City actually issued the United States' first Social Impact Bond.

The New York City effort brought together a strategic partnership including not only the city but also:

- MDRC, a nonprofit, nonpartisan education and social policy research and education organization created in 1974 by the Ford Foundation;
- The Osborne Association, the nonprofit organization founded in 1933 to continue the work of Thomas Matt Osborne, the "prophet of prison reform";
- The Bloomberg Philanthropies, the umbrella organization including all of former New York City Mayor Michael Bloomberg's charitable activities; and
- Global investment bank Goldman Sachs.

Goldman Sachs' loan in August 2012 funded therapeutic services to sixteen-to-eighteen-year-olds incarcerated on Rikers Island, the prison that claims the bulk of the city's billion-dollar corrections budget. The structure of the loan reflects the fact that government is ill-suited to fund preventative interventions, but also responds sensitively to stakeholders' demands, seen throughout the social sector, that the success of an intervention strategy be evidenced by empirical results. The business deal was put together this way:

1. Goldman Sachs funded a $9.6 million multi-draw loan in favor of MDRC.
2. MDRC, experienced in building alliances around public and private investors to test innovative policy ideas, doled out the

proceeds to The Osborne Association, recognized for its skill and experience in providing social services to incarcerated youth.

3. MDRC, as a financial intermediary, oversees the project's operation and will be responsible to make any loan payments eventually owed back to Goldman Sachs.

4. The Vera Institute of Justice, another independent nonprofit, will evaluate the project's success at reducing recidivism among participating Rikers Island inmates over the twenty-four-month period following their release.

5. New York City will make "success payments" to MDRC based on the cost savings the city realizes from the project.

6. MDRC will then repay the Goldman Sachs loan out of the success payments.

7. Over time, Bloomberg Philanthropies will have made a $7.2 million grant to MDRC, guaranteeing a portion of the loan to mitigate Goldman Sachs' risk while requiring some of Goldman Sachs' capital always to remain on the hook.

8. Whatever may remain unused of the guarantee fund will stay with MDRC to support future intervention strategies.

Like other Social Impact Bond efforts, the New York City experiment is not without a substantial downside. But that downside is cushioned by the strength of the consortium and its members' shared commitment to benefit one another. Goldman Sachs, drawing upon its core competency, carefully evaluated the intervention's efficacy and the capabilities of both The Osborne Association and MDRC. The contracts underpinning the various transactions were carefully harmonized to respect the needs of the parties and to align their incentives. Contractual safeguards were added to address contingencies that might crop up. But it's the integrity, track records, and professionalism of the parties that justify cautious optimism about the fate of the Rikers Island Social Impact Bond.

PAY FOR SUCCESS GAINS TRACTION

On the heels of the Rikers Island initiative, private and institutional investors joined forces to fund a five-and-a-half-year, $13.5 million program to expand the re-entry employment work of The Center for Employment opportunities in New York City and Rochester, New York. If the program achieves its goals in reducing recidivism and securing employment for 2,000 ex-offenders over a four-year period, investors stand to see returns as high as 12 percent annually. For investors to be repaid, the program will need to cut recidivism by 8 percent and increase employment by 5 percent. If all goes as well as the investors hope, the public sector could realize as much as $7.8 million in savings.

The universe of investors is itself noteworthy, including thought leaders former U.S. Treasury Secretary Larry Summers; hedge fund founder Bill Ackman's Pershing Square Foundation; James Lee Sorenson, the founder of the James Lee Sorenson Global Impact Investing Center at the University of Utah's David Eccles School of Business; and billionaire and trader John Arnold's foundation, committed to the notion that philanthropy should be transformational and entrepreneurial. They were obviously sold by the project's potential, as were the federal and state governments.

The U.S. Department of Labor awarded the state a $12 million grant for the project, its largest award under a national competition for Pay for Success, and additional funds were included in the state's 2013–2014 budget. To Governor Andrew Cuomo, the public-private partnership is a "win-win": "By assisting these individuals, who are often at risk of becoming repeat offenders, to become members of society, we can make New York's communities safer and more prosperous for years to come."

Similarly structured efforts are underway in Colorado, Connecticut, Illinois, New York, Ohio, and South Carolina, and in Fresno and Santa Clara County, California, each with a different mission—to expand high-quality early childhood education, to help seniors avoid nursing homes, to prevent asthma- and diabetes-related hospitalization, to address chronic homelessness, and to achieve other worthy social goals.

In 2014, Illinois became the first state to implement a Pay for Success initiative to improve outcomes for at-risk youth involved in both the child welfare and juvenile justice systems and the first to partner with a network of community providers for service delivery. Third Sector, a nonprofit advisory firm focused on the Pay for Success sector, is working with One Hope United—a century-old federation of agencies safeguarding the welfare of vulnerable children through a variety of community-based and in-home programs—in partnership with the Conscience Community Network—a collaboration of seven service providers with deep ties to the state: Lawrence Hall Youth Services, Maryville Academy, OMNI Youth Services, SGA Youth & Family Services, UCAN, Youth Outreach Services, and One Hope United itself—to provide community alternatives to institutional care for dually involved youth.

Social Finance, Inc., a U.S. nonprofit dedicated to mobilizing investment capital to drive social progress, is partnering with the District of Columbia to develop and launch the nation's first Pay for Success initiative focused on reducing teen pregnancy. And Bank of America is assessing the use of innovative social financing and other Pay for Success programs to address critical shortfalls in the funding of effective re-integration and ongoing support services for military veterans. Meanwhile, outside the United States, Social Impact Bond proposals are in development, among other places, in Uganda, to reduce sleeping sickness; in Colombia, to avoid teen pregnancy; and in Mozambique, to fight malaria.

WHERE SOCIAL IMPACT BONDS WORK

As the Social Impact Bond and its progeny take root in other cities, counties, states, and countries, service providers and impact investors alike are assessing whether or not the financing strategy might work for them.

Will Social Impact Bond Investing Make Sense?

1. *Define the social problem.* The starting point is to define the social problem intended to be targeted and to identify the population to be supported.

2. *Time the intervention.* It then must be determined at what point it's best to intervene and which services will most likely improve social outcomes.

3. *The proper programs.* These will have to be demonstrated based on their effectiveness and costs.

4. *Establish the metrics.* Operationally practical social metrics that stand as proxies for impact will have to be identified, along with a measurement methodology that's reasonably acceptable to investors.

5. *Test the value proposition.* Anticipated cost savings for improved social outcomes must be estimated.

6. *Make the case.* A financial model must be structured that delivers both savings to the government and a reasonable return to investors.

THE SOCIAL IMPACT BOND'S PROGENY

Some social entrepreneurs and impact investors aren't waiting for government to act on the Social Impact Bond. They see merit in entering into private contracts that can achieve some of the same purposes, but which don't require enabling legislation or the costs and burdens of a publicly sanctioned structure.

One such approach involves two distinct groups of funders upon which a nonprofit service provider might rely. The first group consists of impact investors intent on funding social innovation within the nonprofit. Those investors agree to support an innovative pilot project in return for the nonprofit's promise to peg their financial returns to agreed-on social benchmarks. If the pilot fails, the nonprofit will owe them nothing. If it succeeds, their investment will generate returns based on the level of that success.

That's where the second group of funders comes in. These are the nonprofit's major donors. Periodically asked for recurring donations to support "the cause," they welcome a unique opportunity to stand ready to fund an outcome only if and when it's demonstrably achieved. These investors meet the nonprofit's obligations to the impact investors unless, as is likely, the latter decline payment, opting instead to see their funds re-invested in the nonprofit's now successful programming.

Before long, government debt investments in small and medium-sized enterprises may be complemented by "conditionally guaranteed impact bonds," private debt investments that promote economic development with a government guarantee conditioned upon mission success as measured by contractually agreed-on social metrics. Up-front "pay for performance grants" might be made by private actors to designated nonprofits to help them address a social problem of specific interest to grantors. For example, if a company is especially concerned about a localized social issue, it might advance funding to address it with its investment recovered from the government if—and only if—measurable success is achieved.

EMPOWERING THE SOCIAL SECTOR

As the Social Impact Bond garners increasing attention within the global impact investing community, government is moving away from its historic role as monopoly supplier, increasingly replaced by market-driven participants who value outcomes over inputs and processes. The social sector and those who fund it will become increasingly empowered—and so will those they serve.

CHAPTER NINE

Building and Rebuilding Communities

We might not think of North Dakota as a wellspring of financial innovation, but perhaps we should.

The Bank of North Dakota is America's only state-owned deposit bank. It has operated since 1919, enduring several of the financial sector's most harrowing banking crises. Other state-owned banks have been chartered to support infrastructure projects (so-called "infrastructure banks" that have been proposed at the federal level as well), but North Dakota's bank acts just like a private bank, yet far more willing to open up capital for commercial projects. Many of the projects jump-started by the bank would almost certainly be turned away by the larger, out-of-state banks. "The Bank of North Dakota was formed nearly 100 years ago because of the belief that North Dakota's farmers were being exploited with high interest rates," said Eric Hardmeyer, the bank's president, in an op-ed for *The New York Times*. "Since nine of ten North Dakotans were farmers, this issue galvanized voters and lawmakers." It still does.

Located in a part of the country one wouldn't expect to be fertile territory for socialized banks, the Bank of North Dakota has built political ramparts around itself. If it had taken on too much risk, the bank would have collapsed from its own weight, and few in North Dakota would have mourned its loss. Attempts at privatizing the bank have been few and futile. The relatively free flow of credit in the state has been credited in part for the state's low unemployment rate, which, as of October 2013, stood at an unheard of 2.7 percent. North Dakota's natural gas reserves have also been credited with lowering the state's unemployment rate, yet nearby Wyoming also has a wealth of energy resources, and its unemployment rate has consistently stood well above that of North Dakota since the 2008 financial crisis.

The Bank of North Dakota now holds $4 billion in assets and has turned in $300 million to the state's treasury. Has the bank crowded out other private banks? To the contrary, North Dakota has more than four times the number of private banks per capita as the national average. This is because the bank's mandate is to *support* North Dakota's economy, including its private banks, leveraging their lending capacities. For that reason, among others, the Bank of North Dakota is not seen as a threat; indeed, the North Dakota Bankers Association has applauded the Bank of North Dakota's very existence.

Alone and in collaboration with other financial institutions, the bank finances commercial projects, but also helps finance agricultural development projects, student loans for state residents, and loans following natural disasters, such as a recent spate of floods around Fargo. In other words, if the community needs it, the Bank of North Dakota is there to respond. That is what it has been chartered to do since 1919.

We have long ago accepted the reality that capital can travel around the world and back again at the click of a button. Today, businesses regularly seek capital from loan officers working for major banking institutions based in Charlotte or on Wall Street, while investors deposit their money into ventures about which they know little and care less. This self-evident truth has led some to choose an alternative paradigm: community capital. Community capital circulates around a local area, supporting businesses and ventures in one's own town or city. A dollar spent does *not* get divided and shipped across the globe. Dinner comes from the farm a few miles down the road. The person loaning money knows the debtor beyond his or her credit score.

The Bank of North Dakota has already been a pioneer in community capital. It sowed the seeds for a movement that didn't truly begin to bloom until the 1970s, culminating with the passage of the Community Reinvestment Act (CRA) of 1977. The CRA was designed to spur commercial banks to invest in community development in low-income areas. This was accomplished through the Federal Deposit Insurance Corporation's requirement that FDIC-insured banks serve all areas in which they do business as a prerequisite for receiving insurance on their accounts. Banks are given CRA ratings based on evaluations of how well they are serving low-income neighborhoods. Such ratings took on even greater significance during the wave of bank mergers in the 1990s, when it became clear that regulatory approval would be expedited if the merging banks had strong records of CRA performance.

Community capital was given another boost in 1994 with the passage of the Riegle Community Development and Regulatory Improvement Act, which established Community Development Financial Institutions, or CDFIs. These financial institutions are certified by the U.S. Treasury's CDFI Fund and are mandated to provide financial services to underserved markets. The U.S. Treasury not only regulates CDFIs, but also provides them with debt and equity capital—funds authorized under the Community Reinvestment Act—which invariably attracts private capital. CDFIs can be operated as for-profit or nonprofit financial institutions, as long as the mission comports with the intent of the Riegle Act. Two decades after the Act became law, the approximately 1,000 CDFIs certified in the United States have collectively become the clearinghouse for community capital. More than $1.3 billion in CDFI funds have been awarded and invested since 1994. Nearly 600 CDFIs are loan funds, with another 200 operating as credit unions.

Just before he signed the Riegle Act into law, President Clinton took a moment to describe the South Shore Community Bank in Chicago, a bank that would soon be among the first certified CDFIs. "Anyone who ever heard me give a talk anywhere probably knows that in almost every speech I talked about the South Shore Bank in Chicago, a place where I visited, got to know, and got to understand," Clinton said. "I've long admired the way they've steered private investments into previously underprivileged neighborhoods, to previously undercapitalized, underutilized Americans, proving that a bank can be a remarkable source for hope, and still make money."

Clinton was right about the South Shore Bank, which was renamed ShoreBank in 2000. Opening its doors in 1973, the bank skillfully and profitably lent to low-income neighborhoods in and around Chicago. In the 1990s, it began not only seeing urban renewal as a part of its core mission, but also began to incorporate environmental protection into its operations. All the while, ShoreBank was profitable. By 2008, as the storm clouds began to gather, ShoreBank had amassed more than $2.6 billion in assets. (The story, however, did not end happily; more on that later in this chapter.)

This concept of community capital is the driving force behind organizations like ShoreBank. It also drives organizations like Mountain BizWorks, an investment fund founded in 1989 to invest in small businesses in and around Western North Carolina. Mountain BizWorks is now a certified CDFI that invests as little as $1,000 and as much as $150,000.

Community capital guides the California HealthCare Foundation (CHCF). Based in the Bay Area, the CHCF has grown its endowment to about $700 million, granting about $35 million each year to organizations dedicated to improving the Golden State's health care system and supporting the implementation of the Affordable Care Act.

Community capital has also led the Illinois Finance Fund to launch in 1988 and provide below-market loans to support development projects in the most blighted areas of Chicago. The Illinois Finance Fund has since expanded to neighboring states, rebranded as simply "IFF" and certified as a CDFI. Over nearly three decades, IFF has leveraged more than $1 billion to support community development in Chicago and across the Midwest.

Community capital is what drives RSF Social Finance and its president and CEO, Don Shaffer, a man who learned about high finance as a country club caddy, eavesdropping on conversations of stockbrokers and Wall Street executives. Shaffer now commands a fund that has lent more than $275 million over its thirty-year history, mostly to social enterprises focused on sustainable agriculture and food systems. RSF Social Finance now holds $120 million in assets. To date, RSF has recovered every last penny it has lent for its network of more than 1,600 investors. It was under Shaffer's leadership that RSF introduced "RSF Prime," a new way of determining the interest rate charged to RSF borrowers. The RSF Prime rate is calculated after every quarter, determined through collaboration with all stakeholders—RSF's investors, borrowers, and managers. This collaborative approach to setting borrowing rates has received universal acclaim, especially when compared to the simple metric RSF other lenders still use as their benchmark, the current LIBOR or the thirteen-week Treasury bill rate. "I think that what we're seeing is tremendous demand from individuals who are questioning core assumptions of Wall Street, where the trust factor is very low," Shaffer told the *Huffington Post*.

And community capital is how Local Initiatives Support Corporation (LISC) "helps neighbors build communities." LISC, the largest community development support organization in the country, assembles private and public resources and directs them to locally defined priorities. By expanding investment in housing, increasing family income and wealth, stimulating economic development, improving access to quality education, and supporting healthy environments and lifestyles, LISC's "Building Sustainable Communities" strategy has helped grow the middle class and brighten the future for low-income neighborhoods throughout the nation. In 2013 alone, the organization invested $776 million, which leveraged $2.3 billion in total development. Its accomplishments include 11,850 affordable homes and apartments, two million square feet of retail and community space, thirteen schools, six child care facilities, and eighteen playing fields. It's hard to argue with Michael Rubinger, LISC's president and CEO, who claims, "I think we're on the right course."

•••

According to the Oakland, California–based Business Alliance for Local Living Economies (BALLE), community capital also comes from individuals, like the shoppers at the farmers market or wealthy investors taking ownership stakes in local businesses; donor-advised funds, tax-advantaged conduits where individuals can deposit cash or securities and then have a role in deciding which charities should benefit from them; foundations, particularly those with a regional focus; community "mission-driven banks" like the Bank of North Dakota; credit unions, which tend to charge low fees and are mindful of community needs; CDFIs; venture capitalists; "angel investors," wealthy individuals who use *their own* money to jump-start new companies; and, finally, the government.

DONOR-ADVISED FUNDS

Donor-advised funds were first introduced about seventy years ago. Here's how they work: a donor deposits cash into the fund. Although the donor can deduct the donation when the fund receives it, the fund will make distributions at a time and to a recipient the donor prefers. In the meantime, the cash is invested for growth and stability. The donor can thus accelerate his or her tax deduction, yet more leisurely pace the distributions of cash to designated charities while altogether avoiding the bookkeeping and administration associated with often complex charitable giving strategies. If instead of donating cash to the fund, the donor contributes appreciated securities, he or she avoids the capital gains tax on their sale yet receives a charitable deduction equal to the value of the securities when they're contributed. Donor-advised funds are very popular for donors looking to direct their wealth toward a charitable organization in their own community.

Donors can open up a donor-advised fund with as little as $5,000. Fidelity Investments, the Vanguard Group, and Charles Schwab's Schwab Charitable Division have become the largest participants in this space. More than one in every ten dollars donated to charitable organizations comes from donor-advised funds, according to the National Philanthropic Trust. Assets in donor-advised funds totaled more than $45 billion in 2012, 18 percent more than they held in 2011.

THE ROLE FOUNDATIONS PLAY

Foundations provide the next leg of community capital. In 1930 William Keith Kellogg, founder of the world-famous breakfast cereal company, decided to put some of his capital to use in his community. He founded what would become the W.K. Kellogg Foundation, which initially distributed its capital in and around Battle Creek, Michigan—the home of the foundation and the cereal company. One of its initial grantees was the Michigan Community Health Project, which built a network of health clinics and community hospitals around the Battle Creek area. The Kellogg Foundation also took an interest in building K–12 education in south central Michigan; in 1931, the Kellogg Foundation opened the Ann J. Kellogg School, named after W.K. Kellogg's mother. The Ann J. Kellogg School was among the first to mainstream students with disabilities in the general student population. During World War II the federal government urged the Kellogg Foundation to expand its operations outside of Battle Creek, and it enthusiastically did so. Today the Kellogg Foundation holds assets of $7 billion, making it one of the largest philanthropic foundations in the United States. While it funds efforts in other communities—including projects in the Mississippi Delta, northeastern Brazil, and Haiti—the Kellogg Foundation remains rooted in Battle Creek, a town of only about 51,000 people.

The Calvert Foundation is another pioneering fund. Founded in 1995 and headquartered in the Washington, D.C., area, the foundation has invested more than $240 million in communities across the world through its Community Investment Note. Calvert's impact is generated by taking investors' capital and loaning it to more than 250 nonprofit organizations supporting affordable housing and community development. Investors can purchase a note with as little as $1,000. The note works like a certificate of deposit or a bond: the investor locks his or her money up for a set period of time—the note provides the option of anywhere between one to twenty years—and receives annual interest during that time period, after which principal is returned. Over its nearly twenty years, the Calvert Community Investment Note has not lost a single dollar of principal.

According to BALLE, just 22 percent of bank assets in the United States are held at small- to medium-sized banks. Yet more than half, 54 percent, of all lending to small businesses, is done by those same small- to medium-sized banks. These statistics demonstrate the alchemy of community capital.

The community capital movement that gave birth to CDFIs remains in full force today, largely because of the financial crisis of 2008. Media titan Arianna Huffington has recently led a "Move Your Money" project, asking followers to move their assets from the largest banks and deposit their money into community banks and credit unions. The organizers of the Move Your Money project proudly claim that they are responsible for moving four million accounts out of the "Too Big to Fail" banks. The logic of the movement can be debated, but the potential for smaller community banks and CDFIs to harness the animus currently directed toward Wall Street is clear. In April of 2011, as the Move Your Money movement gained support, Massachusetts treasurer Steven Grossman announced that he would move $100 million of state funds into community banks in the Bay State on the condition that the banks loan out the money to small businesses. Flanked by small town mayors and small business owners, Grossman added that he intended to move another $100 million shortly after the first transfer was completed.

BALLE identifies venture capitalists and angel investors as other large sources of community capital. Take the story of the California Clean Energy Fund (CalCEF). The fund began in 2001 after the California Public Utilities Commission and Pacific Gas & Electric, then going through Chapter 11 proceedings, agreed to set aside $30 million to support the development of clean energy in California. The settlement emerged from the flotsam of the state's energy crisis, which forced rolling blackouts on hundreds of thousands of Californians and played no small part in the 2003 recall of Governor Gray Davis. The $30 million set aside during the PG&E bankruptcy was to help ensure that the state had another source of energy, preventing even the possibility of a repeat of 2001's energy debacle. Enter CalCEF in 2004. CalCEF is an angel investing fund, commissioned to support startup renewable energy providers. Since it opened its doors, CalCEF has provided seed capital for renewable energy ventures all over the state, helping California become the undisputed hub of renewable energy innovation.

There also exists a clear role for government in driving community capital. The use of the New Markets Tax Credit by the Nonprofit Finance Fund, based in New York, illustrates the point. Since its founding in 1980, the Nonprofit Finance Fund has existed for the sole purpose of connecting money to social ventures, including, in recent years, impact investments. The Nonprofit Finance Fund holds more than $80 million in assets and, to date, has provided more than $287 million in financing for organizations that support their mission—organizations like the Urban Health Plan, a network of federally qualified community health centers.

In April of 2011, the Urban Health Plan announced plans to break ground on a new 54,000-square-foot health clinic in the Bronx borough of New York City at a price tag of $55 million. When it's opened in 2016, the facility should dramatically expand the number of medical services provided in one of the poorest neighborhoods in New York. Paloma Hernandez, the president and CEO of Urban Health Plan, estimates that the new facility could help serve at least 20,000 new patients. To help the plan for the facility become reality, the Nonprofit Finance Fund provided $2 million in leveraged debt and $15.5 million in federal tax grants under the New Markets Tax Credit program.

The New Markets Tax Credit was signed into law in 2000 and provides a powerful incentive to lure investments into disadvantaged communities like the South Bronx. The tax credit works in three steps:

1. First, the investor must be qualified as a Community Development Entity by the U.S. Treasury's CDFI fund.

2. The qualifying entity must then submit an application for the tax credit. The process for becoming certified is competitive; the Treasury's reviewers make certain that proposed investments have a profound impact on the communities the tax credit is intended to serve. Demand for the tax credit far exceeds the tax credits allocated, about $3.5 billion in 2013.

3. Once approved to receive the tax credit, the certified entity is then authorized to raise a certain dollar amount to invest. For entities that qualify, an investment like the one into the

Urban Health Plan facility reduces federal taxes by 39 percent of the investment made. If, for example, a $100 investment is made, the entity can write off $39 from its tax bill. For its $15 million investment, the Nonprofit Finance Fund was eligible for a $5.85 million tax write-off, which the Nonprofit Finance Fund would pass on to their investors. That's how powerful the New Markets Tax Credit is.

The Nonprofit Finance Fund's investment helped bring other partners to the table, including three different CDFIs and Goldman Sachs. The facility also received grant money from the American Reinvestment and Recovery Act, better known as President Obama's 2009 economic stimulus plan. The story of the Urban Health Plan hasn't ended, and won't for some time. If the project does not meet standards for impact set by the Treasury—jobs created, patients served, to name two metrics—investors could be forced to repay their tax credit. To avoid this disastrous outcome, the Nonprofit Finance Fund must rigorously verify that the project is compliant with the applicable impact standards, still more evidence of the value and importance of impact measurement.

LESSONS LEARNED

Why such organizations invest community capital should now be clear, but one must appreciate exactly *how* they invest community capital to replicate successes and avoid failures.

The Chicago-based ShoreBank, described earlier in this chapter, is one ignominious example of how a well-intentioned organization can collapse from the weight of oversight. In 2010, with losses from the recession totaling hundreds of millions of dollars, the bank was declared insolvent and closed its doors for good. Even with $150 million in commitments from Bank of America, Goldman Sachs, JP Morgan, and Citigroup to help keep the bank open, the FDIC forced its closure, fearing even greater losses to its insurance fund. The FDIC would soon sell the bank's remaining deposits to the newly formed Urban Partnership Bank, which could only operate ShoreBank's operations at half the scale. It was a devastating end to ShoreBank, but it did not mar the bank's venerable legacy in Chicago.

ShoreBank's downfall is complex, and the nuances of its cause are subject to debate, but without question, over its life, the bank safely and successfully extended hundreds of millions of dollars of credit to businesses and people who never would have received such credit from larger banks. It also left a set of lessons for bankers operating in the community capital space. ShoreBank was a victim of its board's lax oversight of the loans it was approving, and maybe, too, a victim of lax oversight by the FDIC. At the very least, the story of ShoreBank provides a reminder of the risks inherent in lending to those without a long track record of success, as noble as such a practice may be, a lesson lenders will not soon forget.

For the safety and stability of community banking, borrowers and lenders are turning to various methods of "credit enhancement" to lower borrowing costs for the former and contain risk for the latter. Loan Loss Reserves (LLRs) are one way of doing that. When a bank makes a series of loans, it will account for potential defaults by putting aside a certain amount for its LLRs. The reserves are monies from which lenders can draw in the event of a default. If there are no defaults, or fewer defaults than anticipated, the money then returns to the asset side of the balance sheet. Similarly, lenders can also take out loan guarantees, insurance against default that provides 100 percent recapitalization if borrowers do not repay their loans. More risk-averse investors can take on senior debt positions, giving them first priority for repayment in the event the borrower liquidates.

Finally, Debt Service Reserves (DSRs) are stockpiles of capital used during business fluctuations. Farmers frequently rely on DSRs to provide debt service payments during the "off season." May the lessons of ShoreBank empower lenders and borrowers to manage the risks of community investment even more successfully and embrace its extraordinary potential to drive positive social change.

CHAPTER TEN

Investing for Impact

Walk into the Merchandise Mart in Chicago, a massive art deco building once owned by Joseph P. Kennedy, Sr., the bigger-than-life founder of the Kennedy dynasty, and take the elevator to the twelfth floor. When you get there, look down the hall. It seems to stretch for several city blocks. (It, in fact, does.) This was once the largest building in the world. At the end of the hall, you'll see a bright neon sign. It reads "1871," the year the city of Chicago burned in the great fire. For most Chicagoans, 1871 now refers to a place, not a year. It has become Chicago's innovation hearth. At 1871, young entrepreneurs bring their ideas to a group of established business managers and, if their ideas are good enough, they build their businesses with the help of their peers and mentors. The 50,000-square-foot offices of 1871 resemble a college student lounge. The median age couldn't be any higher than twenty-two or twenty-three. The dress code is anything goes.

In this room that overlooks the Chicago River, several multi-billion-dollar businesses will emerge in the coming years. You needn't take my word for it. Notice the J.P. Morgan bankers roaming through the cubicles. Or the visits from the Mayor of Chicago, Rahm Emanuel, that seem so routine that few even bother to take off their headphones when he stops by. Or the almost weekly visits from members of Congress. Even British Prime Minister David Cameron introduced himself to 1871 during a 2012 visit to Chicago. Perhaps most important, notice the constant presence of investors looking for just the right opportunity among these twenty-somethings.

This is the fruition of a vision of 1871's founders, who include J.B. Pritzker—a brother of U.S. Secretary of Commerce Penny

Pritzker and a scion of the family that launched the Hyatt hotel chain—when they organized the innovation hub in 2012. At one central location, Chicago's best innovators collaborate and build businesses that will rebuild Chicago's economy, which at the time I write this, has an unemployment rate higher than 10 percent. Where they once competed for positions on Wall Street, some of the smartest students at the Kellogg School of Management at Northwestern University and the Booth School of Business at the University of Chicago now compete to incubate their ideas at 1871.

One way to get there is to land a spot with Impact Engine, a sixteen-week program to train mission-focused entrepreneurs targeting climate and the environment, education, financial services, food and agriculture, health and wellness, and workforce development. The startups accepted into the program exchange 7 percent of the equity in their companies, not only for co-working space at 1871, but also for $25,000 in seed capital, access to dedicated mentors, business workshops, and seminars, the opportunity to present before prospective investors at "Demo Day," *pro bono* legal services, and fundraising support. Impact Engine is the brainchild of professors at the Kellogg and Booth schools and uber-entrepreneur Chuck Templeton, the founder of Open Table, a website that enables users to reserve tables at popular restaurants, among a host of successful entrepreneurial ventures.

The businesses of Impact Engine work inside 1871, but theirs are different from the non–Impact Engine businesses. "What we want to have is every time a company is making money, they're actually solving a problem or they're addressing the mission that they've gone after to try and solve," Templeton said of Impact Engine. He now serves as chairman of its board.

Impact Engine is Chicago's top impact accelerator. Since 2012, it has "graduated" sixteen companies from its program which, all told, raised more than $9.1 million in seed and Series A funding.

Impact Engine's inaugural class of entrepreneurs included Eileen Murphy, a former English teacher in the Chicago Public School District. Dissatisfied with the archaic instructional material provided by the major academic publishers—McGraw-Hill, Scholastic, and Pearson, to name a few—Murphy turned in her resignation in 2012 and set about building a company that would introduce the most technologically advanced instructional material into public schools in the poorest neighborhoods. Her opus, ThinkCERCA, is a web-based platform that enables teachers to assign students readings with a follow-up quiz, challenging them to make claims and defend those claims with evidence provided in the text. "I felt there were not enough companies in the market to make products that actually work," Murphy said. The ThinkCERCA technology doesn't just work; it dazzles. With ThinkCERCA, teachers can tailor their assignments for ten different reading levels. For example, add ThinkCERCA to the curriculum of a classroom with two groups of students, one reading at the ninth-grade level and the other at a much lower level. With ThinkCERCA, the teacher can assign each group of students an individualized set of problems that matches their current abilities. The program allows the teacher to challenge each student without losing those who are reading at below-grade levels.

Early in the process of developing ThinkCERCA, Murphy and her team faced the choice of becoming a for-profit or a nonprofit entity. It was the ability of the market to force discipline on ThinkCERCA that tipped the balance. "In the world of for-profit companies, basically, customers are more critical and hold higher standards for quality," Murphy said.

The same could be said of the investors—so-called "angel investors"—who would eventually get ThinkCERCA off the ground. Murphy was fortunate. Her initial investors were introduced to the company through Impact Engine. There wasn't much "cold calling" in the initial stages of developing her business. After the initial round of raising capital, ThinkCERCA had raised about $685,000. After successfully introducing the program, demand quickly rose, and Murphy set out to raise more, soon amassing more than $1 million in early-stage capital. ThinkCERCA's big break came when the company won a $250,000 grant from The Bill and Melinda Gates Foundation. With ThinkCERCA growing its business, its benevolent reach will extend into classrooms across the country, just as its early-stage funders intended.

To date, more than 10,000 students have used ThinkCERCA. As Murphy continues to seek capital, she frequently approaches prospective investors who are not satisfied by simply gaining a financial return on their money. These investors are "impact investors."

An unstated convention of the market is that we invest money to make money, and donate money, if we so choose, to drive positive social change. Until recently, we haven't been able to find an overlap in the capital market Venn diagram. No longer. Impact investing is investing with a mission. It's an investment strategy that merges profit-seeking with philanthropy. When an impact investor invests, he or she seeks a financial return *and* a social return—to make money *and* help clean the air we breathe, or feed the hungry, or build better schools. An impact investor does not put profit in conflict with social progress. He or she seeks opportunities with companies that help build a sustainable and equitable future, support developing markets, combat global climate change, and build a portfolio while he or she is at it.

An impact investor provides capital to strengthen companies so they may expand their work and increase the value of the impact investor's interests. Yet, the point cannot be emphasized enough: Impact investing is not charity.

Impact businesses should not be confused with socially responsible businesses, those whose practices contribute to a more just and sustainable world. Impact businesses create positive impact through the very activity by which they earn revenue.

ZipCar, a company that takes cars off the roads (and carbon out of the atmosphere) as it expands its car-sharing business, is an impact business. So is Revolution Foods, an Oakland, California–based company that provides natural, organic foods for schools. Tesla is a impact business. FirstSolar is as well. And, of course, Eileen Murphy's ThinkCERCA is an impact business. As these businesses grow, their social impact is strengthened. Lauren Bush Lauren (granddaughter of George H.W., niece of George W., and daughter-in-law of Ralph) summarily explained the impact business model to *The New York Times* in describing her own company, FEED Projects, a company that raises money for world hunger initiatives through selling their chichi clothing and tote bags. "Our business model tackles poverty through consumerism," she said.

Impact investing is an investment strategy that supports impact businesses. The community of impact investors is diverse, but the largest investors are development finance institutions (DFIs) such as the U.S. Overseas Private Investment Corporation; large foundations, including the W.K. Kellogg Foundation; commercial banks; investment funds; and high-net-worth individuals. These investors are driving the impact investing market closer and closer to the mainstream capital markets. If they aren't oriented around a certain community, institutional investors will frequently be galvanized around the impact they would like to generate—such as strengthening public education or creating job opportunities in low-income communities—and then decide on their approach and, with it, their investments.

Impact investing is not limited to the equity market. Fixed-income investments, such as a municipal bond supporting construction of a new school or an environmental restoration project, certainly qualify as impact investments. In 2008, the World Bank began issuing Green Bonds to support projects combating global climate change. As this book goes to press, the World Bank has issued more than $4.5 billion in Green Bonds. An investment in a Green Bond is an impact investment. Depositing money into a Community Development Financial Institution (CDFI) is an impact investment. Investments in CDFIs can take the form of simple cash deposits that help finance low-income housing development or a grocery store in a community devoid of fresh produce and meats (a so-called "food desert"). CDFIs like the Mississippi-based Hope Credit Union have been vital to rebuilding efforts in the Gulf since Hurricane Katrina, opening credit to small businesses and housing developments that many larger banks were unlikely to finance.

For more than fifty years, foundations have been making "program-related investments" (PRIs), rather than simply giving their money away in grants. In 1968 the Ford Foundation, after extensive lobbying of Congress to allow their use, became the first foundation to invest for impact instead of giving their money away. This win-win proposition is made even better by its treatment under the U.S. tax code. Program-related investments satisfy a federal requirement that foundations give away at least 5 percent of their net assets annually to maintain their tax status. PRIs give foundations the option of acting like a socially impactful bank or social venture capitalist. For example, a PRI might invest in an affordable housing unit in a blighted neighborhood, drawing in other investors in the process. Once the money has been returned with interest, the foundation reinvests it for impact, and that virtuous cycle continues unabated. PRIs are guided by the same general rules that define impact investing. As long as PRIs advance the mission of the foundation, it can support its goals and grow, rather than simply giving away its capital.

Impact investments have frequently been categorized by the targeted impacts they seek. In impact investing parlance, investments can seek "bottom of the pyramid" impact, a term that references Franklin D. Roosevelt's "Forgotten Man" radio address in 1932: "These unhappy times call for the building of plans that rest upon the forgotten ... the forgotten man at the bottom of the economic pyramid." Bottom of the pyramid investments are designed to help the some four billion people who survive on less than $2.50 a day. Impact investments can seek to support community development, such as the Calvert Foundation's Community Investment Note. Investments in public health, such as in anti-malaria nets deployed in the most at-risk regions of the African continent, or capital financing of potable water delivery systems, are other examples of impact investments.

THE ORIGIN OF IMPACT INVESTING

It is difficult to establish the provenance of the impact investing market—when it was born and who was responsible for it. John Wesley, founder of the Methodist church, preached of the responsibility of his followers to "the right use of money" in his *The Use of Money*, published in 1744:

> In the present state of mankind, it is an excellent gift of God, answering the noblest ends. In the hands of his children, it is food for the hungry, drink for the thirsty, raiment for the naked: It gives to the traveler and the stranger where to lay his head. By it we may supply the place of an husband to the widow, and of a father to the fatherless ... It is therefore of the highest concern that all who fear God know how to employ this valuable talent; that they be instructed how it may answer these glorious ends, and in the highest degree.

In 1948 British Prime Minister Chester Attlee commissioned the formation of the Colonial Development Corporation (CDC), a development finance institution launched to help rebuild its colonies in Africa and Asia most adversely impacted by the war. The CDC invested in commercially sustainable farming, and after many of the colonies in which it invested split from Great Britain, the CDC was renamed the Commonwealth Development Corporation. The mission remained the same: investing in some of the poorest regions of the globe. The organization is still around today, having been renamed once again in 1999 as the CDC Group. The World Bank's International Finance Corporation was created in 1956 with a mission parallel to the CDC's—to help spur investment in low-income, developing regions of the globe. It, too, is still active and thriving. As of 2014 the IFC carries a portfolio of $49.6 billion with investments in more than 100 different countries.

Of course, many for-profit ventures have also seen themselves supporting social missions. However, until recently, a comprehensive framework for investing capital into impactful businesses has not existed.

In the 1990s, the impact investing community slowly began to emerge. Bill Gates would call the idea of generating social progress through commerce "creative capitalism." Other names for the idea included "social finance" and "blended value." By the early 2000s, major business schools (including the Harvard Business

School) would begin incorporating social entrepreneurship into their curriculums, an absurd notion just years earlier. Funds would be introduced with the stated mission of impacting society while generating a financial return.

Committed to introducing the power of the marketplace to the world of philanthropy, eBay founder Pierre Omidyar and his then-fiancé Pam founded the Omidyar Network in 2004, soon after Omidyar's 178 million eBay shares spiked in value from $18 to $54 immediately after eBay's initial public offering. At thirty-one, Omidyar was a billionaire. His net worth now exceeds $8 billion, making him the 162nd richest person on earth, according to *Forbes* magazine. "It [his wealth] was clearly far more than we would ever need, and it had accumulated very quickly.... We felt we had a responsibility to make sure those resources got put to good use," Omidyar would later recall in a *Harvard Business Review* piece he penned.

What began as a traditional family foundation would soon become a thought leader. Initially filed publically as a §501(c)3 charitable organization, the Omidyar Network would quickly launch a limited liability company from which it would make investments that would seek both financial returns and social impact. "We were breaking new ground here—our attorneys had never seen anything like this," Omidyar said. "Today there's a name for people who make investments that can produce both impact and profit: impact investors.... But at the time, there was no name for what we were trying to do." They began by investing in organizations that provide financial services for underserved regions (called "microfinance"), and expanded to other missions. Throughout the early 2000s, the Omidyar Network would grow alongside its contemporaries, such as the Calvert Foundation, the IGNIA Fund, the Acumen Fund, and Root Capital.

Another impact fund, the Monterey, Mexico–based IGNIA, was developed to fund housing for families who earn less than $10,000 a year. Among its investors: the Omidyar Network and J.P. Morgan. Remarkably, as the financial market started to recover from the disastrous financial events of 2008, the number of new impact funds more than doubled from 2009 to 2010, from twenty to forty-four, according to a report by the Duke University Center for the Advancement of Social Entrepreneurship. Sixty more impact funds were created in 2011.

Still, as of 2007, the framework for an impact investing market had yet to be built. The industry was bereft of any organization to direct and coordinate the market. That began to change in October of that year, when the Rockefeller Foundation brought together a group of investors in Italy to seek ways to increase efficiency in the social sector and support the growing impact investing community. It was during this meeting that the nascent community settled on the "impact investing" nomenclature, formally defining the idea as "using profit-seeking investment to generate social and environment good." Shortly after the meeting, the Rockefeller Foundation's board of trustees approved a plan to invest $38 million to help launch what has become a new industry.

What later emerged from Rockefeller's efforts was the Global Impact Investing Network (the GIIN), which was formally introduced at the September 2009 Clinton Global Initiative meeting in New York. Since its formation, the GIIN has provided the underpinnings of the market. It operates with a focus on three missions. First, the GIIN seeks to build and expand the community of investors participating in the industry. Through its Investors' Council, the GIIN has brought together more than fifty private foundations, pension funds, banks, and institutional investors participating in impact investing and has supported a dialogue among these organizations on what has worked and what has not. The Investors' Council membership list reads like a "Who's Who" of foundations: the W.G. Kellogg Foundation, the Ford Foundation, The Bill and Melinda Gates Foundation, and other prominent institutions.

The GIIN has also sought to raise the profile of impact investing and provide strategic direction for the fledgling industry. It aggregates research on the strategy and regularly produces reports on the state of the market. The GIIN's ImpactBase serves as a database for impact investment funds, where investors can search for opportunities with an easily accessible online search tool. Also, it hosts a job board for opportunities in the field along with a site with updates on recent large-scale impact investing deals.

Finally, the GIIN directs (and continues to revise) a set of standard definitions and impact metrics called the Impact Reporting and Investing Standards (IRIS). The development of the IRIS standards was the product of a collaboration among the Rockefeller Foundation, the Acumen Fund, and B Lab, before turning over administration of IRIS to the GIIN. IRIS provides the impact investing market's version of the "generally accepted accounting principles" (GAAP), the rules and regulations for financial accounting to which wholly commercial ventures are subject. Companies fanned throughout the world and across sectors report their social outcomes using the IRIS taxonomy on a public registry hosted by the GIIN. With the IRIS standards, one company's environmental performance can be measured against another's, even if the two are not of the same sector. Other impact factors can also be evaluated by using the IRIS taxonomy to benchmark performance: workplace equality, impact on the water table, and creation of jobs for low-income people, to name a few.

A third-party evaluator, established in tandem with IRIS but operated independent of it, was introduced to the impact investing market with the founding of the Global Impact Investing Rating System or GIIRS (pronounced "gears"), now operated by B Lab. Using the IRIS taxonomy, GIIRS rates debt and equity issuers and impact funds on their social and environmental performance using a five-star scale, providing investors with another level of transparency. The scores are based on responses to a comprehensive assessment—verified by random on-site reviews by an independent third party—that looks at the respondents' corporate governance. Environmental impact, impact of their surrounding communities, and the treatment of their workforces. A growing number of managers see value in receiving the GIIRS imprimatur; companies pay between $2,500 and $15,000 to have their social and environmental performance rated.

The issue of third-party impact verification is one that continues to vex the impact investing market. A study by the GIIN and J.P. Morgan found that, although 98 percent of impact investors consider impact measurement to be at least "somewhat important," only 64 percent reported using third-party ratings for their investment decisions; the rest used only their own internal systems or no metric at all to measure social and environmental impact. Thus, the potential for IRIS and GIIRS to drive growth in the impact investing sector could be immense. If successful, IRIS could provide a wealth of data and a common set of rules and barometers of impact, while GIIRS could give real meaning to that data through its competitive ratings. With these tools, impact investors can move beyond anecdotal evidence of success, enabling impact investors instead to learn collectively with cold, hard numbers.

IMPACT INVESTING TAKES ROOT

The financial markets didn't always have a bad reputation. Before the likes of Bernie Madoff and the outrageous post-bailout bonuses to bank executives, the industry was seen as an engine for economic security and social upliftment. It can be so again. No other industry can mobilize capital as effectively as the financial markets. Neither can the nonprofit community nor the state. Impact investing provides the financial services industry a chance to demonstrate its value beyond simply making money. Perhaps one day it can even begin to erase the memories of the financial crisis.

It is no accident that the impact investing market got off the ground as the smoke was clearing from the events of 2008. We are in the midst of the largest transfer of wealth in the history of the world. The Baby Boomers will soon pass on their wealth to a far more socially conscious Millennial generation, a generation that will carry the memories of the 2008 financial collapse with them for the rest of their lives. As the public's faith in the global financial markets continue to dwell on a historic low, the impact investing market holds the promise of reallocating billions of dollars away from the most toxic assets and into a market that funds solutions to the world's most exigent problems. These are the times when the need for social innovation could not be clearer or greater.

Fifteen nonprofit organizations are started every day. According to the IRS, foundations in the United States hold more than $640 billion in assets. As of 2014, 1.4 million nonprofit organizations are operating in the United States, 11 percent more than were operating in 2000, according to the National Center for Charitable Statistics. More than 10 percent of the U.S. non-governmental workforce is employed by a nonprofit. And yet more than forty million Americans live in poverty, according to the Census Bureau.

The grim truth is that enough help is not on the way from existing public institutions. Governments are continuing to have their budgets trimmed and squeezed, leaving little public money to increase foreign aid or to expand the welfare state at home. A 2012 report produced by Accenture estimated that an additional $940 billion of public money will need to be spent in the United States before 2025, just to keep up with the growing demand for social services. It's the cruelest paradox: As the need for government assistance increases, the dollars available to provide that assistance are shrinking fast.

The trend of austere government budgets couldn't come at a worse time for the social sector. Americans are justly proud of our status as the most productive labor force in the world, yet one can't help but wonder whether we have become *too* productive to maintain a robust labor market. The value of labor continues to be driven downward by technology. News for which we once paid a subscription fee can now be accessed online without charge, or even from a 140-character tweet. Newspaper reporters have suffered the plight of travel agents, rendered virtually obsolete by technology.

The same could be said about many other vocations. As we marvel at the possibility of self-driving cars actually becoming a reality on American highways, consider what will become of the bus drivers, taxi drivers, and chauffeurs once they find their jobs are threatened by automation, as so many workers have in the manufacturing sector. The pace of innovation in recent history has been breathtaking, but let's not delude ourselves: automation has also left too many workers disposable. Making matters worse is that, as our workplace becomes more automated, our workforce is becoming older. By 2020, one-fifth of our population will be older than sixty-five. What will come of our labor force in the next twenty or thirty years is beyond the scope of this book, but it is clear that, as our workforce navigates this transition, the nation's safety net must become stronger, not weaker.

Surely there must be a better way to provide aid, care, and ultimately self-sufficiency to our most vulnerable—and we must find that way. To maximize impact, nonprofit organizations must achieve scale, yet they are challenged by large donors to reduce overhead to such a degree that expanding operations often becomes impracticable.

Follow this thought experiment: If a talented manager is given two job offers—one at a $75,000 annual salary with a nonprofit, the other at $250,000 with a large corporation—wouldn't it make more sense for that manager to take the latter opportunity and write the former organization a large check? This is the unintended consequence of narrowly focusing on overhead: efforts to recruit top-level talent and to bridle scale operations. In no industry but the nonprofit industry does it take so much money to make money. According to such sources as the Nonprofit Overhead Cost Project, nearly one-third of every dollar raised in the nonprofit sector is lost in the fundraising process. Consistent with the recommendations of experts in nonprofit financial management, including the Nonprofit Finance Fund, nonprofit organizations frequently carry three months of working capital on a rolling basis, for many making long-term operation a tenuous proposition at best.

With such unrelenting focus and public scrutiny on reducing overhead costs, too much of the §501(c)(3) nonprofit model, many would argue, now seems focused on keeping operations lean than on producing impactful outcomes. The impact investing market provides an alternative universe where business development is welcomed. In the world of impact investing, providing salaries to attract the best talent can be done without reservation or opprobrium. It is where capitalists go to be philanthropic and still be capitalists. If the product is good and the business is sustainable, the money will raise itself.

Despite the allure of an efficient market for impact investors, we are a long way from realizing the potential of impact investing. In 2010, a study by J.P. Morgan (an interested party through its involvement in the formation of the Global Impact Investment Network) projected that the impact investing market might grow to $1 trillion by 2020. It was a staggering projection, one that seemed unrealistic and even a bit quixotic. J.P. Morgan and the GIIN's May 2014 report tallied the amount of social impact money at about $46 billion, representing a 20 percent increase over 2013, but a tiny share of the capital markets overall. While the $1 trillion number may appear to be a chimera, growth in the impact investing market will be exponential once the necessary components of an efficient, functioning market are established. Only then will impact investing be introduced into the mainstream global marketplace, where as much as 5 percent of assets under management are allocated to impact investments. (Foundations typically distribute a larger portion of their assets than the required 5 percent. According to the Foundation Source, the nation's largest provider of support and advisory services for private foundations, in 2013, foundations, on average, gave away about 7 percent of their net assets, with smaller foundations giving away much more of their money—about 14 percent—than larger foundations.)

What are those components? It's self-evident that impact investing needs investors. It needs intermediaries, or funds that can aggregate investment opportunities—receive and distribute capital. The opportunities must be mature and sustainable, with the ability to compensate risk. The market requires resources that have been slow to emerge, such as a unified set of matrices by which to evaluate growth and impact and an efficient, transparent exchange. Once all of these elements are in place, the final element will flood the market—and that element, of course, is capital.

The next two chapters will explore how impact investing works, and how it can break through to the mainstream financial markets. Understanding the impact investing process is essential for any individual or institution wishing to enter the market, from the initial planning stages to the transaction, through the evaluation process, and finally the exit from the investment. Those who understand this process in the world of conventional investing must understand that the impact investing process is far different. If J.P. Morgan's trillion-dollar projection proves to be accurate, impact investing will soon be a part of nearly all conversations between financial advisors and their clients, but we are far from that point. How we will get there is the subject of Chapter 11.

CHAPTER ELEVEN

How Impact Investing Works — and Why

LeapFrog Investments is often described as the first microinsurance fund, and its ambition has never waned. When it was launched in 2008, the company set out to insure more than twenty-five million people in its first ten years, focusing on the lowest income areas of Africa and Asia. LeapFrog hoped to provide a measure of financial security to people who never knew what that meant. Its initial backers included J.P. Morgan and TIAA-CREF, and it was recognized at the 2009 Clinton Global Initiative as it began to take off. Bill Clinton himself called LeapFrog the "insurer to the poor." As of April 2014, LeapFrog Investments is a $300 million fund, vowing to provide financial services for "the next billion" consumers who never before had access to financial services.

But LeapFrog does not directly provide financial services at all. Rather, it helps fund financial services companies that do, never losing sight of the risks it takes on. Among its first investments was a $6.7 million stake in AllLife, a life insurance company providing insurance to people living with AIDS or HIV. The investment would come with this expectation: that the insured submit to regular blood tests to verify that he or she was taking anti-retroviral drugs as prescribed. This small measure of due diligence illustrates the many steps LeapFrog takes to improve the odds that its impact investments will work, both financially and socially. The company's management begins with careful underwriting. Every proposed investee must demonstrate accountability (like LeapFrog did with AllLife), a strong management team, a clear investment strategy, and the reasonable achievability of an available "exit." No capital can change hands before these requirements are met.

In the impact investing market, the due diligence process is generally far more rigorous, and far more critical to ultimate success, than in the conventional financial markets, where every investment has a process in which the opportunity and its associated risks are evaluated and a strategy is put in place to achieve maximum profitability. However, the process of vetting an impact investment, seeking both financial and social returns, looks markedly different.

Building the right management team means first finding the right people and ensuring they work together cooperatively. Impact investing often brings together professionals in finance and the nonprofit sector. The cultural differences between the two can be vast, and bridging those differences isn't easily accomplished. As Pierre Omidyar recalled, writing in the September 2011 issue of the *Harvard Business Review*:

> The way a program officer does due diligence for a foundation is vastly different from the way an investment analyst does it for a venture capital firm. The main difference is that the two view risk in very different ways. Program officers are expected to be much more risk averse: If a foundation makes a grant to an organization that doesn't succeed, it's considered a big mistake. In contrast, the very best venture capitalists are happy if they get two out of ten investments right, and they get incredible financial rewards.

It isn't just the cultural differences that make bringing these two disparate factions together so difficult. For venture capitalists, an investment for a period of five to seven years often *requires* a return of more than 30 percent. If the venture were to fall short of that expectation, it would be seen as a failure. In the world of impact investments, the expected financial return is more forgiving, since the venture is also seeking a social return. In many cases the expected return is between 10 to 25 percent, below that of the expected returns of most venture capital funds. A 2011 study led by Professor Linda Darragh, then of the University of Chicago's Booth School of Business, and Nurkholisoh Aman, an economist at the Central Bank of Indonesia, looked at twenty different impact investing funds focusing on emerging markets. Only three of the twenty funds Darragh and Aman surveyed expected returns comparable to those of traditional venture capital funds.

A similar study performed by J.P. Morgan in 2010 surveyed impact investors on the returns they expected from debt instruments and equity holdings in developed and emerging markets. J.P. Morgan found that impact investors realized returns in line with benchmarks in emerging markets, but struggled to meet benchmarks in developed markets. The difference was attributed to burdensome regulation in more developed markets, such as tax incentives there designed to encourage socially impactful investments in ventures likely to deliver lower returns.

Firmly establishing a time horizon for the investment is just as important as managing investors' expectations about returns. Frequently, managers more concerned about the social impact of an investment can seek to extend its term of investment as long as possible, maximizing impact but sacrificing financial return. Impact funds often carry investments longer than the seven to ten years that venture capital funds typically target for exit.

Any projections of return must take into account the geographic market in which the capital will be invested. The study led by Darragh and Aman asked impact investors which due diligence factors most concerned them. Respondents to the survey most frequently ranked geography as one of the most important factors to consider before investing, along with the target industry and the management team. Specifically, the investors were concerned about the stability of the region they are investing in—taxation, corruption, intellectual property protection, the size of the market, and the general ease of doing business there. With many New York and San Francisco–based investors deploying capital in places like Latin America and Sub-Saharan Africa, these concerns are not easily allayed.

This proves to be one of the biggest challenges of impact investing. Where capital is in the developed markets, the need is in the emerging markets. "You've got to raise the capital, and people are going to feel more comfortable giving you money if you are just a few blocks away from them," noted Álvaro Rodríguez Arregui, co-founder of the Ignia Partners, in an interview with the *Stanford Social Innovation Review*.

A 2011 GIIN case study on an investment in Tanzanian agriculture illustrates the minefield of barriers inherent in bridging the developed market's capital supply with the emerging market's capital demand. The study looked at an investment launched by the Lion's Head Global Partners, based in the U.K., and the Calvert Foundation into Mtanga Farms. At the time of the investment, about 150,000 farmers were cultivating potatoes in Tanzania, most at a very small scale, and many of the potatoes farmed were diseased and inedible. By multiplying the potato yield in Tanzania, as the investment sought to do, Mtanga Farms could dramatically improve the lot of Tanzania's one million people deemed to be "food insecure," according to the International Food Policy Research Institute.

Regional concerns were dominant in evaluating Mtanga Farms. A senior partner at Lion's Head Global Partners, Clemens Calice, traveled to the region to evaluate the investee. During his trip he found that a similar project to provide clean seed to farmers in Kenya tripled the local potato yields and doubled the income of small potato farmers. He also discovered tall barriers to enter the market standing in their way: Tanzanian government officials required that the clean seeds be evaluated with five seasons of in-country trials before they would permit the potatoes to be harvested commercially. This was overcome when Calice and his team found a pre-existing treaty signed by the East African Community—an intergovernmental organization comprising of Kenya, Tanzania, Burundi, Rwanda, and Uganda—that required trials done in one EAC country to be accepted in another. Thus, the project in Kenya was, in fact, lawfully evaluated, obviating the need to start the five-season process again.

THE FORM OF THE INVESTMENT

The next step for an impact investor is to ask what form the investment should take: debt, equity, grant, loan guarantee, or a combination of two or more of them? "Venture capital firms by definition invest in companies seeking an injection of equity capital. Not so, with impact investment funds," Darragh and Aman noted. "Current impact investment firms can provide their portfolio companies with a combination of grants, debt, equity, loan guarantees, and combinations thereof. This diverse range of investment types appears to indicate the desire to achieve social returns over financial returns, since some of these investment vehicles offer minimum financial returns." Nearly all of the funds Darragh and Aman surveyed included equity in the capital structure; about half of the funds held equity positions alone.

An institutional investor should consider the advantages of taking an equity stake in an impact investment. Holding large equity stakes empowers the investor to exercise control over the venture. Frequently, businesses in their early stages are offering shares because they are ready to fund an operation that could help them scale. However, equity is junior in priority if the business were to liquidate, exposing owners to greater risk than bondholders take on. The business is not contractually obligated to pay stockholders, as it is with bondholders, so debt is safer, but it doesn't necessarily entitle the bondholder a seat at the table where key decisions are made. For many institutional investors more interested in the impact the venture generates than the financial return they hope to receive, this may be an unacceptable tradeoff.

But one ought not assume that equity positions are the only way impact investing affords one the opportunity to effectively generate a social impact. Recent empirical evidence demonstrates otherwise. For instance, The Bill and Melinda Gates Foundation, convinced that the Houston-based Knowledge Is Power Program (KIPP) charter schools had achieved a replicable model for public schools, underwrote $30 million in loan guarantees for the school in 2009. The guarantees allowed KIPP to issue $67 million in bonds, while paying significantly less in interest with the backing of the Gates Foundation. At the time of the bond issuance, KIPP estimated that it would save $10 million in interest payments over the thirty-five-year life of the bonds. The bond issuance allowed KIPP to open twenty-seven new schools supporting more than 15,000 new students. Since the first KIPP school opened in 1994, more than 90 percent of KIPP graduates have gone on to college. And the organization would be able to expand its operations without costing its investors, in this case the Gates Foundation, a dollar. Indeed, the loan guarantees allowed the Gates Foundation, whose corpus decreased 20 percent in 2008, to generate significant impact without eating into its assets. According to a 2014 GIIN survey of impact investors, one out of five respondents reported that they, too, offered credit enhancements to their investees.

Moreover, creative impact investors have successfully combined the values of debt and equity. For example, the London-based Bridges Social Ventures Fund gave a £1 million loan to the HCT Group, a transportation company that provides low-cost transportation services for commuters who are unable to use conventional transportation services. HCT provides around seventeen million passenger trips a year for disabled, low-income, and senior citizens. But this loan was not like most. One of its stipulations provided that Bridges Social Ventures receive a small percentage of the revenues earned by HCT, giving the investment an equity-like feature without the risks of equity.

Before deciding on the class of financing, investors should first decide on their goals, the Ignia Partners' Álvaro Rodríguez Arregui argued in the *Stanford Social Innovation Review*. "The first thing they say is 'we provide grants,' or 'we provide equity,' or 'we provide loans.' That's not the right approach. You need to first look at the issue the organization is trying to address, look at what intervention is required to solve that issue, and then look at what type of capital is required."

MANAGING RISK

Then there is the issue of managing risk, an issue the industry has been slow to acknowledge. It is unlikely that large numbers of investors will forego compensation for the risk they are taking in the impact investing market. Investors seeking financial gain must be compensated for risking their capital on ventures without much track record; and the impact investing market, of course, doesn't have a long track record of success. (Indeed, there is a danger of over-forgiving risk, creating a dilatory effect of undermining discipline and ultimately distorting the market that allows the best ideas to scale.) This chicken-and-egg dilemma has been approached in two ways, each with some success: (1) making impact investments less risky and (2) systematically securing riskier capital from investors more willing to take on additional risk.

Until a long track record of success can be touted, impact investments will need to offer at least the potential for sufficient returns for investors to justify taking on additional risk. Alas, we don't have ten years to demonstrate the stability of the market, and nobody is going to capture the next Google in the impact investing market. This leads us to approach the risk conundrum from a different flank. As a January 2014 report issued jointly by Bank of America Merrill Lynch and Bridges Ventures LLP noted, "While demonstrating a track record of sufficient financial return is one way to bring supply-and-demand into line ... another approach is to adjust the risk side of the equation—to 'de-risk' impact investment." The authors of the report unpack risk into five subsets: the risk of losing the principal investment, the risk of not being able to exit the investment, the risk that the investment will generate insufficient impact, the risk of prohibitive transaction costs, and the irreducible risk a young market presents (a so-called "unquantifiable risk," because little data on past performance exists). The report persuasively goes on to propose to de-risk the market by addressing each subset:

- Provide downside protection through collateralization, or pledging pools of assets (real estate or securities) in the event of default, and providing third-party guarantees.
- Reduce the risk of being able to exit the investment by building trading platforms and increasing the number of brokers participating in the market, making the assets more liquid.
- Reduce the transaction costs of impact investments by bundling investments, selling investment opportunities as a combined unit.

- Make evidence of impact more robust and supported by a credible methodology for verifying impact.

- Compensate for the lack of a track record by luring well-established managers to partner with impact investors.

The second strategy for managing risk in the impact investing market involves pairing investors who seek first a financial gain with investors who prioritize the social impact they are generating. Establishing a yin-yang relationship between "financial first" investors and "impact first" investors within impact funds has been essential to support impact businesses through the venture phase of business development. Once this yin-yang relationship is established, the financial first and impact first investors take their roles in the "capital stack." Financial first investors, in demanding a necessary return for the risk they are assuming, take on investment tranches that enable them to receive that return, typically debt. This gives them relative safety. If a business liquidates, they are first to receive their principal back. Impact first investors, in turn, take on more risky equity positions. The tradeoff for the impact first investors is that they are empowered to demand tougher standards for impact. Unlike the debt holders, they have voting rights and can exercise those rights to demand stronger impact. Without strong fiduciary responsibilities to maximize financial return, these impact first investors typically come from foundations and high-net-worth individuals.

Building a stable impact investment would then require identifying who the impact first investors and the financial first investors are, and how they approach the market. The distinction is not always clean. Take, for example, Acumen, a New York–based fund, founded in 2001 with an explicit mission of alleviating worldwide poverty. Investors participating in the Acumen fund are frequently impact first investors. Acumen operates by taking large stock positions, even majority positions, in early-stage impact ventures. Its investments typically range from $250,000 to $3 million. These positions expose Acumen to significant risk, but enable fund managers to exert real control over a venture. Acumen clearly states its intention on its website: "Our aim in investing patient capital is not to seek high returns, but rather to jump-start the creation of enterprises that improve the ability of the poor to live with dignity."

Compare Acumen's approach to an asset manager like Blue-Orchard, a fund whose client base has a nearly equal proportion of institutional investors and high-net-worth individuals. BlueOrchard's Dexia Microfinance Fund was launched to provide capital for microfinancing banks in Africa, Asia, and Latin America. They have exclusively done so through debt instruments, having made equity investments only in institutions with at least a three-year track record. Investments typically target a return of around 1 to 2 percent above the current LIBOR. These are hallmarks of a financial first investment: stable, but not overly ambitious returns; safety of principal; and little managerial control of the impact business eventually receiving the capital.

Yet, we should not view financial first investors as solely interested in safer debt instruments. An investment into ProCredit Holding, for example, can be seen as a financial first investment. ProCredit was founded in 1998, and has since grown to manage a nearly $6 billion loan portfolio, operating through twenty-one banks in Eastern Europe, Latin America, and Africa. The firm is a microfinance bank; the loans it issues are typically around $8,000. Its large stockholders include institutional investors like the World Bank's International Finance Group and TIAA-CREF, the largest manager of retirement funds for the academic and research sector.

What makes an investment in ProCredit a financial first investment is that it prioritizes return while providing relative safety. When ProCredit opened a bank in the Congo, a region in the African continent the size of Western Europe but a market with just eleven banks, it gave itself eight years and targeted a 15 percent return on equity. Similarly, Bridges Ventures Social Entrepreneurs Fund, a fund tailored for impact first investors that raised nearly £12 million (about $20 million) in 2009, insists that prospective investees present a sustainable business model before they are eligible for funding.

Finally, it's worth noting that impact first investors may morph into financial first investors once they mature. This parallels the impact investing market as a whole. (More on this phenomenon later in Chapter 12.) For many institutional investors, their capital originates from foundations and high-net-worth individuals who are willing to concede a market rate of return, if they know their capital is generating real impact. However, over time, these investors may seek a better return, especially if they can do so while maintaining—and even strengthening—their social impact. It is a verity of the impact investing market that, as more impact funds earn market-rate returns for their investors, more capital will gravitate toward those funds.

JUDGING INVESTMENT PERFORMANCE

Evaluating the successes and failures of an investment is essential both to value it and to hold its managers accountable. This is the next step in the impact investing process. Evaluation does not come cheap. The transaction costs associated with verifying impact can render an investment unfeasible, if the investment isn't large enough. "If I make a $2 million investment, and the investors are paying me a 2 percent management fee, that's $40,000 a year," said Ignia Partner's Rodríguez Arregui. "With that money I can pay an analyst and part of the overhead costs to monitor that investment. But if I invest $200,000 and I get a 2 percent fee, that's only $4,000. With $4,000 I can pay the electricity, but I can't support the overhead to do this activity."

Compensating impact investing fund managers requires different incentive packages than those seen in conventional private equity funds, where general partners are compensated by the financial performance of the fund and nothing else. Not so with impact investing funds. Compensation for impact investing fund managers is tied to a bundle of performance metrics—often including environmental and social metrics along with financial metrics.

Consider Aureos Capital's Africa Health Fund, which invests in organizations providing health care services for bottom of the pyramid communities. It is one of seventeen funds operated by

Aureos Capital. The fund's manager earns bonuses only if he or she hits its impact targets. As his or her base compensation, the manager is entitled to "carried interest" of 15 percent of profits made from the fund, assuming it achieves its financial hurdle. Then impact is measured. If half of the people served by the fund have a household income of less than $3,000 per year, the manager will receive an additional 5 percent. If 70 percent of the people served live on less than $3,000 per year, the manager receives an additional 15 percent. Limited partners at Aureos Capital pay a third party to measure the impact achieved by the fund.

QUANTIFYING SOCIAL RETURNS

But we must also define precisely what impact is. This brings us to the final, and perhaps most important, component of a mature impact investing market.

A stock market provides one comprehensive and unified metric to quantify a stock's value. That metric is price. If the efficiency of the market is to be believed, all the variables that enter into valuing a share of Microsoft—the strength of its leadership, earnings, cash flows, projections of future cash flows, and so forth—might tell us on a given day that Microsoft's common shares are more valuable than Intel's. Of course, the NASDAQ evaluates the value of companies only in financial terms. What, then, if we add the variable of social and environmental impact? How can we fairly compare the performance of impact businesses in terms that quantify financial performance and impact?

These questions continue to flummox the impact investing community. Quantifying impact is difficult in theory, and even more so in practice.

- To measure impact, we must first consider what outcome would have been produced in the absence of the activity.
- We also need to consider what intervention might have been displaced, such as an investment in a charity or foundation.

- Is the product that the investee produces necessarily superior to the alternative? For example, can we necessarily quantify the marginal impact generated by a company that produces anti-malarial mosquito nets against other organizations combating the malaria epidemic?

Paul Brest, director of the Stanford Center on Philanthropy and Civil Society, and Kelly Born of the William and Flora Hewlett Foundation reflected on the notion of social return in a piece in the *Stanford Social Innovation Review* in 2013. In noting that "a particular investment has impact only if it increases the quantity or quality of the enterprise's social outcomes beyond what would otherwise have occurred," Brest and Born cast doubt that other investors would turn down such opportunities if they earned comparable financial returns. They then acknowledge that only "someone with distinctive knowledge about the risk and potential social and financial returns of a particular opportunity may make an investment that others would pass up. The question of investment impact is of obvious importance to investors who want to make a difference."

If the industry cannot solve this riddle soon, impact ventures will invariably fall into the habit of trumping up claims of impact. Leaving organizations to record and advertise success in anecdotal form would risk undermining the promise of impact investing. While the industry continues to refine social impact measurement approaches, investment fund managers turn instead to third-party evaluators who quantify the impact funds are generating. The potential conflict of interest, where the evaluators are being paid by the evaluated, is both obvious and problematic.

With help from the Rockefeller Foundation, B Lab, itself a nonprofit organization, was founded, in part, to promote the growth of impact investing through use of an objective rating and analytics system. B Lab operates GIIRS, the rating system discussed in Chapter 10 that evaluates companies' environmental impact and the treatment of their workforces. B Lab also issues "B Corp" certifications to companies that score high enough on a comprehensive sustainability assessment, one that is separate but similar to its points-based GIIRS assessments. To date, more than 1,000 companies across sixty industries and more than thirty countries have been certified as B Corps.

The B Corp certification effort is laudable, but it lacks the ability to compare social performance across sectors or to quantify financial and social performance. The GIIRS rating system comes closer. Under GIIRS, a five-star company has generated a greater positive social impact than a company earning only four stars. Yet even GIIRS cannot precisely quantify social performance like the NASDAQ and NYSE can quantify financial performance. This ability to quantify social performance precisely—and, with it, the ability to provide a comprehensive financial and social valuation of the company—remains conspicuously absent from the impact investing market.

CASHING OUT

The final step in the impact investing process concerns exiting the investment. In 2004, Trillium Asset Management, a Boston-based investment advisory firm dedicated exclusively to socially responsible and impact investing, brought together six of its investors to go in on a $1.5 million deal with EcoEnergy International, a leading developer of hydro and wind power. Four years later, Trillum had built a textbook case for how to make impact investing successful. When EcoEnergy was sold to Suez Energy in 2008, Trillium had earned two and a half times its initial investment. This smooth and profitable exit from the investment is not frequently replicated.

Financial returns can be realized from an initial investment in one of three ways: an investor's stake is acquired in a private transaction; the company issues an initial public offering, liquidating some or all of the initial investment at a greater value than its cost; or the company buys back the investor's stake in the venture. These are all possible exits from an impact investment, as they would be in any conventional investment. Yet, they are infrequently seen in the impact investing marketplace. This dearth of off-ramps in impact investing continues to trouble many institutional investors, and will certainly inhibit growth in the coming years if more reliable avenues for exits are not built into the industry.

Could such an off-ramp be built with an impact investing exchange, parallel to the NASDAQ? If such an exchange were built, could doing so introduce mainstream investors into the impact investing market? Several recently created platforms come close to meeting the objective of a public exchange. If ultimately successful, one or more of these platforms could provide the impact investing market with stable off-ramps for investors to exit their investments—akin to the off-ramps that exist in the conventional capital markets.

One platform launched in 2010, Mission Markets, marked the first step toward a social exchange. Mission Markets is an over-the-counter, online trading platform operated by Bendigo Securities LLC. Accredited investors can log onto Mission Markets to view a full description of an issuer's mission, as well as the issuer's GIIRS ratings and IRIS impact indicators. However, Mission Markets was not created with the intent of becoming a public platform. Only accredited investors can participate.

In June of 2013, the Social Stock Exchange (SSE) opened in London. The SSE is a more public platform than Mission Markets, allowing both accredited and unaccredited investors to participate. The SSE has received financial support from the British government to get off the ground. The name is a misnomer of sorts—it is not an exchange. Instead, it provides a portal from which to trade securities of companies that generate impact. A few months after the SSE was launched, another similar exchange, the Social Venture Connexion (the SVX) opened in Toronto. Only accredited investors and only issuers that meet the SVX's standards for impact may participate in the exchange. Only companies that meet standards developed by B Lab in certifying B Corporations can be included in the Social Venture Connexion. Once investors decide they would like to invest, all transactions are effected outside of the SVX.

The only truly public social stock exchange will soon be found in Singapore. When Impact Exchange Asia (IIX) is fully operational, it will include securities issued by for-profit companies and debt issuances from nonprofit organizations, but the IIX will insist that issuers demonstrate a social mission before they will be permitted to be listed. Building and sustaining the IIX will be a challenge. There are more than a few concerns that the necessary investor base is not yet ready and that the number of investment-ready social enterprises is not yet large enough to sustain the IIX.

THE CHALLENGES OF AN IMPACT INVESTING MARKET

At the moment, visions of a rolling scroll on CNBC of stock prices of impact businesses need to be tempered. Exchanges are open only to foundations, endowments, and accredited investors—and absent a major change in securities regulations, the exchanges will remain the domain of accredited investors for some time. The purpose of these exchanges is not to open the doors of impact investing to retail investors or even to pump more capital into the market; rather, these exchanges and those like them provide an ability to assess and compare impact across the industry.

Still, there will come a time when all of these components of the market are established: a large community of investors ready to make deals, a pipeline of sustainable businesses, and a dedicated platform for the cross-sector evaluation of impact. Once they are, the final issue of capital might solve itself after the infrastructure exists to support it. It is apparent that consumers are ready to embrace and support socially minded businesses. Recent surveys by Edelman, a public relations firm, and the Hope Foundation have found overwhelming majorities of investors expressing interest in impact investing, validating J.P. Morgan's ambitious projections for the market.

Of course, the challenges of the impact investing market are not limited to the necessary infrastructure needed to support the $1 trillion in assets J.P. Morgan projects could enter the market by 2020. Beyond the issues of infrastructure, the development of a mature impact investing market will depend on building a public perception that good social performance increases a company's value. On average, 80 percent of the market value of a Standard & Poor's 500 company is intangible—meaning nothing of any book value. What, then, is shareholder value if not a product of public perception?

How does it change if we view social performance as a component of market value? CVS certainly did not decide in February of 2014 to stop selling cigarettes at all of its stores solely out of altruistic concern for public health. Unalloyed charity does not inspire the California-based TOMS shoes to donate one pair of shoes to children in the poorest regions of the globe for every pair it sells over the counter. These decisions are driven by a fundamental view of the market that did not exist until recently. This emerging view of the market is the raison d'être for the immense talent coming into the impact investing community from the most elite of business schools.

It will probably not take long until this view works its way through the financial-services industry. When it does, financial advisors will hasten to become fluent in the language of impact investing. A 2013 survey by the CFA Association asked financial advisors whether they had even heard of impact investing; 66 percent responded that they had not. Investors who don't have much familiarity with the market rely on their advisors to give them informed advice; if their advisors, in fact, are not informed, a transaction of any size is prohibited. When their advisors become informed, as they inevitably will, impact investing will fully gain its rightful position in the investment marketplace.

CHAPTER TWELVE

Impact Investing

Pursuing Its Destiny

Each year the impact investing community comes together at the Fort Mason Center in San Francisco for the annual "SOCAP"— Social Capital Markets conference. SOCAP was founded by three visionaries: Kevin Jones, the founder of Good Capital, a venture capital firm that invests in social enterprises, and a member of the team launching the first U.S. node by the Hub, a network of more than a dozen work spaces for social entrepreneurs in cities across the world from Cairo to London; Rose Lee Harden, an Episcopal priest who ran Habitat for Humanity's Jackson, Mississippi, affiliate; and Tim Freundlich, who organized the Giving Fund, a $60 million impact investment–based donor fund, and went on to expand it into Impact Assets, which he serves as president.

SOCAP connects global innovators—socially conscious individual investors, foundations, institutions, and social entrepreneurs—to bolster the market at the nexus of money and meaning. They share ideas, collaborate, and go home inspired and empowered by their peers. Once a small conference held next door to Fisherman's Wharf, SOCAP now attracts some 2,000 attendees from more than fifty countries.

You might find Andrew Wolk at SOCAP. Wolk is the founder of Root Cause, a Boston-based consulting company specially purposed to serve nonprofits, foundations, donors, and governments on social innovation. Unhappy with the lack of coordination in the social innovation space, Wolk founded Root Cause in 2003 to be a clearinghouse of ideas and best practices for his clients. The next year he helped launch the Social Innovation Forum, a market of social innovators committed to supporting a dialogue on what works and what doesn't. "Too often, competing factors—such as political agenda, lack of information or agreement on program performance, and relationships taking precedence over data—hinder the decision-making process that drives investment and growth in the private sector," Wolk wrote in a 2012 opinion piece for the *Stanford Social Innovation Review*. "Developing social impact markets is a way to better allocate our limited resources."

You might also find people like Bill Drayton at SOCAP. Drayton, the founder and CEO of the Ashoka Support Network, a community of social entrepreneurs, has worked his entire adult life in advancing social progress. As a young man, he worked for the U.S. Environmental Protection Agency where, among other accomplishments, he was involved in writing a proposal for emissions trading, which later became the basis for the Kyoto Protocol. After leaving the EPA, Drayton worked part-time for McKinsey while he launched Ashoka. The network would soon become a platform from which new solutions could be spawned to solve social problems. Drayton didn't just start a network of social entrepreneurs; he is widely credited with having invented the term "social entrepreneurship." These entrepreneurs could start nonprofit or for-profit ventures, as long as they innovated to solve problems. Ashoka is now the largest network of social entrepreneurs in the world. It provides startup financing, training, technical support, and the network of its more than 3,000 active fellows in seventy different countries.

Ashoka was the first, but there are now many other organizations like Ashoka—including the Skoll Foundation, the Unreasonable Institute ("We exist to give entrepreneurs tackling the world's greatest challenges an 'unreasonable advantage'"), and Impact Engine in Chicago—that exist to bring the impact investing community together. They support the growth of impact entrepreneurs and, most importantly, feed the growing demand for investment-ready businesses.

At least until recently, the market has been ineffective in matching investors with capital to a pipeline of reasonably safe and sustainable deals. Finding few investment opportunities, the Tony Elumelu Foundation, an organization dedicated to supporting entrepreneurs in the African continent, recently put down its checkbooks and became more active in developing and incubating businesses before providing seed capital. This need for incubating businesses before they seek capital is the logic behind Impact Engine. It is also the dirty work that for so long few in the impact industry market seemed eager to do. "It is as if impact investors are lined up around the proverbial water pump waiting for the flood of deals, while no one is actually priming the pump!" noted Matt Bannick and Paula Goldman, two executives of the Omidyar Network, in a 2012 article in the *Stanford Social Innovation Review*.

No longer. The first step in the process of bringing impact investing into the mainstream is a fait accompli: social entrepreneurs are finding networks of mentors who can turn the best ideas into reality and, remarkably, many of these mentors come from competitors. This is the nature of the impact investing market. Each year at SOCAP, you'll find a community of people who could easily be doing business against each other instead doing business with each other. The people here seem as invested in growing the social innovation sector as they are in growing their own businesses.

The energy harnessed each year at SOCAP can only go so far. If J.P. Morgan's projection that the impact investing market could reach $1 trillion in assets by 2020 is to be achieved, the market will have to grow exponentially in the coming years. The first step in achieving such growth, coordinating innovation and building a generation of social entrepreneurs, is already happening at forums like SOCAP. But that is only the first of many hurdles in the race to a $1 trillion market.

THE IMPORTANCE OF PUBLIC POLICY

A 2013 report by Maximilian Martin, founder and CEO of the Switzerland-based strategy firm Impact Economy, organized policy levers around three primary objectives: stimulating the supply of potential impact investing deals, directing and leveraging public capital to grow the market, and regulating demand for impact businesses.

The role of public policy in supporting the growth of impact investing cannot be overstated. For perspective, consider the 1978 Employee Retirement Income Security Act (ERISA). One provision, little noticed when the act was signed into law by President Jimmy Carter, permitted pension funds to invest in venture capital. In 1980, as the law was being enacted, the venture capital sector held an estimated $600 million in assets. Four years later, more than $3 billion was invested into venture capital, enabling Apple, among other early-stage businesses, to take flight. The United States is now the unquestioned leader in the venture capital space.

In Washington, a boost to the supply of impact investments came from a small provision in the Jumpstart Our Business Startups (JOBS) Act. Unlike most orders of business in Washington, the JOBS Act passed with overwhelming bipartisan support, clearing the Republican-led House in March of 2012, and weeks later doing the same in the Democratic-led Senate. The JOBS Act did many things. It exempted issuers from registering small equity offerings with the SEC. It eased restrictions on issuers soliciting and advertising securities offerings. And it instructed the SEC to issue guidelines on "crowdfunding," raising capital—debt and equity—for early-stage businesses through the Internet. For the first time, businesses can raise up to $1 million under a significantly pared-down set of disclosures that are still required for larger public offerings.

As this book goes to press, the regulations surrounding crowd-funding have yet to be issued. That hasn't stopped a number of platforms from getting a head start. From 2011 to 2013, the crowdfunding platform MicroVentures raised more than $16 million for tech startups, taking more than 2,000 applications from companies seeking startup capital and winnowing them down to fewer than forty investment opportunities. The SEC is well past the congressionally mandated deadline for issuing the regulations, although in October of 2013, the Commission proposed a set of rules that were to have been finalized in early 2014 (but were not). The proposed rules can only be seen as cautionary, and more than a bit restrictive. The issuer would have to file annual reports to the SEC until all securities have been sold or dissolved. Included in those reports would be an exhaustive introduction of the company, detailed explanations of what the company plans to do with the money, and biographies of the company's top executives. Additionally, a company raising more than $500,000 would be required to produce audited financial statements. In short, while the restrictions around crowdfunding are less onerous than those governing conventional security offerings, the crowdfunding market will hardly be anarchic.

Until the crowdfunding regulations are finalized, federal law generally prohibits issuers from raising capital from more than thirty-five non-accredited investors. By law, accredited investors must have a minimum of $1 million in net worth, or have earned $200,000 the previous two years. Before the JOBS Act, the law prevented non-accredited investors from losing significant wealth in companies destined to fail; it also served to starve startups from significant sources of capital. Soon non-accredited investors will be in the game, but they, too, will not be without restrictions. The JOBS Act prevents non-accredited investors from investing more than 5 percent of their income, or $2,000, whichever is greater. Regulations surrounding the issuers are equally onerous, perhaps prohibitively so. Issuers must verify that their investors are accredited and that they have not exceeded their limits.

Could crowdfunding nourish the impact investing market enough to break into the mainstream? The promise of crowdfunding to jump-start legions of new businesses is immense. The success of crowdfunded ventures will almost certainly rest on the alchemy of social media to expand the reach of startups. Or, as Devin Thorpe of *Forbes* magazine put it, "If you only have 78 Facebook friends and you've never understood what Twitter is for, building a successful crowdfunding campaign will be a challenge." Yet it would be irresponsible to be purblind to its risks. Through crowdfunding, startup entrepreneurs will bypass the humbling process of raising funds from friends, family members, and venture capitalists and instead pitch their businesses to investors on the web. If it goes well, crowdfunding will provide entrepreneurs with a massive new stream of capital; if it doesn't, legions of unsophisticated investors could become targets of fraud, virtually outside the auspices of the SEC. It's worth considering that many of these startups and early-stage businesses will likely turn to crowdfunding for capital only after they have been turned away from multiple venture capitalists, suggesting they may not have sustainable businesses. The sharks are circling the market. Six months after the JOBS Act was signed into law, the North American Securities Administrators Association found nearly 9,000 website domains that included the term "crowdfunding," ten times the number that existed just before the law was enacted.

Both in the United States and in Europe, governments have taken notice of the ability of the private sector to do their work for them and invested public monies into the emergent impact investing market. In September of 2009, President Obama commissioned the White House Office of Social Innovation and Civic Participation, a clearinghouse of ideas and federal dollars directed toward efficient social organizations. Two years later, Obama introduced the Startup America Initiative, a massive effort to mobilize federal resources to support early-stage businesses; included in the Startup America strategy was a $1 billion impact investing fund, administered by the U.S. Small Business Administration.

In April of 2012, British Prime Minister David Cameron launched Big Society Capital, providing £600 million to help support a "well capitalized and sustainable social investment market," according to its vision statement. Among Big Society Capital's first investments was a pledge of £450,000 for social impact bonds to finance a support program for school kids in East London. If the program failed, investors would be left with nothing, but if the program succeeded, the investors would be made whole with interest. It would be logical to expect Cameron, having found his way to 10 Downing Street promising (and delivering on) austerity, to nix discretionary spending programs like Big Society Capital. In fact, just the opposite has happened. Seeking to support the social sector with as much efficiency and as little money as possible, Big Society Capital has provided financing for a broad array of social services, from affordable housing units and job programs to homeless shelters. Certainly among the current generation of global leaders, Cameron has led the cause of impact investing.

In June of 2013 the British government hosted leaders throughout the industry for the first G8 Social Impact Investing Forum in London. Prime Minister Cameron, in touting his Big Society Capital, told attendees, "We've got a great idea here that can transform our societies, by using the power of finance to tackle the most difficult social problems. Problems that have frustrated government after government, country after country, generation after generation. Issues like drug abuse, youth unemployment, homelessness, and even global poverty. The potential for social investment is that big." It was during the G8 Forum that the Obama Administration threw both arms around impact investing, introducing its National Impact Initiative, the U.S. government's most expansive impact investing venture to date. As a part of the initiative, the U.S. Agency for International Development is partnering with their British counterparts, the U.K.'s Department for International Development, in a $25 million a year fund to finance anti-poverty strategies in the developing world. The National Impact Initiative would also fund a round of small business loans directed at impact ventures.

The clearest and most effective example of a policy regulating demand came in 2012 when the British Parliament passed the Social Value Act, requiring government officials to account for social and environmental impact when issuing government contracts. The measure drew support from the Labour and Conservative parties alike and from Prime Minister Cameron. Remarkably, the bill was passed without much notice by the British press, given that the law has the potential to transform the way government procurement is done (and not just in the U.K.). The law is sure to give rise to some creative proposals, highlighting and perhaps exaggerating social benefits of service providers. Yet, it is equally likely to benefit organizations that had genuinely been reducing the negative environmental impact of their business operations long before the Social Value Act.

A similar law could be enacted in the United States. It seems only logical that, if presented with a bid that undercuts the alternative but produces more pollution, it may be in the government's interest to issue the contract to the higher-bid service provider. Indeed, a more limited version of the Social Value Act has already been implemented by the most unlikely source: the U.S. military. In 2007, House Democrats inserted a provision into the Department of Defense budget requiring that 25 percent of all electricity used by the military come from renewable energy sources. The military is the largest single user of energy in the United States, and now they are leveraging their market power to drive demand for renewable energy. In no small part due to this mandate, renewable energy usage in the United States has nearly tripled since the 2007 DoD budget was passed.

THE INSTITUTIONAL INVESTORS WEIGH IN

James Gifford, an ambitious Ph.D. student in economics, had an idea: ask large capital managers to sign onto a set of principles guiding how they manage their money. The initiative was launched in 2006, and Gifford later convinced the United Nations to help spearhead it. It was called the Principles for Responsible Investment Initiative. The exponential growth of the Principles for Responsible Investment Initiative has provided yet another indication of impact investing's longevity. The Principles for Responsible Investment Initiative enlisted signatories to uphold six principles of impactful investing, which were written in collaboration with the world's twenty largest asset managers:

1. We will incorporate ESG (environmental, social, and governance) issues into investment analysis and decision-making processes.

2. We will be active owners and incorporate ESG issues into our ownership policies and practices.

3. We will seek appropriate disclosure on ESG issues by the entities in which we invest.

4. We will promote acceptance and implementation of the Principles within the investment industry.

5. We will work together to enhance our effectiveness in implementing the Principles.

6. We will each report on our activities and progress towards implementing the Principles.

They initially enlisted fifty signatories, but would soon gain steam. "Before the PRI, the number of organizations reporting on responsible investment in any systematic way could be counted on two hands," Gifford wrote in 2013. "In 2007, 104 signatories participated in the first PRI reporting and assessment process. The next year, 156. Then 276, 433, and in 2011, 545." The PRI now has more than 1,200 signatories, including 800 asset managers, who collectively hold more than $34 trillion in assets.

This virtuous cycle has begun to spin for the impact investing market. The bulge bracket banks have begun to take notice, leading the way for more retail investors to enter the market. This final phase of the process is ongoing and accelerating. In recent years the SOCAP conference has drawn greater interest and participation from the likes of Bank of America, Goldman Sachs, Credit Suisse, and other large banks.

Of the major multi-national banks, J.P. Morgan Chase was the first to recognize the opportunity, opening its Social Finance Department in 2007. J.P. Morgan Social Finance now offers a diverse impact investment portfolio and provides thought leadership for the market. Recently, it partnered with The Bill and Melinda Gates Foundation and Lion's Head Global Partners to bring the Global Health Investment Fund (GHIF) to market. The GHIF holds $108 million in assets, supporting the introduction of health products into markets where they can make the strongest impact.

Deutsche Bank has operated its $10 million Impact Investment Fund since 2011. Goldman Sachs has also recently jumped into the impact investing market, launching its GS Social Impact Fund in November of 2013. Appearing at the left-leaning Center for American Progress in Washington, Goldman Sachs CEO Lloyd Blankfein said that the fund would begin with $250 million, but predicted that "if it works, it'll get bigger and bigger and bigger, and have a life of its own."

Other bulge bracket banks provide impact investing advising services, although they call it by their own names: UBS and Bank of America Merrill Lynch call it "values-based investing." In April of 2012, Morgan Stanley introduced its Investing with Impact platform, enabling retail investors to build an impact investing sleeve in their portfolios. With Investing with Impact, Morgan Stanley began providing interested investors with information on financial return and detailed information on social and environmental impact.

This issue of market accessibility is being further attenuated by the development of social indexes. The RBS Social Enterprise 100 Index was introduced in 2010 to track impactful enterprises of all kinds. In spite of the name, the index has 863 organizations, as of March of 2014. Two other popular indices also provide the value of diversification while advancing the social mission: the Dow Jones Sustainability Index and the FTSE4Good.

Impact investing appears to be at an inflection point, where the market could soon accelerate toward the $1 trillion goalpost or languish as just a good, but ultimately unworkable idea. It is one thing for the concept to be embraced on paper, yet another for actual impact investing deals to materialize in significant size and number. There is clear potential for impact investing to become not just an investment strategy but an asset class, like hedge funds and emerging market funds, recognizable to institutional and retail investors alike. But it will no doubt be a long slog before we see a mature market. In the end, impact investing could be destined for desuetude once the twenty-somethings who have given the field such promise confront their first $200,000-a-year offer in something decidedly less impactful. The ability for the market to evolve will determine its ultimate fate.

The ability to build all of the components of a financial market is critical to allowing the industry to scale. So, too, is the ability for investors to transcend the massive cultural differences between the financial industry and the nonprofit sector. Can any one fund manager satisfy investors seeking a financial return before a social return and investors seeking the opposite? Integrating Wall Street with the nonprofit sector probably won't be seamless. It appears unlikely that the ruthless culture of the financial industry—with its strict adherence to the numbers and lack of filial affection for underperforming managers—will be fully embraced by professionals who have spent decades in the nonprofit sector. The process of persuading both spheres to cooperate with one another will surely be a long one.

There is also the issue of competition. To the extent that the impact investing industry seeks to displace the nonprofit sector—not a goal embraced by many—it will need to persuade legions of fiercely loyal donors to abandon the causes many have supported their entire adult lives. If polling data is to be believed, that will be an impossible task. A 2010 Hope Foundation survey of investors found that, of those investors expressing interest in impact investing, just 10 percent would invest dollars that could instead be donated to a nonprofit, absent an impact investing opportunity. Yet, if these investors were to participate in the impact investing market, more than half of the respondents, 56 percent, said they would turn dollars away from conventional investments to direct them toward impact investments. The finding indicated that impact businesses must compete in the conventional capital market, not the nonprofit market. Additionally, the Hope Foundation survey confirmed what many professionals in the nonprofit sector already knew: donors are almost implacably loyal to the nonprofits they support. Nearly 80 percent of respondents said they were "100 percent loyal" to the nonprofits they donate to, and few respondents expressed any interest in finding out how the nonprofits they supported actually performed. The clear takeaway from the Hope Foundation survey was that, to achieve critical mass, the impact investing community needs to compete with conventional investment vehicles and resist targeting the nonprofit sector. Donors are so loyal to their favorite nonprofit organizations that they are comfortable losing 100 percent of their principal capital before they are willing to consider investing in an organization that will return their money with interest and still generate a comparable impact. Submarket rates of return in the impact investing market will not be compared against simply giving away your money. So the likelihood is that donations and investments will always co-exist, as they should.

Finally, there's this reality: not many people know what impact investing is. Given the role of financial advisors as gatekeepers to the market, information on impact investing must go through them first. Impact investing is finding its way to the desks of financial advisors, but the older generation appears uninterested. A 2012 survey of more than 1,000 financial advisors, sponsored by the Rockefeller Foundation and Deutsche Bank, found common characteristics of advisors who were interested in impact investing—they were far more likely to be younger and far more likely to be female. Only 30 percent of advisors with more than fifteen years in the business expressed interest in these investments, while 51 percent of advisors with more than three years but less than ten years said they would be interested. Female advisors were 25 percent more likely than their male counterparts to be interested in recommending investments that could "provide financial returns and environmental and social benefits."

THE GROWTH TRAJECTORY IS CLEAR

Clearly, we are at the front end of the evolution of the market. But there are plenty of indications that impact investing may indeed change how capital is invested in both the for-profit and nonprofit sectors, and soon. As ambitious as J.P. Morgan's projection is that the impact investing market could reach $1 trillion in invested capital by 2020, even if the industry achieves that lofty goal, only $1 in $900 in financial assets will be invested in impact ventures. That's about .1 percent of all invested capital. When seen from that perspective, reaching the $1 trillion target may be achievable. The growth trajectory of this industry is clear. In 2010, J.P. Morgan counted 1,105 impact investing deals amounting to $2.5 billion; the next year, they found 2,213 deals totaling $4.3 billion.

First, consider the demand to provide services for the bottom of the pyramid. The J.P. Morgan report I've referenced also estimated that as much as $786 billion would be needed to provide affordable housing worldwide, another $13 billion to provide clean water for rural communities, and as much as $10 billion to provide primary education to each and every child. Then consider how much capital will flow into reducing carbon emissions, if only out of sheer necessity. Investments in renewable energy are expected to continue and accelerate their current breakneck pace, projected to nearly triple globally, from $115 billion in 2008 to $318 billion in 2018. Given the alarming need to curb global carbon emissions, this is somewhat settling news. We don't have a choice but to not serve the bottom of the pyramid and to solve global climate change. These are investments that will need to be made if we are to maintain the long-term sustainability of humanity.

This awareness of the market, as slow as it has been to reach retail investors and financial advisors, has certainly weaved its way through major foundations. In 2009, The Bill and Melinda Gates Foundation committed an eye-popping $400 million for program-related investments to support impact investing initiatives. (The loan guarantee provided to the KIPP charter school in Houston was a part of this massive program-related investment.)

The potential precedent of the impact investing industry's growth trajectory is that of the microfinance industry, an industry that emerged in the 1970s to provide financial services to the poorest regions of the globe with loans as small as a few hundred dollars. For two decades, the microfinance industry toiled as a little-noticed idea confined to think tanks, foreign service officers, and the like. It was not until the 1990s that the industry began to demonstrate profitability and slowly introduce itself to the mainstream markets. It has been, and continues to be, buoyed by the purchasing power of government. The U.S. Overseas Private Investment Corporation (OPIC), an investment fund for the U.S. government to support developmental finance, carries a portfolio weighted heavily with microfinance institutions. After more than thirty years of development, the microfinance market has extended loans to more than 200 million people and has achieved stable annual returns.

A long view of the development of the market is essential. For close observers, the coming years in the impact investing market are certain to bring seemingly endless fits and starts, ideas that hold the potential to be the next Google, only to be tossed into the wastebasket, and moments where the trajectory of the market may for a short time point down toward zero, not up toward $1 trillion. Even in failure, their efforts are significant if they in some way enable future market innovation. Muhammad Yunus' Grameen Bank, founded in 1983, took fifteen years to reach one million customers. In walking the trail Grameen charted for microfinance institutions, the Chennai, India–based Equitas Holdings tallied its first one million customers within five years after opening its doors in 2007. Nonetheless, if the standard pattern holds true, we would expect plenty of businesses to fail before the learning curve flattens enough to enable the next generation of firms to scale the industry.

The microfinance market followed the familiar "S-curve," marking the pace of growth against time. The curve begins with an innovation slowly entering a market, pushed by a group of persistent innovators and risk-loving investors. Once the innovation has been perfected, growth quickly accelerates. Once the innovation matures, marginal growth decreases, but only after the market has been saturated. It would be logical to expect that the impact investing market will follow a similar trajectory, and that we are on the front end of this process. We might then wonder when that critical moment, when an innovation has been perfected and growth accelerates, will come for impact investing.

As the Omidyar Network's Matt Bannick and Paula Goodman noted in the *Stanford Social Innovation Review* in September of 2013: "Market scalers enter a sector after a generic model has been de-risked. They accelerate the growth of a sector by scaling as individual firms. They may also tend to refine and enhance the generic model." It goes without saying that the firms Bannick and Goodman call "market scalers" will enjoy a far larger pool of capital than the far riskier innovators. This awareness should guide observers of the market as they watch how early-stage innovators navigate the capital markets—including the crowdfunding platforms soon to be introduced—and the later-stage businesses that follow. If the S-curve applies to the impact investing market, it will be the market scalers that provide that critical moment where the market breaks out of the doldrums of early-stage development.

It will be the Millennials, the eighty million or so people born in the United States between 1980 and 2000, who will likely bring impact investing mainstream. Accenture, the global strategy firm, estimates that more than $30 trillion in financial and non-financial assets will transfer from Baby Boomers to Millennials over the next thirty to forty years, and that 10 percent of the total wealth in the United States will change hands every five years between 2031 and 2045. The accelerating rate at which wealth will shift to the next generation will become a defining issue for wealth managers and for the impact investing universe. According to the Spectrum Group, the Washington, D.C.–based counseling firm, the Millennials will be our first impact investing generation; already, 45 percent of affluent Millennials want to put their wealth to use in helping others and consider social responsibility a factor when making investment decisions.

Millennials experienced the September 11 attacks, both first-hand and from afar; they experienced the international turmoil of the Arab Spring and wars in Iraq and Afghanistan; they have been personally affected by the housing meltdown and two boom-and-bust cycles; they feel the threat of terrorism; they have seen political dysfunction in Washington and in their home states; and they are activists for personal rights, including gay marriage and health care. They also know that economic injustice and power disparities have robbed millions of sustainable livelihoods and, with it, hope.

Millennials, a growing number of whom are social entrepreneurs in their own right, embrace the power of capital to drive positive social change. As the market is demanding that financial advisors gain expertise in the science and art of impact investing, as impact measurement becomes more reliable, and as impact investing knowledge and research become more accessible, Millennials, with their new-found wealth and their shared experiences across borders and cultures, are sure to put vast resources to work in pursuit of both financial and social returns and, to their credit, lead the way for others to follow suit.

CHAPTER THIRTEEN

Keeping Score

What Success Looks Like

Charmaine Bowman was twenty-three years old when her mother died of cancer. Depressed and alone, Charmaine self-medicated with drugs, resulting in addiction that led to her incarceration. She hit rock bottom when she gave birth to her daughter, Aniya, in prison. When Charmaine was released in 2009, she needed help getting back on her feet. She turned to A Safe Haven Foundation, a Chicago-based nonprofit organization that empowers families and individuals experiencing homelessness or crisis to achieve sustainable self-sufficiency.

A Safe Haven provided Charmaine with integrated recovery services that gave her a new start: Charmaine received addiction treatment and participated in morning meditation, twelve-step meetings, and pre-employment classes. She also learned marketable job skills through one of A Safe Haven's workforce development programs. With help from A Safe Haven Foundation, in time Charmaine transitioned to her own apartment, found stable employment, and reunited with her sons, Anthony and Alex.

If corporations seeking to maximize shareholder value define success by the amount of profits they earn, using financial statements and accounting tools to benchmark and demonstrate achievement, how can enterprises whose primary or secondary motive is positive change measure—and prove—success? Charmaine can tell us how A Safe Haven Foundation impacted her life, but is Charmaine's story enough to tell A Safe Haven's management and stakeholders whether—and to what extent—it's succeeding in achieving its social mission?

Unlike the traditional profit-driven business, an enterprise in the business of producing an intangible bottom line—social good—cannot measure success in terms of dollars alone. In addition to demonstrating profitability—or at least financial sustainability—mission-driven ventures must show that they're making progress toward achieving their social missions. They must demonstrate their *social impact*.

This chapter and the two that follow explore the concept of measuring social impact. We'll begin by defining the "social impact" that mission-driven ventures are called upon to measure. Next, we'll examine who's making that call and why, concluding with a focus on the global push for, and development of, a universal framework for defining, tracking, and measuring social impact. Throughout these three chapters about measuring social impact, we'll introduce you to mission-driven ventures that have benefited from effective impact measurement, illustrating why reliable metrics are so important.

A SAFE HAVEN'S SOCIAL IMPACT

The concept of measuring or evaluating social impact can include a wide range of definitions and use varying terminology. For purposes of this book, when we talk about measuring social impact, we mean tracking and quantifying the long-term changes that are attributable to an organization's activities and programs—how the world is different because those activities and programs exist.

That information is both necessary and desirable for social entrepreneurs who seek to scale their more successful programs and tweak their less successful ones, as well as donors and investors who increasingly support results over mere intentions. Measuring social impact is different from measuring performance, which involves monitoring and measuring inputs, outputs, and immediate outcomes. That's not to say, however, that a mission-driven venture does not need to measure these elements of performance. Indeed, inputs, outputs, and outcomes are essential ingredients in the recipe for social impact.

Think of social impact like baking a loaf of bread. You start with a recipe, just as a social venture begins with an idea of what it hopes to achieve. From there you measure and mix the ingredients—flour, sugar, yeast, and so forth. The ingredients for the bread are analogous to the mission-driven venture's *inputs*—its funds, staff and volunteers, and all of the other resources that go into its activities and programs. The bread dough (and once it's baked, the loaf itself) is analogous to the venture's *outputs*—the number of people it serves, or whatever metric makes sense to indicate the results of the venture's activities. When a hungry child eats the bread, her full stomach is like the venture's *outcome*—the ultimate change the mission-driven venture is trying to make in the world.

Social impact is the greater, long-term effect of the venture's activities on its intended beneficiaries, as well as on the community as a whole, that results from its inputs, activities, and outputs. The social impact of the bread in our example might be an increase in a child's health, happiness, and general well-being as a result of having eaten bread when she was hungry, as well as the benefit to her community that otherwise would have had to find food for the child or deal with the consequences of having a hungry child running around.

Would the improvement in the child's health, happiness, and general well-being have happened if she did not eat the bread? Would she have eventually found food elsewhere? What if, instead of eating a loaf of bread, she ate a sandwich made with that bread, still receiving the benefits of a full stomach? How, and to what extent, could those benefits then be attributed to the bread, independent of the other components of the sandwich? These questions highlight one of the many challenges to measuring social impact that we address in this trilogy of chapters—determining the counterfactual: What would have happened anyway, regardless of the social venture's intervention.

At the end of the day, the mission-driven venture needs to show that its inputs generate desired outputs, and that its outputs are not only connected to, but also are the cause of, measureable, long-term outcomes. This process is called the impact value chain, as shown in Figure 13.1.

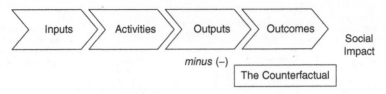

FIGURE 13.1   Impact Value Chain

Neli Vazquez-Rowland and her husband Brian Rowland, founders of A Safe Haven Foundation, understand Charmaine's story all too well. Brian's battle with addiction opened their eyes to a need for integrated recovery services. The Rowlands—both employed in the financial sector at the time—had resources that gave them options for Brian's treatment. Yet they realized that not everyone suffering from addiction is so fortunate. Upon recognizing this tremendous gap in treatment options, the couple took a leap of faith and founded A Safe Haven Foundation in 1994.

A Safe Haven's quantifiable social impact continues to reassure Neli and Brian that they made the right choice when they took that leap of faith. With over 350 employees, an annual budget of $30 million, and a network of thirty-four locations, A Safe Haven now offers integrated supportive housing, case management, addiction treatment, education, and life skills development within a network of affordable housing, industry training, and job placement services. These are examples of A Safe Haven's inputs (employees, financial resources, and housing facilities) and its activities (case management, addiction treatment, and education).

The organization has served more than 55,000 clients like Charmaine, providing services daily to 1,200 people in need. In 2011, A Safe Haven provided 5,275 individual and group treatment sessions, including 14,714 hours of treatment across A Safe Haven programs. As a result, 82 percent of individuals who needed treatment that year successfully completed A Safe Haven recovery programs. These are examples of A Safe Haven's measurable outputs.

One way of addressing the counterfactual is to measure outputs against a relevant industry standard benchmark. A Safe Haven boasts a 15.4 percent recidivism rate compared to 51.3 percent for

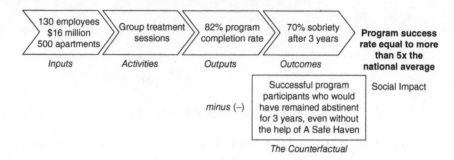

FIGURE 13.2   A Safe Haven's Value Chain

the State of Illinois, and 70 percent of the program's participants remain sober for three years—more than five times the national average. The organization also has some of the United States' highest job placement and retention rates, as measured by the U.S. Department of Labor. These are examples of A Safe Haven's quantifiable outcomes, measured against relevant benchmarks to demonstrate its social impact.

Figure 13.2 depicts how A Safe Haven's inputs, outputs, and outcomes lead to measurable social impact for clients like Charmaine.

Charmaine now wakes up early every morning to take Aniya to daycare and get to work, and in the evening she attends financial literacy classes and the daycare's parent committee meetings. Charmaine talks about the pride she feels when she can point to the flowers she planted throughout the City of Chicago through one of A Safe Haven's workforce development program and say, "'I did that.' It gives you an accomplishment," Charmaine says. "It builds your self-esteem. It makes you feel good."

This is A Safe Haven's social impact, and the reason Neli and Brian Rowland will never look back.

CREDITING THE CAUSES OF POSITIVE SOCIAL CHANGE

Halfway around the world, Richard and Erin Wilobo also feel the impact of social enterprise. The Wilobos are two of the 1.4 million people who were displaced by armed conflict and civil strife in the Gulu district of Northern Uganda. After living in a refugee camp for twelve years, they returned to their ravaged village to find their home had been burned to the ground. Before fleeing that home, Richard had been a smallholder cotton farmer with a reliable source of income from a nearby ginnery. But that ginnery—the only commercial ginnery in the Gulu district—had now lain dormant for many years. Without even the few assets they once had, and with minimal access to seeds, markets, or credit, Richard and Erin, along with their neighbors, struggled to rebuild their lives and community.

Enter Gulu Agricultural Development Company (GADC). With a social impact loan, GADC was able to reopen the commercial cotton ginnery in the Gulu district, stimulating cotton growth and creating economic opportunities for more than 40,000 smallholder farmers like Richard.

In addition to providing a market for his cotton, GADC trained Richard on effective harvesting and sorting techniques. Richard and the other farmers in his village now produce quality cotton that they sell for premium prices. Just a few years before GADC reopened the commercial ginnery, virtually every school in the Gulu district was empty. But now, most of the farmers in Richard's group are able to afford school fees to send at least some of their children back to school. With proceeds from the prior year's cotton harvest, Richard plans to replace the livestock he left behind—an investment that will provide him, Erin, and their six children a source of food as well as savings as they rebuild their lives. Conditions are still tough, but access to export cotton markets though GADC is helping Richard and other farmers in the Gulu district rebuild their lives in Northern Uganda.

GADC is a client of Root Capital, a nonprofit social investment fund that supports rural prosperity in poor, environmentally vulnerable places in Africa and Latin America. Root Capital lends funds, delivers financial training, and strengthens market connections for small and growing agricultural businesses like GADC that help build sustainable livelihoods for producers like Richard.

In its report, *Roadmap for Impact*, Root Capital tells the story of how its loan to GADC helped the displaced farmers of Northern Uganda rebuild their lives, and how such stories affect Root Capital and its stakeholders. Then Root Capital digs deeper: "And yet, such stories raise as many questions as they answer. How many of the 600,000+ farmers that Root Capital has reached over the past decade have similar stories? How do we know whether Root Capital's loan made a difference for them?" Further, how does Root Capital know whether 600,000 farmer households is a lot or a little, given the human and financial resources it has invested, and what does it mean to "reach" a farmer?

Even more challenging: How does Root Capital know that its work *caused* the positive changes in the lives of farmers like Richard, and that the farmers' lives would not have improved anyway?

Root Capital recognizes that, while output metrics and personal stories like Richard and Erin's are an important starting point, to answer these questions—to really evaluate and demonstrate its impact—requires a step further. To answer the most difficult of these questions requires a comparison of the outcomes that Root Capital measures to what would have happened in the absence of its involvement.

In contrast to A Safe Haven Foundation, which can assess at least some of its outcomes relative to an industry standard, such as the overall rate of recidivism in the community it serves, a relevant benchmark is not always available to mission-driven ventures, particularly for those that, like Root Capital, serve developing countries. In such cases, determining the counterfactual can be a significant undertaking, and often an impossible one at that.

A version of the counterfactual also exists when changes occur over a long period of time or when several organizations contribute toward the same cause, as in the case of the sandwich in our bread example. Consider a natural disaster, for instance. How does an organization that contributes food and medical supplies to the victims of a tsunami or a hurricane measure its distinctive contribution isolated from others of the same character? In those situations, it is nearly impossible to attribute all or even a quantifiable part of the outcome to the original activity. The passage of time, or introduction of such other forces affecting the intended beneficiary, also create variables that make it tricky to determine direct causality.

Challenges with measuring social impact also arise when the changes that mission-driven ventures seek to implement—such as the long-term improvements in a program recipient's overall well-being—are unobservable. Even when those changes are discernible, they are often not quantifiable. What's more, even when the changes are measurable, they are often denominated in different cultural and economic "currencies," making direct comparison and benchmarking impossible. When attempting to compare the performance of one organization or program against that of another (for example, comparing the impact of supplying low-income families with bednets against the impact of researching a malaria vaccine), if the two organizations are not using the same approach or model to address the same social issue, applying comparable inputs with the same objectives, then using the same metrics to compare one organization to the other is like comparing apples and oranges.

We introduce you to these challenges, acknowledging the reality that quantifying something that, in many cases, is entirely qualitative is at best an approximation. Much like an accountant subtracts costs from revenues to determine a company's net profits, hundreds of methods, tools, and frameworks take a formulaic, approach to measuring social impact. But what goes into the revenue column when the objective is to generate not only money, but also social good? Unlike black and white accounting measures, the various means of measuring an intangible outcome like social good are necessarily imperfect.

Yet, the need for measurable indications of a mission-driven venture's social impact is undeniable (as discussed in the next chapter). Thus, we use the most relevant and reliable information we can find about what's happened in the past to make our best guess about what might have happened had we not intervened. We subtract the latter from the former, and what's left is our *social impact*—a metric that, in practice, is far less precise than it often appears when it's the product of a meticulous, albeit simplistic, formula.

Nevertheless, without applying some formula or tool to discern and define outcome data, there would be no meaningful way of understanding a mission-driven venture's social impact. The social sector has reached a consensus that measuring social impact is imperative, and an imprecise conception of social impact is better than no perception at all. However, the matters of what to measure and how to measure it are still hot potato items—compounding the difficult task at hand. Even the question of where to start in designing an impact measurement system is up in the air.

For instance, Mission Measurement, a consulting and strategy firm that focuses on measuring the success of social strategies, starts with the end in mind. Beginning with a clear articulation of the organization's mission—the outcomes that the organization seeks to achieve—Mission Measurement then works with the organization to develop practical, relevant metrics that will demonstrate its progress toward achieving those outcomes.

Root Cause, a nonprofit research and consulting firm that helps leaders from the nonprofit, government, and business sectors work together to bring effective solutions to longstanding social problems, recommends a different approach. Root Cause first looks to reliable information about the targeted issue. After researching the social issue and understanding the most effective approaches to addressing it, Root Cause then helps the organization to develop indicators to evaluate how effectively it is implementing the recommended, proven approach.

Still, despite rigorous efforts to design *the gold standard* method for measuring impact, the reality is that there is not one method that works best across the board. Finding the best starting point is often just another challenge to measuring social impact. Indeed, from determining what to measure and how to measure it, to tracking and defining indiscernible outcomes and predicting what would or could happen in a different reality—quantifying, tracking, and reporting the data to demonstrate the connections between inputs, outputs, and long-term social impact can be a daunting task.

REDF AND SOCIAL RETURN ON INVESTMENT

Focused efforts continue to be made around the world and across sectors to resolve, or at least manage, some of the challenges to effective impact measurement, and a number of tools have been developed to help with the task. Impact pioneers, such as the Rockefeller Foundation, Root Capital, Acumen Fund, and B Lab, continue to push the conversation about social metrics forward by employing innovative strategies to overcome those hurdles that remain.

The Roberts Enterprise Development Fund (REDF), a nonprofit social venture fund that invests in social enterprises engaged in workforce development, led one of the early efforts to quantify social outcomes with its Social Return on Investment (SROI) methodology. At its core, SROI places a monetary value on outcomes so they can be added up and compared with the investment made, resulting in a ratio of total benefits (a sum of all outcomes) to total investments that is analogous to the accounting and financial return on investment (ROI) ratio used to predict commercial returns on investment.

REDF developed the methodology to demonstrate the blended social and economic value accrued to society compared to the total investments for each of the social enterprises in its portfolio. Having co-founded and headed a global private equity investment firm prior to launching REDF, George R. Roberts understood the utility of the ROI metric in the commercial sector. With this acumen and experience in his back pocket, he established REDF in 1997 to undertake venture philanthropy in support of job development programs.

You can take a man out of the commercial investment market, but you can't take the commercial investor mindset out of the man. Roberts, being such a man, structured REDF from such a mindset, with the expected return measured in people employed and lives changed. He recalls, "I could see how the power and proven practices of the business world could be applied to this problem [of persistent joblessness] to bring real solutions." This meant applying an investment-like approach and making a commitment to measure results.

REDF developed its SROI framework in the late 1990s, and in 2000, the framework was shared through publication of SROI Reports and several SROI methodology documents and tools. REDF no longer uses its SROI methodology, but the core concepts of that framework have since inspired several other widely used approaches to measuring social impact.

Workforce development programs are particularly amenable to the SROI methodology due to the quantifiable nature of their outcomes. A modern application of the SROI methodology to workforce development programming is seen in The Cara Program, a Chicago-based nonprofit organization that provides job training and placement services to individuals affected by homelessness and poverty. In fiscal year 2014 alone, Cara created or secured 648 jobs for its students, with a retention rate of 78 percent in the initial job placement after one year.

Using the SROI methodology, The Cara Program can tell donors and impact investors exactly how much good their money will produce: for every dollar invested in The Cara Program, $5.02 is produced over a five-year time horizon.

That calculation is based on the organization's one-year social impact, which is essentially the sum of (a) annualized contributions to society made by the program's employed students (tax contributions, Social Security, sales taxes paid) and (b) annualized cost savings to society (from avoiding expenses such as shelter costs, cash assistance, unemployment benefits, health care costs, food stamps, re-arrest costs, and the like).

As employed members of society, the program's students pay income taxes and Social Security taxes. They also have more disposable income to purchase items on which they pay sales tax. The Cara Program includes all of these taxes, which are determined by applying the applicable tax rates for a given year to each student's income earned in that year to determine its employed students' annualized contributions to society.

Based on 2010 tax rates, The Cara Program determined that payments made by its employed students in 2010 consisted of $857,659 in federal and state taxes and $295,416 in Social Security taxes. Based on the findings of a 2010 Consumer Expenditure Survey conducted by the Bureau of Labor Statistics, the organization assumes that its students spend an average of 28 percent of their total income on purchases subject to sales tax. Multiplying this number by the applicable city tax rate, The Cara Program is able to determine that its employed students also contributed $127,581 to society through the payment of sales tax.

The Cara Program's annualized savings to society in costs avoided as a result of its students' employment include the costs for Temporary Assistance for Needy Families, Medicaid, food stamps, unemployment, health care, substance abuse treatment, housing, and recidivism and re-arrests for prison and jail. The Cara Program determines these numbers by reference to statistical reports, studies, and other published material that is relevant, timely, and applicable to its employed students.

ROOT CAPITAL AND ITS "SOCIAL AND ENVIRONMENTAL SCORECARD"

Root Capital tackles the obstacles to effective impact measurement, including the irreducible uncertainty involved with measuring human issues, by employing a unique GPS-like approach. Like a global positioning system that combines information from multiple sources to measure three dimensions of location (latitude, longitude, and elevation), thereby overcoming each individual source's own limitations and triangulating highly accurate estimates of a position, Root Capital interprets impact information as having three primary dimensions—type, scale, and depth—and uses different tools and metrics, or *impact satellites*, to triangulate and piece together information about each dimension to create a whole, integrated picture of an investment's social impact.

Type of impact includes the nature of the impact(s) on each person, organization, or ecosystem, articulated as outputs or, ideally, as outcomes; *scale of impact* is the number of people, organizations, or ecological units affected; and *depth of impact* is the amount or intensity of change in subjectively experienced well-being. In theory, the total impact of a loan can be measured by adding together, for each type of impact, the changes in well-being (depth of impact) for all people affected (scale of impact). Root Capital's loan officers evaluate prospective clients along each of these three dimensions of impact using the fund's unique Social and Environmental Scorecards to assign value to the investment, thereby allowing it to be compared against benchmarks and other available investment options.

ACUMEN FUND AND ITS "BEST ALTERNATIVE CHARITABLE OPTION"

Acumen Fund, a nonprofit global venture fund with a diverse portfolio of investments in social enterprises in Africa and Asia, also employs an innovative method to evaluating the social impact of its investments. Recognizing the challenge of determining an absolute return across a broad spectrum of investments, Acumen Fund informs its portfolio decision making by assessing whether the investment will "outperform" the best plausible alternative.

Acumen Fund developed its Best Alternative Charitable Option (BACO) methodology in 2004 to help portfolio managers assess the prospective merit of an individual investment opportunity versus making a charitable grant. The approach quantifies a potential investment's social output and compares it to the universe of existing charitable options for that explicit social issue, essentially asking: "For each dollar invested, how much social output will this generate over the life of the investment relative to the best alternative charitable option?" Using this approach, Acumen Fund can compare efficiencies across investments (for example, an investment in malaria bednets was sixteen times more cost-effective than the charitable alternatives, while the low-income housing investment is only twice as cost-effective as the alternatives).

One limitation to the BACO methodology, however, is that it does not resolve the "apples to oranges" problem of identifying which investment is more cost-effective at impacting poverty more generally (for example, a loan to a social enterprise that supplies malaria bednets, or a grant to research a malaria vaccine). There are other confines to the BACO methodology as well, and SROI and Root Capital's GPS approach are also not without limitations. But these metrics are, nevertheless, useful tools within the bounds of those limitations. More importantly—and the reason they are featured here—is that they represent some of the many innovative approaches that have spurred conversation about just how one goes about measuring social impact.

Stories like Charmaine Bowman's and Richard Wilobo's demonstrate the heart and soul of the "social impact" that mission-driven ventures are called upon to measure. Despite the challenges and imperfection in measuring results like Charmaine's sense of accomplishment and Richard's self-sufficiency, the demand for measurable and quantifiable evidence of a program's success has never been stronger—a demand that mission-driven ventures from every sector are meeting in ever more sophisticated ways.

CHAPTER FOURTEEN

Answering the Call

The Demand for Social Metrics

A Safe Haven is now a national model for social and economic development. In 2013, Neli Vazquez-Rowland was recognized as a "Champion of Change" by the White House for creating one of America's most successful organizations dealing with homelessness, unemployment, and addiction.

Success begets success. A Safe Haven has recently turned its attention to helping veterans as well—Brian Rowland himself is an Army veteran—partnering with the VA to offer housing, warm meals, employment, and other services to Chicago's homeless veterans.

The organization has come a long way from what the Rowlands envisioned in 1994 when they first bought and rehabbed an abandoned apartment building, turning it into a residential treatment facility. Their plan was to rent out apartments to people who were recovering from drug or alcohol addiction for a year, and then sell the renovated building when the market improved. But that plan changed when the Rowlands saw the impact they were making. So they continued to offer housing and services to people in recovery, financing operations out of their own pockets.

Over time, and as more people showed up at A Safe Haven in need of housing and recovery services, the Rowlands saw that to really help people help themselves, A Safe Haven would need to provide residents with a comprehensive, integrated path to self-sufficiency and independence. All that they could personally give to A Safe Haven would still not be enough to support their vision of providing additional services like long-term treatment, education, life skills training, job training, employment, and affordable housing. After five years of growth, it was time for A Safe Haven to seek outside funding.

With backgrounds in finance, the Rowlands knew that stories like Charmaine Bowman's would not be enough to secure the financial commitments they needed to expand A Safe Haven's services. Outside funders would need measurable evidence of the impact that their money could achieve through the A Safe Haven model.

Traditional businesses that operate exclusively to make a profit routinely engage in performance measurement to answer the questions: Are we making a profit? and If so, how much profit are we making? The answers to these questions are relevant to a range of outside stakeholders: shareholders who own stock in the corporation, lenders who extend credit to the company, suppliers who have long-term contracts with the company, and often many others. They are also important drivers of strategy within the company. Perhaps most important, management uses performance indicators to identify inefficiencies and profit centers so it can make informed decisions to strengthen the company's bottom line.

Fortunately, the Rowlands' business acumen drove their work from the beginning. "With our background as investment bankers, we know how to measure what we do," says Neli. An early investment in state-of-the-art information technology allowed them to track A Safe Haven's residents, providing information from the start that would inform their decisions as the operation evolved.

Ultimately, that investment also helped them secure the outside funding they needed to expand A Safe Haven's impact. In 1999, A Safe Haven Foundation commissioned researchers at Northwestern University to assess the data they had collected over the first five years of operations. "We felt it wouldn't be appropriate to approach a state funding agency without an empirical study showing that our approach worked," Neli says. "In other words, we wanted to be able to give them data to allow them to make a good business decision for taxpayers." The study, which was published in the *American Journal of Public Health*, proved that A Safe Haven's approach was effective. "The government can lock people up for $100 a day or put kids in foster care for $30,000 a year,"

Neli explains. "Our average cost is $80 a day." As they had hoped, the results of the Northwestern study opened the door to critical resources: a contract with the Illinois Department of Corrections to provide transitional housing for nonviolent ex-offenders—A Safe Haven's first source of outside funding.

Just as it is essential for a traditional for-profit corporation to understand its bottom line, a mission-driven venture must also understand whether and to what extent it is achieving its mission. The functions that social impact metrics serve in the social sector parallel the functions of profitability indicators in the traditional business sector. As the Rowlands saw, one important purpose of social impact metrics is to secure funding for social programs and thereby build their organization's capacity.

Indeed, the role that metrics play in attracting funding from outside sources and accounting to these external stakeholders is a significant one, but *external accountability* is just one of three critical roles that social impact metrics play. Other key functions of impact metrics are to enable *internal decision making* and to contribute to *shared outcomes*—the sector-wide body of knowledge of what works and what doesn't work in solving the world's most vexing social problems.

SCALING SUCCESS

Just as measures of financial performance metrics inform managers of profit-driven businesses about the efficiency and scalability of business operations, social impact metrics provide mission-driven ventures—and those whose decisions drive them—with an indication of whether, and to what extent, the mission-driven venture is succeeding at achieving its mission. With reliable evidence of a program's impact on the intended beneficiaries, a social venture's management team can make informed decisions that propel continuous improvement.

Case in Point: BUILD

If you ask twelve-year-old Jermeisha what it's like growing up in the Fifth City neighborhood in Chicago's West Side, she'll tell you that it's "not safe at all. You see gangbangers, drug dealers, people fighting and robbing, and kids getting shot because they are in the wrong place at the wrong time." Jermeisha's neighborhood is one of the focus communities of Broader Urban Involvement and Leadership Development (BUILD), a youth development organization that helps at-risk youth in Chicago's low-income, high-crime neighborhoods to rise above the influence of drugs, gangs, and violence.

Founded in 1969 as a gang intervention program working with fewer than 200 gang-affiliated youth in one Chicago community, BUILD now serves more than 4,127 youth annually in eleven of Chicago's toughest neighborhoods. BUILD's success over four decades reflects its ability to evolve along with the communities it serves. By continually assessing the evolving challenges that place youth at risk, BUILD is able to offer programs that most effectively help kids overcome them.

Today, youth violence is an epidemic in Chicago, with nearly two-thirds of murders involving gangs and almost half of homicide victims being twenty-five or younger. The communities that BUILD serves are in the heart of the crossfire. In the first half of 2012 alone, gang-related violence contributed to a 38 percent increase in Chicago's 2012 homicide rate. While the city's overall homicide rate declined in 2013, the proportion of those murders that were gang-related increased. During the 2011–2012 school year, twenty-four Chicago Public School students were killed—and another 319 were shot—as a result of gang wars in BUILD's focus neighborhoods. After that school year, CPS stopped releasing information about gun-related violence involving students.

BUILD staff members reach out to youth who are at risk for gang recruitment and/or of being victims of gang violence, engaging them in activities that provide an alternative to that lifestyle. The rapport that staff members develop with at-risk youth through recreational and athletic activities allows staff to guide young people like Jermeisha away from violence and crime and toward involvement with BUILD's tutoring, counseling, substance abuse treatment, and job training programs.

At school, Jermeisha stands less of a chance of being caught in the crossfire of gang wars. Yet, she doesn't feel entirely safe there either. While she might be out of range for bullets from drive-by shootings, at school she is most vulnerable to attacks of another nature: bullying. When she used to get caught up in fighting, Jermeisha's dad would tell her: "You're too pretty to be fighting!" Yet, her classmates tease her about the way she looks and dresses, leaving Jermeisha feeling discouraged—a precarious state in which to be amidst gang recruitment efforts that promise loyalty, protection, and a sense of belonging.

While the primary risks facing BUILD's youth—gangs, drugs, and poverty—have remained the same throughout the years, the sources of those risks are ever-changing. In 2010, BUILD undertook a project to streamline its intake and data-collection processes to track key performance metrics using Efforts to Outcomes (ETO), a performance management software tool developed by Social Solutions that helps grantees track and report efforts to funders. An external evaluator helped identify common goals across BUILD's programs, translating goals into measureable outcomes around which BUILD tailored its data-collection efforts. Using ETO to track and analyze participant and program progress also provided the insight that BUILD needed to improve its programs. Before long, the results of the data collected through ETO revealed critical gaps in BUILD's programming that were hindering its efforts to keep youth safe.

In particular, BUILD learned that the sources of risk facing its focus communities had evolved to include mental health issues, HIV/AIDS, and obesity, as well as bullying, a problem frequently associated with persons struggling with these health-related concerns. The data that BUILD collected using ETO revealed that 10 percent of BUILD participants identified as LGBTQ, 25 percent reported having used addictive substances, and 32 percent reported they are not able to effectively manage their anger. Additionally, one in ten BUILD youth—like Jermeisha—stated that they do not feel good about themselves. This critical data highlighted the shifting needs and demographics of the communities that BUILD serves.

BUILD used that information to strategically reallocate resources and develop new programs and services to meet the evolved needs of its participants. For instance, BUILD recently added a health and wellness component to its program model to address mental and physical health issues. Through its BUILDing Healthy Futures program, youth receive counseling services, health education, case management, and access to external health partners.

The new program's impact was quickly evident for BUILD participants like Jermeisha, whose feelings of discouragement blurred the lines between the safe and dangerous places in her life. She was feeling disheartened when she met Mr. Ramiro, a youth development specialist from BUILD. "He helped me with my homework, my problems, and my attitude," she says. Jermeisha also talks about Ms. Angella, another BUILD specialist: "[She] showed me that you can be happier with different types of attitudes. Now I'm trying to be a good girl, a better person." Jermeisha likes BUILD and the caring adults she's met there. "Just like my dad," she says, "they tell me 'you're too beautiful for bad attitudes!'"

The flexibility that ETO offers in designing data management systems to track unique program characteristics makes it a widely used tool for internal tracking and assessment of program performance. For BUILD, the software tells program operators that last year, 85 percent of BUILD program participants were educated on the importance of diet, exercise, and healthy relationships. Every participant increased his or her understanding of the body mass index (BMI), and 41 percent showed an improvement in their BMI. "I didn't know how bad fat and sugar was until this program," says Charlie, a program participant. "I knew it was bad for you, but it didn't make ME fat, so I was cool with it. But now that I know how bad those things are and what protein and carbs really are, I'm going be at my all-time best."

Understanding the evolving needs of the youth in Chicago's gang-ridden neighborhoods allows BUILD to offer programs that keep the organizing on track to achieve its mission. Its success has received local and national recognition. Locally, the Chicago Community Trust lists BUILD as an example of an "exemplary program" for prevention and intervention. Nationally, the Office of Juvenile Justice and Delinquency Prevention (OJJDP) designates BUILD as a "promising practice" and lists it as one of five program models worthy of replication. In line with that designation, the BUILD model has recently been replicated in Minneapolis, Tucson, Houston, and Corpus Christi.

SHARED-OUTCOMES NETWORKS

The Rockefeller Foundation understands that the world's greatest challenges cannot be solved alone. In contrast to the traditional for-profit sector in which efficiencies are often jealously safeguarded to maintain a competitive advantage, the social sector thrives on shared experiences of what works, what doesn't work, and what could work better, with mission-driven ventures collaborating within and across sectors to achieve maximum impact.

Especially in developing countries, social problems often involve a complex mix of stakeholders whose interdependence spans sectors and geographies. The Rockefeller Foundation—along with other global philanthropists, including The Bill & Melinda Gates Foundation—are increasingly recognizing the opportunity to achieve sustained and transformational change by collaborating with grantees and partners in developing countries to establish a common vision of the problem, outcomes, and indicators for success.

Robert Picciotto, a former vice president at the World Bank and now a professor at Kings College London, described the opportunity at the Future of Philanthropy and Development forum held in Billagio, Italy, a few years ago: "The philanthropic enterprise will not fulfill its potential unless it identifies and taps into its distinctive comparative advantage and coordinates its interventions with other development actors."

By establishing networks, alliances, and coalitions of stakeholders from governments, foundations, civil society, and private businesses, a shared outcomes approach not only mobilizes a vast range of resources, but also brings empowerment—and a sense of ownership—to a broad cross-section of stakeholders engaged in the collective effort.

Judith Rodin, president of the Rockefeller Foundation, and Nancy MacPherson, managing director of evaluation at the

Foundation, describe key elements of an effective evaluation practice for shared outcomes as: (1) embracing a broader set of voices in framing approaches to evaluation; (2) viewing collaboration and partnerships between developed and developing areas as mutually beneficial toward a common goal of expanding and sharing evaluation knowledge as a public good aimed at achieving better development outcomes; (3) recognizing the need to address issues of accountability, transparency, ethics, culture, and independence; and (4) addressing asymmetries in individual and institutional capacities for undertaking, driving, and owning evaluation in developing regions by promoting opportunities for professional excellence, networks, and sustained global partnerships in the discipline of development evaluation.

A critical component of an effective shared-outcomes network that touches upon all four of those elements is the reliance on the boots-on-the-ground evaluators to provide information and facilitate the implementation of program objectives. Foundations and other development agencies partner with monitoring and evaluation (M&E) groups and specialists (known to the Rockefeller Foundation as "critical friends") who work with grantees to identify key evaluation points, help to set up monitoring systems, and provide support in monitoring and analyzing data. M&E partners build trust with grantees, acting as a conduit by which grantees seek and use feedback to make improvements throughout the life of the work. Another important data-collection tool is the use of independent evaluator teams who provide an objective assessment of progress toward meeting program goals.

Case in Point: The Campaign to Eradicate Polio

Two-year-old Abubarkar Al Hassan is the unfortunate victim of a social program in need of improvement. Abubarkar was tagged as Nigeria's first polio victim of 2013. Sadly, he's unlikely to be the last Nigerian child to endure lifelong paralysis from contracting polio, despite worldwide efforts over the last twenty-five years to eradicate the crippling disease.

In 1988, the U.S. Centers for Disease Control and Prevention, Rotary International, UNICEF, the World Health Organization, and the governments of many countries joined forces toward the goal of eradicating polio. Spearheaded through the Global Polio Eradication Initiative (GPEI), their combined efforts eliminated the disease in the Americas, Europe, and most of Asia by 2000, and in recent years, the number of polio cases elsewhere has been below 1,000. Yet, despite being so close to the finish line, eradicating polio in the last three countries in which it remains—Nigeria, Pakistan, and Afghanistan—has been slow and fraught with challenges.

The eradication of polio is also a top propriety of The Bill & Melinda Gates Foundation, a key supporter of the GPEI. So when the steadfast accounting of the reported polio cases—data collected as part of the campaign's impact measurement system—revealed that something was amiss in these countries, Bill Gates visited northern Nigeria in an effort to understand why polio persists there when even densely crowded countries with poor sanitation and large mobile populations had achieved the goal. In his 2013 Annual Letter, Bill Gates discusses the challenges in Nigeria and describes how the campaign to eradicate polio is using shared outcomes to keep the vaccination program on course.

In response to the campaign's performance reports in Nigeria, GPEI engaged highly trained, impartial workers to conduct random sampling of villages, checking to see whether the children in those places had been vaccinated. This additional layer of quality monitoring revealed several impediments to the campaign's efforts in Nigeria. For one, the vaccinators had been using incomplete and inaccurate maps to locate the villages that were home to children needing vaccinations. Many smaller settlements were missing from the hand-drawn maps, the distance between villages was off by miles, and many villages were not assigned to any vaccination team.

It was clear that more complete, accurate information was crucial to eradicating polio in Nigeria. The team of workers explored the undocumented areas and, as a result, added 3,000 communities to the immunization campaign. The program in Nigeria is now also working with GPEI's technology partners to utilize high-resolution satellite images to create detailed, accurate maps that allow health workers to reach more children in need of vaccines. These developments are expected to help improve the campaign's performance in Nigeria.

However, a deeper assessment of the country's social dynamics and sentiment toward the vaccine reveals additional hurdles for the campaign.

A conversation with Ramatu Garab, a twenty-eight-year-old Muslim food vendor in Kano—a state in northern Nigeria that has consistently seen a host of polio cases—provides a glimpse into the problem. For Ramatu, the polio vaccine—which she tells a reporter for the Associated Press is used to sterilize Nigerian girls—is part of an evil Western plot to reduce the Nigerian population. Ramatu refuses to let health teams vaccinate her daughter.

Ramatu is not alone in her resistance and fears about the polio vaccine—fears that have persisted throughout Nigeria for more than ten years. In 2003, the Kano state government suspended the vaccines for almost a year while it was tested for infertility hormones with which it was rumored to be laced. The suspension led to an unprecedented number of polio infections and widespread transmission of the disease to countries that had previously eradicated polio within their borders.

Thus, while a persisting hurdle to eradication efforts, the sterilization rumors and resulting fear of the vaccine are not a new problem for the campaign. On the other hand, the brutal murder of nine polio immunization workers in northern Nigeria in February 2013, with eerie resemblance to the murder of nine polio workers in Pakistan the previous December, evidences the development of a new challenge.

Heidi Larson, an anthropologist at the London School of Hygiene and Tropical Medicine who tracks vaccine issues, says that the recent increase in Nigerian resistance is prompted by what's happening in Pakistan. Indeed, while polio remains in Nigeria, there have been more new cases of the disease in 2014 reported in Pakistan than all other countries combined.

The C.I.A.'s efforts to track Osama bin Laden—which involved paying a Pakistani doctor to seek entry to bin Laden's compound on the pretext of vaccinating the children living there—enraged some

Taliban factions in Pakistan. Those factions outlawed vaccines in their areas, leaving around 300,000 children inaccessible to vaccination teams. The Pakistani Taliban has also led attacks on health workers that have resulted in the deaths of nearly forty vaccinators in the last few years.

Negative media coverage and increasing opposition to the vaccine by Islamic representatives further perpetuate a connection between the polio vaccinations and an outside conspiracy.

Sheikh Nasir Muhammed Nasir, imam of Fagge Juma'at Mosque, the largest in Kano, explains the link between the local sentiment against the United States and the region's rejection of the polio vaccine: "There is nothing wrong with the polio vaccine. The major reason why people reject it is the deep-seated suspicion they harbor against the West, particularly the United States, due to its foreign policies in the Muslim world, especially the war in Iraq and Afghanistan."

Suspicion also stems from the campaign's persistent focus on polio vaccines when other easily treatable illnesses plague the local people. As Mamman Nababa, a father of three in Kano, explains: "I can't understand how the West will spend millions of dollars in providing medication against polio for our children while they systematically killed 500,000 Muslim children in Iraq by imposing an embargo that denied them access to basic medicines." Sheikh Nasir Muhammed Nasir adds in reference to the U.S. invasion of Iraq and Afghanistan: "[Muslims here] wonder how the same countries responsible for this colossal carnage can now turn and save lives elsewhere. To them, it doesn't make any sense that you offer to save my children from a crippling disease yet are killing my brothers."

The campaign has modified the eradication efforts before to better account for social dynamics, and with success. Before the rumors of the U.S. conspiracy to eliminate the local people through sterilization, the campaign partnered only with political and health authorities. The challenges brought on by the fear that the vaccine was laced with infertility hormones generated the need for additional community-based support efforts. The polio campaigners in Nigeria began working closely with community and religious leaders to calm fears and promote the vaccine. The results were positive: greater community acceptance and improved understanding of the vaccine led to an increase in vaccinations.

Now, a decade later, better maps and the use of GPS devices are helping vaccinators locate more children who have slipped through the cracks. One can speculate that, had these techniques been employed sooner, two-year-old Abubarkar Al Hassan might have been spared—but that's only because his parents do not reject the vaccine. In fact, all thirteen of Abubarkar's siblings are vaccinated. But will these improvements result in the vaccination of Ramatu Garab's daughter in Kano? Probably not.

The performance metrics for the campaign's efforts in Nigeria and Pakistan once again call for a new approach to vaccination. The impediments of recent years make clear that to achieve eradication of polio in Pakistan—where there were more new cases of the disease in 2014 than in all other countries combined—will require cooperation and coordination among multiple stakeholders at different levels—including the support of local administrative and political leaders. Once again, the campaign has engaged a full spectrum of community leaders in collaboration to resolve the issues preventing the eradication of polio.

Last year, the campaign convened leaders at various levels of Pakistani government and several partnership agencies to review these challenges and devise a plan to overcome them, resulting in a number of new and renewed commitments from stakeholders at various levels. In January 2014, the Global Polio Eradication Emergency Action Plan was endorsed by the National Task Force for Polio Eradication chaired by the prime minister of Pakistan and participating chief ministers, the Governor of the Khyber Pakhtunkhwa region, the Prime Minister of Azad Jammu and Kashmir, and heads of partner agencies.

Tackling the challenges in Pakistan—in particular, the misconceptions driving refusals of the vaccine—will require the joint efforts of all polio partners across civil, social, and private sectors. The campaign reports that, in 2014, partnerships will mainly evolve around fostering closer cooperation with parliamentarians, religious leaders and scholars, media, and private-sector businesses.

In addition, The Bill & Melinda Gates Foundation is making strides in data collection and data sharing to facilitate and support understanding of the shifting dynamics in Nigeria and Pakistan. In particular, the foundation reports that it is working with a consortium of partners to develop an overall decision framework for polio eradication efforts that identifies key decision areas, the data needed to inform decisions, and the staff and partners needed to analyze the data and create models. The Bill & Melinda Gates Foundation is also developing a data access platform at the World Health Organization that will increase access to, and facilitate the sharing of, key polio data that is standardized, quality assured, and readily available to the broad coalition of stakeholders in the campaign to eradicate polio.

The new and renewed efforts from stakeholders are showing some positive results, with the latest reports from Pakistan reflecting a beacon of hope: after two years of banning the vaccine, the militant groups enforcing the ban are asking locals to provide them with vaccines for their own children. Also, in line with the Pakistani government's renewed commitments, the Pakistani Army has recently penetrated areas that were previously inaccessible to health care workers, providing safe access to unvaccinated children in those areas.

These developments, while perhaps only small steps in a long journey, are an example of the results that can be achieved through shared outcomes. I hope the collaborative efforts to understand, address, and ultimately overcome the obstacles to eradicating polio in Pakistan will improve conditions in Nigeria as well—perhaps even convincing Ramatu Garab to vaccinate her daughter in Kano.

Case in Point: Charity:Water

Scott Harrison understands the simple yet powerful connection between demonstrating social impact and generating the support to make it happen. Before founding charity:water, a relatively young organization that raises money to bring clean and safe drinking water to people in developing nations, Scott lived in the fast lane, working as a promoter of New York's club scene—a world away from Shariatpur, Bangladesh, and home to Khadija, a fifth grader at No. 57 Government Primary School and one of the 800 million people on the planet who do not have clean water.

Without running water, Khadija and the more than 300 students at No. 57 Primary School in Bangladesh missed an average of thirty-five full days of school out of the 229-day school year. Absenteeism of female students was particularly prevalent, averaging thirty-three days, sometimes because they were sick from water-related diarrhea, dysentery, or skin diseases, and sometimes to avoid harassment. No. 57 Primary School did not have a bathroom.

At first Khadija and her friends would use the fields close to school, taking turns standing guard for one another. But two people missing class instead of one soon became troublesome, so Khadija and her friends started going by themselves to use the toilets of neighbors who lived near the school. Neighborhood boys would follow Khadija as she walked twenty minutes along the street to strangers' houses, taunting and throwing things at her, one day even crushing stones on her head. The boys would tease her—sometimes about being a girl, but mostly about being poor. "You go to the school for the absolute poor people," they taunted. "You have to go someplace else to get water—to beg for water!"

The school's neighbors also gave the students a hard time about using their private restrooms. Embarrassed, Khadija started missing school to walk home alone and use the toilet at her house. As her time alone on the road increased, so did the harassment. Khadija missed fifteen days of school that year as a result—a low count compared to her classmates.

Back in New York, Scott Harrison found himself "emotionally, spiritually, and morally bankrupt" after living in the fast lane for ten years. While on vacation in Uruguay in 2004, he had an awakening that stirred him to change his life. When Scott returned to New York, he gave up club promoting and volunteered as a photographer for Mercy Ships, a nonprofit organization that provides medical care in developing countries from its fleet of hospital boats.

Scott visited Liberia on his first tour with Mercy Ships, where he witnessed illness and poverty that changed his trajectory. "I fell in love with Liberia and its people," he told *Wired* magazine, "and it dawned on me what an opportunity it would be if my previous [clubbing] contacts could be corralled to make a difference to the people there. These were people living on less in a year than I would blow on a bottle of vodka," he said. "It was shocking, powerful, and an amazing opportunity to do good." So Scott started emailing his long list of nightclub contacts, showing them photographs of the Liberians who came for treatment. "People would reply, saying things like, 'I am sitting at my desk at Chanel and weeping.'"

Scott's trip to Liberia also opened his eyes to the relationship between dirty water and poverty. So when he returned to New York, he threw a party for his thirty-first birthday, charged a $20 cover, and pledged that all the money raised would go to drilling wells in Africa. That night he raised $15,000. True to his promise, Scott used the proceeds from his birthday party to fund the construction and repair of wells in the Bobi refugee camp in northern Uganda, bringing clean water to 30,000 people.

The use of proceeds from Scott's birthday party was by no means inconsequential. But it was what he did next that had the most profound impact—and that ultimately brought Khadija back to school.

"We sent everyone who had been at that party an email with photos of the wells, saying, 'Look what your money has done,'" Scott recalled. "Half of them couldn't even remember being at the party, but they were blown away by the pictures and the difference they had made. It was incredible. I knew then we were on to something." Charity:water had been born.

Charity:water is built on three core principles: educating the public about the developing world; funding projects in the field; and—most significantly—maintaining a connection with donors. The overhead expenses are covered by private investors so that 100 percent of the money raised for water projects goes to water projects, and complete transparency allows donors to see which projects they are helping to fund.

Fast-forward a few years to another thirty-first birthday pledge. True to its roots, charity:water encourages donors to give up their birthdays and ask friends and family members to donate to charity:water rather than buy a birthday gift, just as Scott used the money from his thirty-first birthday party for the initial projects in Uganda. Donors create a fundraising page on the organization's website where they can track in real time how much money has been raised. Every dollar raised is linked to a project, and when the project is completed, each contributor to that project receives a Project Detail Report that shows GPS coordinates, videos, photos, and other details about the project and how it served a community in need.

On Ryan Guard's thirty-first birthday, he donated $31 to charity:water and started his own birthday campaign. Eighteen months later, Ryan met Khadija and learned how his donation helped bring her and her classmates back to school.

Charity:water used Ryan's donation (and the other $3,499 he raised through his birthday campaign), along with other public donations, to fund the installation of separate latrines for boys and girls at Khadija's school. The students and teachers also received training in hand washing, personal and menstrual hygiene, and disease prevention. Waterborne illnesses in the village soon declined by 15 percent. Reports of harassment fell by 8 percent, and school attendance and enrollment increased to 100 percent. Khadija says she feels safer at school. Hers is not an isolated story—across Shariatpur, the increase in girls' attendance has increased as a result of having latrines at the schools.

Because Ryan's donation was used to bring clean drinking water and latrines to the people of Shariatpur, Bangladesh, he and the other donors whose funds went to that project received a Project Detail Report showing GPS coordinates, photos, and other details about Khadija's community—and, of course, Khadija's story.

By connecting donors with the actual communities they help through pictures, personal stories, and GPS coordinates, charity:water demonstrates the outcome of its projects. Neil Hutchinson, founder and managing director of Forward Internet, a London-based venture capital company, and one of charity:water's background investors, described the importance of showing founders the impact of their investment: "What caught my eye was the model of transparency. One hundred percent of what people give goes to the field and you can see what is happening, with the GPS coordinates and so on. I look at donations to charity as an investment and treat them like other investments, and Scott has a very tech approach to charity, delivering data and numbers. You can see a clear return."

Daniel Ek, Spotify founder and long-term donor to charity:water, says it well: "This is a huge change from traditional charity giving where, once you give, you forget. Once people feel part of something good, it actually changes the way they donate in the future."

Scott quotes motivational speaker Simon Sinek, who describes the golden circles of why, how, and what and stresses the importance of every organization knowing its "Why?" "I asked, 'What is our why?' It's not clean water, that's the what. It's not storytelling, that's the how. It's restoring faith to donors, inspiring giving, and inspiring compassion. That is our why."

Making the Cut: Accounting to Investors

Perhaps the loudest call for social impact metrics comes from the developing impact investment industry. The Global Impact Investing Network (GIIN), a nonprofit organization dedicated to increasing the scale of effectiveness of impact investing, recently released an updated definition of "impact investment," revised to include impact measurement as a prominent feature of the practice:

> A hallmark of impact investing is the commitment of the investor to measure and report the social and environmental performance of underlying investments. Impact measurement helps ensure transparency and accountability and is essential to informing the practice of impact investing and building the field.

The update highlighting impact measurement is appropriate and timely, given the growing importance of metrics to the impact investment industry. (The GIIN's prior version of the definition of impact investments was "Investments that are designed to address social or environmental challenges while generating some level of financial profit.")

As the impact investment market has expanded to include a diverse set of investors, each with its own individual risk, return, and impact expectations, as well as a growing number of social impact opportunities, up-front screening of investments to assess their alignment with a fund's investment objectives has evolved as an essential component of the practice.

The impact investing industry is not alone in its call for evidence of social impact. Indeed, outside stakeholders from nearly every segment of the social sector now make that call. In the next chapter, we take a closer look at the evolving need for benchmark metrics that facilitate the type of information that outside stakeholders need to make funding decisions, as well as the tools that they use to apply that knowledge.

CHAPTER FIFTEEN

Toward a Universal Metrics Language

Willy Foote fondly recalls playing folk music with the leader of a vanilla farmer cooperative deep in the cloud forests of the Chimalapas jungle of southern Mexico. Foote also got to know many of the member farmers of the cooperative who labored amidst drug traffickers to improve the lives of the indigenous people, and whose failure in that endeavor ultimately inspired the Root Capital model.

A year earlier, following the 1994 peso devaluation, Foote traded his job with Lehman Brothers for a business journalism fellowship that brought him and his wife on a two-year journey through rural Mexico—a world away from his life as an investment banker. He was in Oaxaca, Mexico, to study and write about the financial crisis and its effects on the Mexican people and the environment when he met the vanilla farmers, who opened his eyes to the daily struggle of farmers who lacked the critical resources that they needed to establish sustainable practices. The vanilla cooperative ultimately failed. "It wasn't because of the drug traffickers," he recalls. "It was because they lacked access to capital and markets and basic business skills."

Foote's friends at the vanilla cooperative—and all of the farmers he met and observed during his time in Mexico—had a profound effect on him that led him to think more deeply about the cycle of rural poverty. Foote had plans to attend Harvard Business School upon completion of his fellowship, where his wife had also been accepted. But as he drove his truck out of Mexico and back to the United States, he realized that he needed to pursue his evolving ideas about ways to link what he calls "the missing middle"—small and growing business (SGBs) like the vanilla cooperative that are too big for microloans and too small and risky for remote commercial banks—to the resources they need to succeed. "I had this growing fear that if I didn't act on my ideas," he says, "I'd lose my sense of urgency."

Willy Foote did not go to Harvard Business School. Instead, he undertook a research project focused on SGB financing for impoverished rural communities. Three months later, Willy had identified a model for reaching "the missing middle," written a business plan, and secured investment funds to launch Root Capital in 1999, the nonprofit social investment fund that would go to help Richard Wilobo rebuild his farming community in northern Uganda (as discussed in Chapter 13).

In its early years, Root Capital had few formal tools or methods for measuring the social impact of its portfolio companies. Willy would hire loan officers who, as he says, "knew how to pick 'em"—meaning their experiences growing up in farming communities or managing the financial components of an agricultural business gave them an intuitive sense of which agricultural businesses would be able to use a loan from Root Capital to stimulate prosperity for rural farmers. Credit evaluations were performed using a Microsoft Word memo in which loan officers would describe the client's social and environmental practices and perceived impact, based on the loan officer's first-hand observations during field-based due diligence. Third-party referrals and the client's social certifications would also play into the mix but, ultimately, a small portfolio made it possible for members of the lending team to know the details of every client without a need for formal assessments of—or reports on—environmental and social issues.

Root Capital grew, and it became necessary to formalize those intuitive practices and apply common standards across the growing portfolio, both for purposes of training new staff and for evaluating potential clients, including those clients outside of Root Capital's specific expertise in the coffee and cocoa sectors. In addition to applying consistent assessment criteria and methods, Root Capital, like its peers in the developing impact investing industry, needed a way to compare the performance of its impact capital across its portfolio. Root Capital had outgrown its ability to rely on the gut of loan officers. It needed standardized metrics for describing and measuring its clients' social impact. To meet this need, the company developed standardized social scorecards and environmental scorecards that loan officers could use to guide evaluations. The scorecards included specific categories focused primarily on observable practices.

In recent years, an impressive array of practitioners, academics, investors, entrepreneurs, and donors has contributed to what is now a sizable and well-developed body of knowledge on how to define, measure, track, and report social impact. Over that time, the conversation about measuring social impact has evolved considerably. From a discussion about whether and to what extent impact metrics matter, to an exploration of how to define, measure, track, and report those metrics, the social sector has made significant advances, including, importantly, the widespread acceptance of the need to measure and report meaningful evidence of social impact.

The evolution of Root Capital and the corresponding development of its need for standardized metrics track the broader conversation about impact metrics within the impact investing industry. Foundations seeking to streamline the assessment and evaluation of grantees have likewise developed standard criteria of program outcomes and indicators of success, as have government agencies. The increased demand for performance metrics over the last twenty years has spawned the development of hundreds of different methods, systems, and tools like Root Capital's scorecards for measuring impact. To the extent there is any uniform application of these methods, systems, and tools, it is generally confined to a particular segment of the social sector, with foundations using one set, governments another, social investors yet another.

The consequence of this disjointed framework is twofold:

First, the mission-driven ventures whose performance is the subject of measurement invest considerable resources in collecting fragmented data on a select few programs or initiatives in order to meet the often-conflicting demands of outside stakeholders, who not only use different reporting systems, but also apply varying definitions to outcomes and indicators of success. Because the ventures typically report outcome and impact data to multiple public and private stakeholders—each of which has its own metrics, reporting requirements, and definitions of success—those who run an organization and need to make well-informed decisions are often left with piecemeal metrics of little value to them or to their stakeholders.

The frustration was reflected in responses to a 2012 study by U.K.-based Inspiring Impact, a collective impact program that aims to embed good impact measurement practices across the U.K. social sector by 2022. The study revealed that over two-thirds of funders ask their grantees for information tailored to the funder. It is not surprising, then, that the surveyed organizations reported that different funders asking for different types of information prevented impact measurement from being used to its full potential.

The second inefficiency that results from a disjointed framework of metrics and measures is that the data reported has no contextual meaning. This limitation is echoed in Root Capital's reflections about stories like Richard and Erin Wilobo's re-establishment in Northern Uganda. Root Capital knows that it has reached more than 600,000 rural farmers like Richard over the past decade, but how does it know whether 600,000 farmer households is a lot or a little, given the human and financial resources it has invested, and what does it mean to "reach" a farmer? Without a benchmark or some other way to draw apples-to-apples comparisons across similar investments, that metric is of little utility not only to Root Capital, but also to its stakeholders.

Indeed, pioneers of impact investing identify the lack of comparability and credibility regarding how funds define, track, and report on the social performance of their investments as major barriers to the growth of the impact investing industry. The benefits of benchmarking are not limited to impact investors, but extend to all sources of social program funding. For every dollar granted to, or invested in, one social program, there is an opportunity cost of not allocating that resource elsewhere. Yet, without a common yardstick by which the alternatives can be measured, there is simply no way to account for that cost in making funding decisions. Effective benchmarking is also essential for the managers of mission-driven ventures to know whether or not resources are being applied to achieve the greatest impact possible.

Ultimately, a framework for making credible comparisons is critical to understanding what works and what does not work.

In addition to widespread agreement that impact metrics are of critical importance, a consensus among the various constituents of the social sector has developed over the last decade about exactly what "meaningful" data looks like. In essence, it must facilitate the ability to draw apples-to-apples comparisons across social programs.

CREATING MORE SOCIAL GOOD

In recent years, the sector's growing interest in performance metrics has been informed by debates about how those measures could facilitate efficiency, transparency, and growth for the sector as a whole—and, ultimately, the creation of more social good—if only they could be *meaningful* in a broader context. Optimism and ambition to reach that full potential have fueled initiatives across the globe toward developing a universal taxonomy of social performance metrics and shared measurement platforms, common platforms through which organizations can report results using standard performance indicators.

For some sectors and social programs (such as workforce development, for example), it makes sense to create this common language by assigning monetary value to social outcomes so they can be added up and compared. REDF's social return on investment was one of the first and most influential of the tools that have been developed based on the core concept of monetizing social outcomes.

But not every social program can be seamlessly reduced to numerical metrics. Thus, efforts have also been made to establish common languages in which qualitative outcomes can be consistently measured and described.

In 2004, the Center for What Works joined forces with the Urban Institute in an early effort to develop a standard taxonomy of qualitative outcomes for the nonprofit sector. The project was initiated amidst a backdrop of increasing demand for nonprofit accountability, heightened government oversight, and growing competition for funding—each accelerating the need to overcome barriers to measurement. As is still the case, nonprofits were facing increasing pressure to account for and improve results, yet they generally had limited capacity or resources for collecting, analyzing, and using data to inform practice. Recognizing the need for a more standardized approach to impact measurement—both for nonprofits and for the organizations that fund their efforts—the Center for What Works and the Urban Institute sought to develop the first sector-wide framework for defining nonprofit program outcomes and indicators of success.

Their work culminated in the Outcome Indicators Project, an online tool that allowed users to browse through common outcomes for fourteen nonprofit program areas and to create customized reports of outcomes and measurable indicators of success relevant to the user's mission. The intention was that service providers would use the framework to identify appropriate and relevant program outputs to measure common program outcomes to benchmark and improve, while grant-makers would use the framework to compare grantees in a common language. The Outcome Indicators Project, which was released in 2007 and includes data from the team's research conducted from 2004 to 2006, is still available at no cost on the Urban Institute's website, but it has not been updated or expanded beyond the initial fourteen program areas.

THE INDUSTRY STEPS UP

Perhaps the strongest push for a universal taxonomy of social impact metrics has come from the impact investing industry—in part, due to the organic expectation of impact investors to see a social return along with a financial one.

In October 2007, the Rockefeller Foundation gathered an international group of fifteen investors who were actively participating in such investment opportunities to discuss the needs of the emerging industry. This group, self-named the Rockefeller Impact Investing Collaborative, identified the lack of clear, consistent impact information as a primary barrier to achieving scalability of the impact investing sector.

The conversation continued in June 2008 when a group of forty investors from around the world convened to discuss and strategize ways in which to expand the newly dubbed impact investing (or social investing) industry. These investors shared a vision of an impact investing market that functioned much like the traditional financial markets. They also agreed that the lack of a common language to describe investment objectives and impact measurement was a significant impediment to making this vision a reality. The group organized itself around a number of initiatives to develop the impact investing marketplace they envisioned, including the creation of a global network of leading investors and a standard framework for assessing social and environmental impact.

Just over a year later, J.P. Morgan, the Rockefeller Foundation, and the United States Agency for International Development (USAID) fulfilled the first initiative by launching the Global Impact Investing Network (GIIN), a nonprofit organization dedicated to increasing the scale and effectiveness of impact investing. The GIIN was tasked to develop the critical infrastructure activities that would facilitate growth of the impact investment marketplace.

At the first Metrics Conference, hosted by the Aspen Network of Development Entrepreneurs (ANDE) in 2009, the bulk of the conversation continued to focus on the need for standardization in industry dialogue about measuring social impact. However, by that time the seeds of change had already begun to sprout. What would soon become the GIIN Investors Council had already planted two more seeds that would fulfill the second initiative developed at the June 2008 conference: one that would grow into the Impact Reporting and Investment Standards (IRIS), and one that would become the Global Impact Investing Rating System (GIIRS), both widely accepted tools for selecting and tracking impact metrics.

IMPACT REPORTING AND INVESTMENT STANDARDS (IRIS)

Establishing a common language to describe performance and ensure consistent measurement across portfolio outcomes was the first step in building the framework for an effective impact investing industry. In 2008, Acumen Fund, B Lab, and the Rocke-feller Foundation joined forces in an effort to develop a universal taxonomy of social and environmental performance metrics. These pioneers of impact investing recognized that, if investors could agree on common definitions of outputs, those metrics would be more transparent and comparable, enabling performance to be compared and benchmarked and for reporting requirements to be streamlined and simplified. The product of this initiative was Impact Reporting and Investment Standards (IRIS), a com-prehensive, but flexible taxonomy of standard definitions and impact metrics that, like financial accounting standards, provides a credible reference for performance reporting. Once the GIIN was launched in 2009, it took over the IRIS initiative and has managed the project ever since.

IRIS offers approximately 400 metrics with standard definitions that provide a consistent method for describing the social, envi-ronmental, and financial performance of an organization receiving impact capital. The taxonomy spans a range of performance objectives and includes sector-specific metrics for areas including agriculture, education, environment, and financial services, among others. Social impact investors can select metrics that are specifi-cally relevant to their particular activities, investment objectives, and stakeholder requirements and apply the same metrics across portfolios to develop a common framework for defining, tracking, and reporting impact metrics.

For example, Root Capital, the nonprofit social investment fund, uses IRIS output metrics within its social and environmental score-cards to evaluate and vet potential clients. It also uses the same metrics to measure the scale of its impact across its portfolio and as a way to hold itself accountable for impact internally and externally.

Root Capital selected four core metrics that make sense for assessing its loans, all of which are made to farmer associations and private businesses that help build sustainable livelihoods by aggregating rural producers in Africa and Latin America. The core metrics that Root Capital uses—number of farmers reached, purchases from rural producers, total revenue of rural SGBs, and hectares under sustainable management—are consistently applied to every investment, enabling relative comparison across the portfolio and over time.

IRIS was designed to facilitate comparability among investments and, indeed, has been widely adopted throughout the impact investing sector. However, social enterprises and nonprofit organizations can also use IRIS to identify appropriate outcome indicators—a purpose that the Center for What Works and the Urban Institute intended the Outcome Indicators Project to serve. In 2012, the GIIN launched a free online registry of IRIS users who publicly list the IRIS metrics they use and track. The IRIS registry can be searched by sector, geography, or impact focus, allowing visitors to gain a sense of what similar ventures find important to measure—a valuable resource for mission-driven ventures seeking to identify which outcomes to measure as an indication of a program's success.

THE GLOBAL IMPACT INVESTING RATING SYSTEM (GIIRS)

While the IRIS catalogue serves as a repository of data collected and reported using the standard IRIS definitions, thereby enabling benchmarking across investment portfolios, it is not an assessment or valuation framework. Rather, a rating system for impact investments called the Global Impact Investing Rating System (GIIRS) was designed to fulfill this complementary role.

Developed by B Lab in 2010 and powered by the B Impact Ratings System, GIIRS was designed in tandem with IRIS and incorporated IRIS metrics into its approach. An average social enterprise will report about twenty IRIS metrics and respond to a number of IRIS-defined questions across the GIIRS assessment. Utilizing the IRIS taxonomy and an organization's reported data, GIIRS assigns relative value to the social performance of impact investments—a GIIRS rating—enabling investors to aggregate impact data across a portfolio, compare impact performance, and screen different investment opportunities.

B ANALYTICS

In 2013, B Lab developed and, in partnership with the GIIN, launched B Analytics, a customizable data platform that helps investors, fund managers, business associations, and other partners collect, analyze, and report data reflecting their impact performance.

B Analytics incorporates data from PULSE—a portfolio data management system developed by Acumen, in collaboration with Salesforce and Google, in 2006 that enabled impact investors to collect, manage, and report on the impact of their investees. With the integration of PULSE, B Analytics is the only fully integrated data platform that enables investors to measure, benchmark, and report on the impact of their portfolios using their own custom impact metrics as well as GIIRS ratings—all built on the IRIS catalogue. B Analytics is the exclusive source of impact data on Certified B Corporations (discussed in Chapter 3) and GIIRS-rated companies and funds.

B Lab also developed the B Impact Assessment, a tool that enables social enterprisers to assesses and benchmark their performance against best practices on employee, community, and environmental impact and compare performance to others who have reported data through B Analytics.

OTHER "UNIVERSAL" STANDARDS

The impact investing industry is not alone in its development of a universal taxonomy and common framework for defining, tracking, and reporting social impact. Rather, a number of other players in the field have established their own "universal" standards—resulting in a plethora of parallel, but different frameworks for evaluating social impact.

For example, the microfinance industry, organized under the Social Performance Task Force (SPTF), an organization consisting of more than 1,500 international members from every microfinance stakeholder group, adopted the *Universal Standards for Social Performance Management* in 2010. This set of metrics—the microfinance industry's first global, shared understanding of social performance management—provides universal industry standards for measuring the social performance of microfinance institutions. The standards are incorporated into the MIX Market reporting platform, a data hub where microfinance institutions and supporting organizations share institutional data to broaden transparency and market insight.

Another example is the *Guidelines on Measuring Subjective Well-Being*—the first set of international guidelines and recommendations on collecting, measuring, and reporting subjective well-being data, which were released in 2013 by the Organisation for Economic Co-Operation and Development (OECD).

2013 also saw the publications of the *Code of Good Impact Practice* and *Funder Principles*—the U.K.'s first sector-wide collaborative resources providing guidelines for nonprofits and grant-makers, respectively, regarding impact metrics and practices. The guidelines were developed by Inspiring Impact, a U.K.-based collective impact program.

THE WORLD TAKES NOTE

Conversations among the world's leaders at the G8 Summit in June 2013 ignited global support for impact investing. Recognizing the growing relevance of impact investing worldwide—a development being driven largely by the G8 countries (Canada, France, Germany, Italy, Japan, the United States, the United Kingdom, and then including Russia)—delegates participated in the G8 Social Impact Investment Forum, a special event organized to focus on social investment. The event was the first of its kind to use the G8 platform to discuss social impact investment, creating an opportunity for the group of 150 industry leaders comprised of senior politicians, government officials, major philanthropists, business and finance executives, social entrepreneurs, and academics—including key players from government, civil society, and the private sector—to share insight on what is needed for the market to operate on a global scale.

The major theme of the day's discussions was a familiar one—the critical need for a common set of tools on social impact measurement. The G8 delegates unanimously agreed that shared standards are crucial to the development of the impact investment market. They also agreed that, while the work around impact assessment has increased in recent years, there is still much work to be done. Coordination among the various impact assessment systems will be necessary to drive the market forward. Bringing social impact investment into the mainstream will require universal adoption of a single common language in which to speak about social impact.

As a member of the U.S. National Advisory Board to the G8 Social Impact Investment Taskforce, and as co-chair of its Impact Measurement Working Group, the GIIN is working hard to make IRIS that universal language. The GIIN has recently partnered with a number of the players in the social impact field to incorporate the IRIS catalogue into the plethora of industry-specific frameworks that currently exist. One such partnership is with the microfinance industry. With the support of the Rockefeller Foundation, the GIIN and the Social Performance Task Force (SPTF) joined forces to incorporate the IRIS catalogue into the *Universal Standards for Social Performance Management* and to introduce it to the MIX Market reporting platform.

Largely as a result of the GIIN's diligent development of such partnerships, the seed of the IRIS catalogue is spreading. However, there is still much work to be done before IRIS becomes the *one* universal language for talking about social impact, particularly outside of the impact investing industry. Nonetheless, the initiative to establish a single framework for defining, tracking, measuring, and reporting social impact metrics is moving full steam ahead. The demand for impact measurement, along with impact investing itself, is market-driven, and market solutions are quickly rising to the challenge.

CHAPTER SIXTEEEN

What the Future May Hold

The Triumph of the Mission-Driven Venture

Gallup, Inc., the global research firm, recently reported that one in five people living in 131 countries, including most of the residents of twenty-seven sub-Saharan African nations, barely survive on $1.25 a day or less, the World Bank's definition of "extreme poverty." The World Bank Group has resolved that the poor must be lifted out of poverty and has set the laudable, but ambitious goal of reducing the rate of extreme poverty to 3 percent or less of the world's population by 2030.

THE POOREST OF THE POOR HAVE REASON FOR HOPE

Despite the stunning implications of the data Gallup has collected from thousands of households, a world virtually free of extreme poverty is, in fact, within our reach. Since 1980 more than one billion people, once poor, are no longer living in poverty. In the past fifteen years alone, nearly fifty developing nations have, on average, enjoyed a 5 percent annual increase in their gross domestic product.

The poorest of the poor have also seen their lives improve. Thanks to job creation and economic development, extreme-poverty households in developing countries actually declined from 52 percent in 1980 to 21 percent in 2010.

Progress can be seen all over the world. Since 1960, India's per capita income has quadrupled, and China's has increased eight-fold. Over the same period, the life expectancy of women in sub-Saharan Africa has jumped from forty-one to fifty-five. Meanwhile, childhood mortality rates have plummeted: UNICEF has reported that ninety-eight children out of 1,000 under the age of five died in Africa in 2012, compared to 177 in 1990. The number of AIDS-related deaths dropped 38 percent in Eastern and Southern Africa between 2005 and 2011, according to the United Nations.

Not surprisingly, the public sector deserves much of the credit for economic and social gains over the last half-century. Governments have consistently supported science and technology, public education, disease control, and environmental protection, all clearly public functions. Foreign aid to the developing world has funded vaccines, family planning, and other life-saving measures that keep people alive, healthy, and productive. For example, the worldwide incidence of malaria has dropped at least 30 percent, mostly because of the publicly supported Global Fund to Fight AIDS, Tuberculosis, and Malaria's wide distribution of bednets; and community health workers are becoming ever more efficient and effective because of a wide range of new smart phone applications funded, in large measure, by the public sector.

THE GROWING ROLE OF BUSINESS

While foreign aid has its important place in the mix, trade, it may be argued, is even more impactful. While aid provides relief to its recipient and esteem to its provider, trade dignifies and empowers both recipient and provider. While aid unsustainably addresses short-term needs, trade maintains a sustainable structure for supply and demand. While aid supports survival, trade enables growth.

As pop economists Steven D. Levitt and Stephen J. Dubner persuasively point out in their iconoclastic bestseller, *Think Like a Freak*:

> Consider poverty and famine: What causes them? A glib answer is the lack of money and food. So theoretically you can fight poverty and famine by airlifting vast amounts of money and food into poor and hungry places. That is pretty much what governments and aid groups have been doing for many years. So why do the same problems persist in the same places? Because poverty is a symptom—of the absence of a workable economy built on credible political, social, and legal institutions.

Only with private investment, entrepreneurship, and free markets can economic growth—and, with it, sustainable gains in individual income and public health—be assured. Were it not for private financing of Africa's infrastructure, for example, the continent's economies would never have seen their annual growth rates jump from 2.3 percent in the 1990s to 5.7 percent in the following decade, nor would the ensuing decline in poverty rates have been possible.

The mainstream capital markets are increasingly willing to step up to support businesses that see scalable market opportunities to meet the daunting challenges of water scarcity, affordable housing, accessible health care, education and training and, most of all, jobs. Such mission-driven ventures will play a key role in making societies fairer, setting the standard for responsibility in the private sector, and empowering communities to revitalize themselves. As Chi Onwurah, a U.K. shadow minister, describes the social enterprise's mandate in an interview with *The Guardian*:

> Social enterprise is, at its heart, a collective enterprise for the benefit of a community. It can be the best of both worlds—economic and social force fusing the dynamism of market forces with the social responsibility of public service. It should be about redressing the balance of power between vested interests and citizens, delivering true localism, community resilience and assets, employee rights and security, while enabling the participatory reform of both the public and private sectors.

SOCIAL ENTERPRISE GAINS INFLUENCE IN THE DEVELOPING WORLD

In much of the developing world, social enterprises are seeing their impact and influence grow.

Consider, for example, the employment challenges facing Africa, where 70 percent of the population is under the age of thirty. By 2040, half the world's youth will be African, mostly women and girls, and almost half of Africa's youth are unemployed.

Social entrepreneurs are also helping African youth become change-makers in their own right. Charles Maisel, among many others, understood the barriers young men in South Africa faced when looking for a job: the economy is informal, so employment tends to be short-term and unstable; and employers often distrust job-seekers and have a tough time matching skills with opportunities. So in 2001, Charles founded Men on the Side of the Road, which developed a database employers could access to see the results of an applicant's skills assessment and confirm his or her references. The social enterprise also built a network of employers in South Africa's townships, creating a market for the unemployed. By understanding the barriers South Africa's youth faced and by creating a market solution to overcome those barriers, Charles empowered them.

Charles Maisel's story is by no means unique. His entrepreneurship signals a global phenomenon.

Facing declines in charitable giving and staggering government budget deficits, even nonprofits are becoming increasingly entrepreneurial, on their own and in combination with other nonprofits, as well as for-profit businesses. Over time, most charities are likely to embrace the social enterprise model—earning revenue in the pursuit of a social purpose and reinvesting profits in business growth, social programs, or both.

BUSINESS RAISES THE BAR

At the same time, traditional businesses will more consistently be held accountable as actors whose conduct drives or retards positive social change. Government procurement practices and policies will reward socially responsible businesses with public contract opportunities, shunning companies that fail to meet their social-justice and environmental obligations. Governments will continue to encourage businesses that employ and train disabled and otherwise economically disadvantaged people. While companies will capitalize on these market opportunities, they will also view them as ways to build their brands, earn customer loyalty, and meaningfully repay the debts they owe their communities for supporting their efforts. Eventually, commercial enterprises will see—and promote—themselves as social enterprises, deploying their capital to earn both financial and social returns.

Already, companies are raising the bar for themselves and their competitors. Dell's 2020 "Legacy of Good Plan" pledges to reduce the company's greenhouse gases by 50 percent and product energy intensity by 80 percent no later than 2020. Coca-Cola published its own goals for 2020, promising to reduce its value-chain carbon emissions by 25 percent, to recover 75 percent of the bottles and cans it distributes, and to replenish all the water the company uses. By 2016, Lego plans to use only renewable energy.

All told, 75 percent of the world's biggest companies have announced multiple social and environmental goals, all driving both competition and performance. Some have gone further still, contractually requiring their suppliers to do no less than they themselves commit. Hewlett-Packard, for example, has set a carbon reduction target of 20 percent for its supply chain, while Wal-Mart is systematically clearing its shelves of products containing ten different toxic chemicals.

Companies that meet their customers' expectations in delivering authentic impact, by partnering with nonprofits, for example, will positively transform their brands and grow their businesses. Although Procter & Gamble's Pampers brand had focused on maternal/newborn tetanus for decades, only when the company joined forces with UNICEF did its commitment pay off. Since 2006, Pampers' sales have spiked while the company helped fund more than 300 million tetanus vaccines in eight countries.

P&G isn't alone. More and more companies are evaluating their performance by measuring environmental sustainability and social responsibility in addition to profits, the so-called "Triple Bottom Line." Echoing a growing theme among major corporations, Andrea Thomas, Wal-Mart, Inc.'s senior vice president for sustainability, described the company's commitment to help people live better around the world this way: "We believe our customers should not have to choose between affordability and sustainability." Good corporate citizenship thus becomes good business.

Nonprofit social enterprises, for-profit social-purpose businesses, and traditional businesses may find themselves competing both for contracts and for consumers. Many nonprofits have launched customer-focused substance abuse recovery centers, literacy initiatives, supportive housing developments, adult day-care facilities, hospices, and supplemental educational services. They have also created employee-focused social enterprises that offer people outside the economic mainstream job training, mentoring, and a path to permanent employment.

GOVERNMENTS REACH OUT TO MISSION-DRIVEN VENTURES

While such initiatives are becoming increasingly popular and successful, governments do more with less by outsourcing to both nonprofit and for-profit contractors, often making indistinguishable those services that are performed *by* government from those performed *for* government. As mission-driven ventures bid for health care, criminal justice, education, and other contracts, their ability to innovate may be compromised. As such contracts are awarded to them, their intentional accountability to the populations they serve could fall victim to pressures imposed by competitive processes that reward the lowest-cost bidder.

In June of 2014, at a White House roundtable on impact investing, more than twenty banks, foundations, and individuals pledged $1.5 billion to fund social ventures, spurring other investors who were sitting on the sidelines to join them. As Jean Case, the Case Foundation's CEO, put it: "I think this is the tip of the iceberg. We know there are many organizations poised to make more and bigger commitments, but didn't feel like the timing was right today to come forward. I love that, because it gives us another bite at the apple, if you will."

At the same time, several government agencies, including the U.S. Agency for International Development (USAID) and the Small Business Administration, made pledges to renew or launch programs that will directly finance entrepreneurs engaged in development or other double-bottom-line activities. The Obama Administration pledged:

- To increase the reach of the $1 billion Small Business Investment Company (SBIC) Impact Fund to mobilize greater private-sector investment in high-impact sectors as well as low-to-moderate income, rural, and economically distressed communities;

- To launch a $60 million USAID loan guarantee facility to encourage lending to businesses that sell environmentally friendly household technologies—from solar lamps to clean cook stoves to water filters—for use by families at the bottom of the pyramid in Africa, Latin America, South Asia, and Southeast Asia; and

- To clarify that mission-driven charitable institutions, including foundations and universities, can use their estimated $750 billion in endowment assets for program-related investments.

MEASUREMENT OF SOCIAL PERFORMANCE BECOMES MORE SOPHISTICATED

In a world where nonprofits, for-profits, and governments seek to deliver social value, the public and the investment and donor communities will demand increasingly sophisticated approaches to the measurement and reporting of social impact. All organizations claiming to address societal problems will be expected to publish annual statements, reporting on their social, environmental, and economic impact; and management will be guided by empirical data justifying decisions to scale successful programs and abandon unsuccessful ones. Similarly, consumers, donors, and investors will make their buying, giving, and investing decisions based on what they know about what works and what does not.

STAKEHOLDERS LOOK TO SUBSTANCE OVER FORM

All of society will follow suit, favoring or disfavoring organizations based on their demonstrated social benefit. Social enterprises will gain little support solely on the basis of their compelling missions; noble intentions simply won't excuse bad business decisions, ineffective strategies, or unsustainable revenue models. Commercial ventures will reject greenwashing as a useless, even counterproductive tactic; and socially and environmentally conscious investors will continue to back those companies whose managerial decisions reflect their own values and rebuff those that don't.

Ethically run commercial businesses and social enterprises will compete head to head, dedicating their finite resources to value propositions that include social outcomes. Those social enterprises that fail to realize meaningful social gains will be harshly judged, and their programs will be scrapped as new models surface and some prove themselves as legitimate drivers of societal values. Funders will reward providers who achieve both financial stability and their stated social and environmental goals, even as Benefit Corporations, L3Cs, Social Impact Bonds, and other emerging structures are tested against legal and market challenges.

Yet, stakeholders will become agnostic about a mission-driven venture's business form, whether for-profit, nonprofit, or hybrid. While entity design will continue to be an important part of a venture's business planning—with funding options, governance and tax considerations, and risk management no less important than ever—success will be measured by an organization's capital efficiency in delivering long-term results in addressing poverty, unemployment, and other social problems. Governments, investors, and donors will seek to support only those mission-driven ventures that achieve the greatest social impact at the lowest cost.

That proof won't come easy. Measuring social impact is expensive, especially for smaller organizations. The expertise, systems, and personnel to do the job credibly will cut into the very resources organizations are duty-bound to dedicate to mission. But all mission-driven ventures will have to prove that their social returns on investment beat their peers' or funding will eventually be lost to them. For that reason, many smaller organizations may join forces with others whose missions are complementary, as together they meet market demands that they quantify and evidence their impact claims. That collaboration may itself spark strategic alliances in the pursuit of shared social objectives.

Improved impact measurement will inexorably lead to greater financial support for mission-driven ventures. No longer will foundations seek to maximize their portfolios' financial returns and then reflexively give their profits away to those operating charities that appear to be making a difference. Instead, foundation managers will track the social impact of all their grants, along with all their mission-related and program-related investments. Their investments will be catalytic, spurring participating investments by their foundation peers and leveraged to attract private-sector investment.

Mission-driven enterprises, for their part, will be held accountable for demonstrable impact. As social outputs are realistically valued, institutional and market-driven investors will increase their commitment to enterprises that offer both financial and social returns. As social enterprises become more investable and financial products are developed to securitize double- or triple-bottom-line opportunities, the largest of financial institutions and their socially conscious customers will join the early movers.

When mission-driven ventures move mainstream, they will have embraced prudent business principles, attracted top-flight executive talent from the private sector, and held themselves to the standards that have always applied to traditional for-profit ventures. Those that live within a budget and compete with tough and hungry commercial competitors—as well as mission-driven ventures—will thereby have become stronger and more sustainable.

SOCIAL CAPITAL TAKES CENTER STAGE

Still greater access to capital, empowering as it is, will trigger market forces that mission-driven ventures should anticipate. Most obvious among them, investments will start to squeeze out grants. Even those ventures that are not well-suited to issue debt instruments or equity shares might be encouraged to do so. The explanation can be found in any basic accounting text: a grant is an expense, once incurred never to be recovered; by contrast, an investment remains an asset on the foundation's balance sheet, to be recovered on an agreed date or when a capital transaction occurs, and then available for reinvestment. Unlike a grant, an investment offers the foundation a financial multiplier effect and, consequently, a social multiplier effect, both irresistible to the foundation manager doing his best to be a good steward of the resources entrusted to him.

As funding shifts from grants to investments, funders may see less reason to encourage innovation, opting instead to stake claims to proven strategies. Similarly, government funding of new ideas may dry up as public resources are made available only for results that save public dollars. For both reasons, mission-driven ventures will be disadvantaged if their results, albeit socially beneficial, cannot easily be monetized. Those whose causes can readily be tied to savings or profits, such as efforts to reduce recidivism, will likely come out ahead.

Although innovation may be compromised, greater demands for impact measurement and reporting—and the expansion of impact investment—will encourage mission-driven ventures to scale up through replication, strategic alliance, and even licensing and franchising, which will allow community-based enterprises to expand their social footprints, diversify their sources of revenue, and maintain their community focus and local control. Social franchising will also become attractive to the broader universe of nonprofits and for-profit businesses with social missions, fostering cooperation and teaching the lessons of social enterprise to the world at large.

THE STAKES GO HIGHER

Bigger and bigger mission-driven enterprises, alone and in concert with others, will tackle increasingly complex social problems. As they gain stature and recognition as job creators, tax generators, and drivers of social change, some will challenge traditional business models and even the traditional corporate culture. Yet, larger for-profit and hybrid mission-driven ventures may also struggle to maintain their social values as they more acutely feel pressure to reward their owners financially.

As mission-driven ventures, irrespective of their form, grow in size and reach, some will find it tougher to remain faithful to their core values and accountable to their diverse stakeholders, putting at risk that which will have distinguished them from other players in the social sector and the business community. Lines between sectors will continue to blur.

But social enterprise has never been about sectors. The mission-driven venture will continue to look past legalistic boundaries and attack the social problems for-profit businesses, nonprofits, and governments, however well-motivated, have been unable to conquer on their own.

Mission-driven ventures won't be judged only by purity of thought, revenue, profit, or even the number of people they serve. It will be their effectiveness as change agents that separates those that earn support and acclaim from those that do not. They will engage and empower commercial businesses to improve their practices; they will lobby governments to change their laws and policies as they help eradicate poverty and unemployment and improve public health and education; and they will leverage their successes, spreading beyond their markets and service areas the solutions they have learned will work.

Some mission-driven ventures will have sufficiently achieved their goals to claim victory and shut down. Others will grow larger and larger. Micro-enterprises will network and collaborate across national borders. Crowdsourcing and crowdfunding will permit still others to connect and reconnect, first around one social issue, then another. Socially conscious leaders of mission-driven ventures throughout a nation, a region, a continent, or the world will galvanize around issues of common concern, sometimes even supplanting political blocs as the preferred method to mobilize public opinion and effect public policy in furtherance of democratization, social justice, equal opportunity, and other social aims.

Some mission-driven ventures will evolve into highly respected and risk-averse charities and private concerns, but others will continue to risk and innovate. Risk won't be shunned, but encouraged by donors and investors who respect the mission-driven venture's research and development function. They will wisely conclude that, without experimentation, our corpus of knowledge simply cannot grow. So, like the foundation's and the venture capitalist's assessment of risk and reward, their measure of social return won't be tied to specific initiatives, but to a mission-driven venture's whole portfolio.

COLLABORATION BECOMES THE WATCHWORD

Now a laboratory committed to discovering workable solutions to social problems, the mission-driven venture will no longer be seen as a business competitor in a zero-sum game. Public, nonprofit, and for-profit participants will join forces to cooperate in their shared mandate to effectively tackle the social problems that plague society. As solutions reveal themselves, they will systematically be introduced into mainstream thought and action.

Social entrepreneurs—the disrupters among us—will take on the most complex of social issues as they embrace or accommodate the legal, business, and market ecosystem in which they find themselves and which they help shape. Mission-driven ventures will create jobs for the disenfranchised and exploit business opportunities which themselves tackle the challenges of water scarcity, energy, and climate change. Their achievement will be recognized not only by their measurable social impact and their financial sustainability, but also by their pivotal role in fostering both a sustainable for-profit sector and a transformative public sector.

The mission-driven venture, no longer bound or defined by legal structures or business models, will have evolved. Funded by impact investors who seek both financial and social returns, they will be judged by their long-term impact; their creativity in networking, collaborating, and germinating innovative ideas; and their influence on the public, private, and social sectors, each more fully assuming its own role as change-maker.

Index

Page references followed by *fig* indicate an illustrated figure; followed by *t* indicate a table.

A

Accenture, 177
Accountability: B Corp Impact Assessment used to ensure stakeholder, 53; B Lab's model law on benefit corporations providing for, 49; B Lab's standards for social and environmental, 15, 53–54; impact investing and required, 147–148; of mission-driven ventures, 230; social impact metrics functioning as external, 194, 208–209
Ackman, Bill, 117
ACT exam, 3
Activia, 80
Acumen Fund: BACO (Best Alternative Charitable Option) developed by, 190–191; growth of, 139; impact investing focus of, 154–155; IRIS standards development role of, 141; PULSE system developed by, 219; social impact metrics support by the, 187
Affordable Care Act (U.S.), 124
Afghanistan War, 177, 202
Africa Health Fund (Aureos Capital), 156–157. *See also* Sub-Saharan Africa
Al Hassan, Abubarkar, 199, 203
AllLife, 147
Ally Bank (formerly GMAC), 64
Aman, Nurkholisoh, 148, 149
American Journal of Public Health, 193
American Red Cross of Greater Chicago, 53
American Reinvestment and Recovery Act (2009), 130
ANDI, 15
"Angel investors," 126, 128
Ann J. Kellogg School, 127
Apple, 84, 166
Arab Spring, 177
Architecture, Urban Design, and Sustainable Development (Cleveland Foundation), 104
Arizmediarrieta (Arizmedi), José María, 91–92, 95
Armani, 84
Arnold, John, 117
Ashoka Support Network, 164
Aspen Network of Development Entrepreneurs (ANDE), 216

Associated Press survey (2013), 1
Association, 29
Association to Advance Collegiate Schools of Business (AACSB), 14
Attlee, Chester, 138
Aureos Capital, 156–157
Australia, Social Benefit Bonds of, 17

B

B Corp Impact Assessment, 53, 219
B Corps certification: B Corp Impact Assessment, 53; ensuring accountability to stakeholders through, 53–54; origins and purpose of, 15, 54, 158, 160; WorkSquare, LLC as Florida's first certified, 6, 15
B Lab: B Corp certification issued by, 6, 15, 53–54, 158, 160; B Corp Impact Assessment of, 53; B Impact Ratings System of, 218; on California's organic cotton industry, 51; on consumers' social and environmental impact concerns, 8; founded to rate social performance of businesses, 158; GIIRS development role of, 218; IRIS standards development role of, 141, 218; model law on benefit corporations by, 49; social and environmental accountability standards of, 15, 53–54; social metrics promoted by, 187; third-party standards followed by, 48
Babson College, 8
Baby Boomers, 142, 177
BACO (Best Alternative Charitable Option) [Acumen Fund], 190–191
Bangladesh: charity:water case study, 204–208; failure of the banking system in, 71–72; Grameen Danone's social impact on, 79–81; independence (1971) of, 69; Muhammad Yunus' journey to establishing microcredit program in, 68–73; oppression and poverty conditions of, 68; Shokti Doi ("Yogurt for Power") sold in, 79–81. *See also* Grameen Bank (Bangladesh)
Bank of America, 64, 118, 130, 171
Bank of America Merrill Lynch, 153, 172
Bank of North Dakota, 121–122, 126
Banks: Ally Bank (formerly GMAC), 64; Bank of America, 64, 118, 130, 171; Bank of America Merrill Lynch, 153, 172; Bank of North Dakota, 121–122, 126; Caja Laboral Popular (Mondragón co-ops bank), 95–96; Citibank, 64, 130; Community Reinvestment Act (CRA) promoting community investment by,

122–123; Deutsche Bank, 171, 174; failure of Bangladesh banking system, 71–72; Federal Reserve Bank of St. Louis, 97; impact investing by, 171–172; increasing SOCAP conference participation by, 171; South Shore Community Bank (Chicago), 123–124, 130–131; "Too Big to Fail," 128; UBS, 172; Urban Partnership Bank, 130; World Bank, 13, 136, 138, 155. *See also* Grameen Bank (Bangladesh)

Bannick, Matt, 165, 176
Barriers to entry, 25
Bartram, Vanessa, 6, 15
BASE, 81
Basque region (Spain): economic and social innovation found in the, 91–92; Mondragón polytechnic school in the, 91–92
BCYI Mildred Community

Center (Boston), 113
Ben and Jerry's Scoop Shop (San Francisco), 4
Benefit Corporations: B Lab's model law on, 49; California Benefit Corporation law on, 46–48; characteristics of, 32*t*–33*t*; Delaware's version of, 29, 49; description and different types of, 16, 29; "general public benefit" mandate of, 46–47, 48–49; legal protections for making shareholder decisions, 48–49; Patagonia, Inc. as example of, 50–52; Public Good Software, Inc. as example of, 52–53; signaling advantages offered by, 30; Sustainability's "Rate the Raters" report on, 48; third-party standard of, 47–48. *See also* Corporations

Berkeley (University of California, Berkeley), 14
Best Alternative Charitable Option (BACO) [Acumen Fund], 190–191
Better Business Bureau, 83
Big Society Capital (UK), 168–169
Bill & Melinda Gates Foundation, 59, 134, 151–152, 171, 175, 198, 200, 204
bin Laden, Osama, 201
Blankfein, Lloyd, 171
Bloomberg, Michael, 17
Bloomberg Philanthropies, 116
Blue Sky (UK), 106
BlueOrchard's Dexia Microfinance Fund, 155
Bobi refugee camp (Uganda), 206
Bono, 84
Booth School of Business (University of Chicago), 133, 148
Born, Kelly, 158
Bosch Group, 10
"Bottom of the pyramid" impact, 137
Bowman, Aniya, 178

Bowman, Charmaine, 178, 181, 182, 191, 193

Boyle, Father Greg ("Father G" or "G-Dog"), 5, 6

Brayton, Bill, 164

Brest, Paul, 158

Bridges Social Ventures Fund, 152

Bridges Ventures LLP, 152

Bridges Ventures's Social Entrepreneurs Fund, 155

Bridgespan Group, 14

"Broad applicability" constituency statutes, 42–43

Buckmaster, Jim, 43, 44

BUILD case study: ETO (Efforts to Outcomes) for tracking performance metrics, 196–197; founding (1969) of BUILD (Broader Urban Involvement and Leadership Development), 195; preventing gang violence focus of BUILD, 195–198; scaling success using

social impact metrics, 194–198

Bureau of Labor Statistics, 188

Burundi, 150

Bush, George H. W., 136

Bush, George W., 136

Business Alliance for Local Living Economies (BALLE) [California], 125–126, 127–128

Business models: comparing impact and socially responsible, 135–136; elements and hypotheses of, 20, 21t; entity design choices to make on, 28–30; hybrid, nonprofit/for-profit, 28–29; for reaching "the missing middle," 211; social venture franchising, 86–87; steps for maximizing prospects of financial success and social impact, 22–26

C

Caja Laboral Popular (Mondragón co-ops bank), 95–96

Calice, Clemens, 150

California: Benefit Corporation law of, 46–48; on benefit corporation's third-party standard, 47–48; Business Alliance for Local Living Economies (BALLE) of, 125–126, 127–128; California Clean Energy Fund (CalCEF) of, 128; California HealthCare Foundation (CHCF) of, 124; Flexible Purpose Corporation law of, 29; organic cotton industry of, 51; Patagonia, Inc. as first benefit corporation in, 50–52; Pay for Success programs in, 117–118

California Clean Energy Fund (CalCEF), 128

California HealthCare Foundation (CHCF), 124

California Public Utilities Commission, 128

Calvert Community Investment Note, 127, 137

Calvert Foundation, 127, 139, 150

Cameron, David, 17, 132, 168–169

Campaign to eradicate polio case study, 199–204

Capital: Chicago's Impact Engine commitment to providing seed, 133, 165; Debt Service Reserves (DSRs), 131; estimating capital costs, 25–26; impact investing challenges in emerging markets, 149–150; Loan Loss Reserves (LLRs), 131; Millennials embracing social change through power of, 177; Mondragón co-ops' entrepreneurial policies on, 96; questions to ask about, 34; SOCODEN providing SCOP co-op access to, 99. See also Community capital; Financial issues; Social capital

Capital costs, 25–26

Capital One, 78

Capitalism: both a brain and a soul required by, 13; impact investing as "creative," 138; reinvented as a force for social good and sustainable, 15–17

The Cara Program, 188–189

Carnegie, Andrew, 7

Carter, Jimmy, 166

case Foundation, 227

Case, Jean, 227

Case Western Reserve University, 100, 102

Cassoy, Andrew, 15

Cause-related marketing: Better Business Bureau's recommendations on, 83; business value of, 81–82; Cone Communications Social Impact Study on, 82–83; description of, 81; (PRODUCT)[RED] use of, 84; Yoplait's "Save Lids to Save Lives" campaign as example of, 83–84

CDC Group (UK), 138

CDFI Funds, 123, 124, 126, 128, 130

Center for American Progress, 171

Center for Medicare and Medical Services, 102

Center for What Works, 214–215, 218

Central Bank of Indonesia, 148

CEO pay debate, 96–97

Ceres Roadmap to Sustainability, 48, 53

CFA Association survey (2013), 162

Chakravati, Manoj, 9

Change-of-control situations: Alabama's standard formula for constituency statutes on, 41–42; constituency statutes on, 41; Iowa's "limited applicability" constituency statute on, 42

Charity:water case study: Khadija's story, 205, 207; origins and focus of, 204–208; Project Detail Reports provided to contributors to, 207

Charles Schwab's Schwab Charitable Division, 126
Chennai (India), 176
Chicago: Chicago Mayor Richard M. Daley's sustainability impact in, 62–64; Impact Engine of, 133, 164; Merchandise Mart in, 132; Millennium Park of, 62–63; OJJDP recognition of BUILD's work to prevent gang violence in, 197–198; A Safe Haven Foundation of, 178; South Shore Community Bank of, 123–124, 130–131. *See also* Illinois
Chicago, Inc. Housing Action Illinois, 64
Chicago Public School District, 133
Chicago Tribune, 62–63
Child labor, 89
Chittagong University (Bangladesh), 69
Chouinard, Yvon, 50–52
Cicilline, David N., 16
Citi Foundation, 78
Citibank, 64, 130
Civil society: changing relationships in

current, 53; Public Good Software, Inc. focus on re-tooling, 52–53
Clegg, Nick, 17
Cleveland: "buy local" strategy of, 101; Evergreen Cooperatives of, 100–104
Cleveland Clinic, 102
Cleveland Foundation, 101, 104
Clinton, Bill, 123, 147
Clinton Global Initiative, 147
Co-operatives. *See* Worker-owned co-operatives
Coca-Cola, 226
Code of Good Impact Practice (2013) [UK], 220
Colonial Development Corporation (CDC) [UK], 138
Colorado's Pay for Success programs, 117–118
Columbia teen pregnancy Social Impact Bond, 118
"Common Threads Initiative" (Patagonia, Inc.), 51
Commonwealth Development Corporation (UK), 138

Community building: Community Reinvestment Act (CRA) promoting bank investment in, 122–123; donor-advised funds used for, 126; examples of community capital financing of, 121–126; lessons learned about funding, 130–131
Community capital sources: "angel investors," 126, 128; Bank of North Dakota, 121–123, 126; Business Alliance for Local Living Economies (BALLE) on, 125–126, 127–128; California Clean Energy Fund (CalCEF), 128; California HealthCare Foundation (CHCF), 124; CDFI Funds used for, 123, 124, 126, 128, 130; donor-advised funds, 126; foundations, 126–127; the government, 129–130; Illinois Finance Fund, 124;

lessons learned about, 130–131; Local Initiatives Support Corporation (LISC), 125; Mountain BizWorks, 124; Nonprofit Finance Fund, 129; RSF Social Finance, 124–125; South Shore Community Bank (Chicago), 123–124, 130–131; venture capitalists, 126, 128. *See also* Capital

Community Contribution Company (C3) [British Columbia, Canada], 30

Community Development Financial Institution (CDFI), 65, 123, 136

Community Interest Company (CIC) [UK], 30

Community Reinvestment Act (CRA) [U.S.], 122–123

Competitive rivalry, 24–25

Cone Communications Social Impact Study, 82–83

Congressional Gold Medal, 68

Connecticut: constituency statute of, 41, 43; Pay for Success programs of, 117–118

Constituency statutes: "broad applicability," 42–43; on corporate takeovers, change-of-control situations, or mergers, 41–43; four different ways of literalizing board's fiduciary duty, 41; "limited applicability," 42

Consumer Expenditure Survey (2010), 188

Control Data Corporation, 8

Control questions, 35

"Corporate Law Corporate Constituency Statutes Hopes and False Fears" (Springer), 45–46

Corporate Social Responsibility (CSR): examples of social change is driven by, 9–11;

public debate over, 12–13

Corporate takeovers: Alabama's standard formula for constituency statutes on, 41–42; constituency statutes on, 41; Iowa's "limited applicability" constituency statute on, 42

Corporation for National and Community Services, 15

Corporations: Delaware's corporate law emphasis on shareholder benefit, 40; for-profit mission-driven ventures organized as, 29; sustainable business, 29, 32t–33t; tax-exempt nonprofit corporation, 32t–33t, 214–215, 226–227; traditional, 32t–33t. *See also* Benefit corporations

Counseling Data L3C case study, 64–66

Craigslist (*eBay v. Newmark* case), 43–46

"Creative capitalism," 138

Credit Suisse, 171

Crowdfunding: mission-driven ventures increasing use of, 232; new regulations permitting, 166; success in raising impact investing funds, 166–168

Crowdsourcing, 232

Cuomo, Andrew, 117

Customer power, 25

Customers: competitive force of the power of, 25; minimum viable product (MVP) to validate interest by, 20; mitigating risk for your, 19–20; positioning by making the case for value proposition to, 24; segmentation of your potential, 23–24; social environmental impact concerns of, 8

CVS, 161–162

Cycle of poverty: description of the, 1; mission-driven ventures used to break the, 1–2

D

Daley, Richard M., 62–64

Dannon (Group Danone in France), 79, 80–81

Darragh, Linda, 148, 149

DataEdge (also Grameen IT Park Limited), 88

David Eccles School of Business (University of Utah), 117

Davis Gray, 128

Debt Service Reserves (DSRs), 131

Decision making: benefit corporation legal protections related to shareholder, 48–49; shareholder primacy doctrine impact on, 40, 43–46; social impact metrics functioning as internal, 194; stakeholder constituency statutes impacting, 41–43

Delaware: benefit corporation version in, 29, 49; corporate law on shareholder primacy in, 40, 43–46; *eBay v. Newmark* case (2010) in, 43–46

Dell's "Legacy of Good Plan" pledges, 226

Democracy. *See* Workplace democracy

Democracy Collaborative (University of Maryland), 101, 103

Department for International Development (UK), 169

Deutsche Bank, 171, 174

Deutsche Bank Impact Investment Fund, 171

Deutsche Bank Research, 77

Developing world: Gallup report on "extreme" poverty in, 222; increasing influence of social enterprise in the, 224–225; reasons for hope by those living in poverty in, 222–223

Development finance institutions (DFIs), 136
Dhaka University (Bangladesh), 68
District of Columbia, 118
Doctrine of shareholder primacy: benefit corporation legal protections related to, 48–49; Delaware's *eBay v. Newmark* case (2010) on, 43–46; description and implications of, 40
Dolores Mission, 5
Donor-advised funds, 126
Dow Jones Sustainability Index, 172
Dubner, Stephen J., 223
Due diligence, 148
Duke University, 14
Duke University Center for the Advancement of Social Entrepreneurship, 140

E
East African Community, 150
eBay, 43–46, 139
eBay v. Newmark (Delaware), 43–46

EcoEnergy International, 159
Edelman, 161
Ek, Daniel, 208
Ellerman, David, 100
Emanuel, Rahm, 132
Emerging markets, 149–150
Employee Ownership Center (Kent State University), 101
Employee Retirement Income Security Act (ERISA), 166
Employees: Rochdale Society of Equitable Pioneers' worker-owner co-operative, 92–93; unequal wages paid to U.S. CEOs versus rank-and-file, 96–97. *See also* Worker-owner co-operatives
Entity design choices, 28–30
Entrepreneurial non-profits. *See* Nonprofit corporations
Environmental protection. *See* Sustainability issues
EPA (U.S. Environmental Protection Agency), 164

Equilar Inc., 96
Erickson, Pam, 11
Estimating capital costs, 25–26
Euclid (Ohio), 102
European Union social co-operatives, 98. *See also* United Kingdom
Evergreen Cooperative Corporation (ECC), 103–104
Evergreen Cooperative Development Fund, 104
Evergreen Cooperatives (Cleveland): Evergreen Cooperatives Laundry, 102; Green City Grocers Cooperative, 102, 103; Leadership in Energy and Environmental Design (LEED), 102; Mondragón model followed by the, 100, 103; Ohio Cooperative Solar (OCS), 102–103; owned and operated by Greater University Circle residents, 101; success of the,

Evergreen Cooperatives (Cleveland) (*continued*) 100–102; unprecedented partnership making up the, 101

Evergreen Cooperatives Laundry, 102

Evergreen Land Trust, 104

Evian, 80

"Expenditure responsibility" requirement, 56–58

Extreme poverty. *See* Poverty

F

Fargo floods (North Dakota), 122

Federal Deposit Insurance Corporation (FDIC), 123, 130, 131

Federal Reserve Bank of St. Louis, 97

FEED Projects, 136

Fidelity Investments, 126

Financial first investors, 154–156

Financial forecasts, 25–26

Financial issues: doctrine of shareholder primacy, 40, 43–46, 48; establishing financial viability of the venture, 25–26; estimating capital costs, 25–26; forecasting the venture finances, 25–26; getting funding for a venture, 38–39; questions to ask about venture expenses, 31; stakeholder constituency statutes impacting decisions on, 41–43; tracking financial performance, 37. *See also* Capital; Profits

Firefox web browser, 10

FirstSolar, 135

"The Five Competitive Forces that Shape Strategy" (Porter), 24–25

501(c)(3) nonprofit status: description of, 7; of Evergreen Cooperative Corporation (ECC), 103; increased financial pressures on, 144; Omidyar Network initially filed as, 139

Flexible Purpose Corporation (California), 29

Food and Agriculture Organization (UN), 13

"Food deserts," 136

Foote, Willy, 210–211

Forbes magazine, 139, 167

Ford Foundation, 137

"Forgotten Man" radio address (Roosevelt, 1932), 137

Forward Internet, 207

Foundation Source, 145

Foundations. *See* Private foundations

France: SCOP (Société coopérative et participative) of, 99; SOCODEN (Société coopérative de dévelopement et d'entraide) of, 99

Franco, Francisco, 92

Freundlich, Tim, 163

Friedman, Milton, 12

FSG (formerly Foundation Strategy Group), 66

FTSE4Good, 172

Funder Principles (2013) [UK], 220

Future of Philanthropy and Development forum (Billagio, Italy), 198

G

"G-Dog" (Father Greg Boyle), 5, 6
G8 Social Impact Investing Forum (2013), 169
G8 Summit (2013), 220
GAAP (generally accepted accounting principles), 141
GADA (Gulu Agricultural Development Company) [Uganda], 183–184
Gallup global poverty report, 222
Gang members: BUILD case study on interventions for, 194–198; Homeboy Industries' employment of former, 5. *See also* Juvenile offender programs
The Gap, 84
Garab, Ramatu, 201, 203
Gates, Bill, 138, 200
Gates Foundation, 59, 134, 151–152, 171, 175, 198, 200, 204

General public benefit mandate: of benefit corporations, 46–47; legal protections for benefit corporation directors related to, 48–49
Ghosh, Shikhar, 19
Gifford, James, 170, 171
GIIN case study on Tanzanian agriculture (2011), 150
GIIN (Global Impact Investing Network), 140–141, 142, 145, 150, 152, 208–209, 216, 221
GIIN impact investor study (2014), 142, 145, 152
GIIRS (Global Impact Investing Rating System), 141–142, 159, 216, 218
Gilbert, Jay Coen, 15
Giving Fund, 163
Global Fund to Fight AIDS, TB, and Malaria, 84, 223
Global Health Investment Fund (GHIF), 171
Global Impact Investing Center (University of Utah), 117, 145

Global Impact Investing Network (GIIN), 140–141, 142, 145, 150, 152, 208–209, 216, 221
Global Polio Eradication Emergency Action Plan (2014), 203
Global Polio Eradication Initiative (GPEI), 200–201
Global Reporting Initiative (GRI), 48, 53
GlobeKids Digital Limited, 88
GMAC (now Ally Bank), 64
Goldman, Paula, 165
Goldman Sachs, 115, 116, 130, 171
Goldman Sachs GS Social Impact Fund, 171
Good Capital, 163
Good corporate citizenship, 226–227
Good Guide Company rating, 53
Goodman, Paula, 176
Google, 175, 219
Government: outsourcing to mission-driven ventures by, 227–228; Pay-for-Success

Government
(*continued*)
model adopted by
the U.S., 17;
shrinking dollars
and increased
need for assistance
from, 143; as
source of
community
capital, 129–130.
See also Obama
Administration
Grameen America, 78,
85
Grameen Bank
(Bangladesh):
continued
expansion of the,
84–85, 176; the
earliest
microcredit
program and birth
of the, 72–73;
economic strategy
followed by, 75–
78; entrepreneur
empowerment by,
88–90; loans made
to women by,
69–70, 88–89;
microcredit
program model of
the, 67–68; "social
business"
approach of,
74–75. *See also*
Bangladesh;
Banks; Microcredit
programs; Yunus,
Muhammad

Grameen Bitek
Limited, 88
Grameen Byabosa
Bikash, 88
Grameen Capital
Management
Limited, 88
Grameen CyberNet
Limited, 88
Grameen-Daffodil IT
Education
Limited, 88
Grameen Danone
Foods Ltd., 79–80,
89
Grameen Fisheries
and Livestock, 89
Grameen Fund, 88
Grameen Health Care
Services, 90
Grameen IT Park
Limited (also
DataEdge), 88
Grameen Kalyan, 90
Grameen Knitwear
Limited, 88
Grameen Shamogree,
87
Grameen Shikkha, 89
Grameen Solutions
Limited
(previously
Grameen
Software), 88
Grameen Star
Education
Limited, 88
Grameen Trust, 77,
84–85
Grameen Uddog, 87

Graziadio School of
Business
(Pepperdine
University), 14
Great Recession, 1
Greater University
Circle (Cleveland),
101, 103, 104
Green America
Business Network,
48
Green Bonds (World
Bank), 136
Green City Grocers
Cooperative
[Evergreen
Cooperatives],
102, 103
Greenseal, 48
Grossman, Steven, 128
Group Danone
(Dannon in the
U.S.), 79, 80–81
GS Social Impact
Fund (Goldman
Sachs), 171
Guard, Ryan, 207
The Guardian, 96, 224
*Guardian Sustainable
Business*, 40
*Guidelines on
Measuring
Subjective Well-
Being* (2013), 220
Gulu district
(Northern
Uganda), 182–183

H
Habitat for Humanity,
163

Harden, Rose Lee, 163
Hardmeyer, Eric, 121
Harrison, Scott, 204–207, 208
Hart, Stuart L., 9
Harvard Business Review, 24, 139, 148
Harvard Business School, 13, 19, 138–139, 210, 211
Harvard University, 14, 63
Hasenstab, Garrett, 11
Hawaii's Sustainable Business Corporation, 29
HCT Group, 152
Her Majesty's Prison Peterborough (England): failures of the, 105–106; Social Impact Bond for recidivism intervention program at, 106–112; "Transforming Rehabilitation" strategy pursued for prisoners of, 110. *See also* Peterborough (England)
Hernandez, Paloma, 129
Hewlett Foundation, 158
Hewlett-Packard, 226

"Hit the ground running" approach, 20, 22
Hitachi Foundation, 6
Homeboy Bakery, 5
Homeboy Diner, 5
Homeboy Farmers Markets, 5
Homeboy Industries, 5–6, 7
Homeboy Plumbing, 5
Homeboy Silkscreen, 5
Homeboy/Homegirl Merchandise, 5
Homegirl Café, 5
Hope Credit union, 136
Hope Foundation, 161
Hope Foundation survey (2010), 173
Hortense, 6
Houlihan, Bart, 15
Housing Action Illinois, 64, 65–66
Howard, Ted, 103
Huffington, Arianna, 128
Huffington Post, 125
Hurricane Katrina, 136
Hutchinson, Neil, 207–208
Hybrid, nonprofit/for-profit business model, 28–29

I
IGNIA Fund, 139
Ignia Partners, 150, 152

IIX (Impact Exchange Asia), 160–161
Illinois: Chicago Mayor Richard M. Daley's sustainability impact in, 62–64; Chicago's South Shore Community Bank in, 123–124, 130–131; constituency statute of, 41, 43; Illinois Finance Fund (IFF) of, 124; Pay for Success programs in, 117–118; Task Force on Social Innovation, Entrepreneurship, and Enterprise of, 16. *See also* Chicago
Illinois Department of Corrections, 194
Illinois Finance Fund (IFF), 124
Impact businesses, 135–136
Impact Economy, 165
Impact Engine (Chicago), 133, 164
Impact Exchange Asia (IIX), 160–161
Impact first investors, 154–155
Impact investing: AllLife, 147; "bottom of the pyramid" impact

Impact investing
(*continued*)
of, 137; CFA
Association
survey (2013) on,
162; Darragh and
Aman study (2011)
of, 148–149; due
diligence process
in, 148; emerging
markets
challenges for,
149–150; examples
and social impact
of, 135–136;
fixed-income
investments using,
136; forms of,
150–152; GIIN
(Global Impact
Investing
Network),
140–141, 142, 145,
150, 152, 208–209,
216, 221; GIIN's
definition of
"impact
investment",
208–209; growth
since the financial
crisis (2008),
142–146; growth
trajectory of,
174–177; history of
Chicago's,
132–135; Hope
Foundation survey
(2010) on, 173;
IGNIA, 139–140;
importance of
public policy for,

165–170;
institutional,
170–174; J.P.
Morgan survey
(2010) of, 149; J.P.
Morgan's estimate
on impact
investing market
by 2020, 161, 165,
174–175; judging
performance of
investment,
156–157;
managing risk
issue of, 152–156;
market challenges
of, 161–162;
Omidyar
Network, 139, 165,
176; origins and
historic
development of,
137–138;
Principles for
Responsible
Initiative on,
170–171;
quantifying social
returns of,
157–159;
requirements of,
147–148; S-curve
growth of, 176;
social
entrepreneurship
through, 138–139.
See also PRIs
(program-related
investments);
Social impact

Impact investing
public policy:
ERISA permitting
venture capital
investing by
pension funds,
166; JOBS Act
providing boost to
impact investing,
166, 167, 168;
Obama's National
Impact Initiative,
169; regulations
permitting
crowdfunding,
166–168; role in
supporting growth
of impact
investing, 165–166;
Startup America
Initiative, 168;
UK's Big Society
Capital, 168–169;
UK's Social Value
Act (2012), 169,
170. *See also* U.S.
legislation
Impact investment
standards: GIIRS
third-party
evaluator of,
141–142, 159, 216,
218; IRIS (Impact
reporting and
Investing
Standards) of, 141,
216–218, 221
Impact investors:
deciding on form
of investing,
150–152;

description of, 135; J.P. Morgan and GIIN study (2014) of, 142, 145, 152; J.P. Morgan survey (2010) of, 149; maturing into financial first investors, 155–156; pairing impact first and financial first, 154–155

Impact Measurement Working Group (G8 social Impact Investment Taskforce), 221

Impact reporting and Investing Standards (IRIS), 141, 216–218, 221

Indian Companies Act (India), 9–10

Individual Development Account program (Juma Ventures), description of, 2–3

Industrial Co-Operative Association, 100

Innovation Centre (TATA Group), 9

Input indicators, 27–28

Inspiring Impact study (2012), 213

Intel, 81

Internal Revenue Service. *See* U.S.

Internal Revenue Service (IRS)

International Co-Operative Alliance's Statement on the Co-Operative Identity, 93–95

International Finance Corporation (World Bank), 138, 155

International Labour Organization, 10

Investors' Council, 140

Iowa's "limited applicability" constituency statute, 42

Iraq War, 177, 202

IRIS (Impact reporting and Investing Standards), 141, 216–218, 221

IS02600, 48

Italy's "social co-operatives," 97–98

J

Jackson, Frank G., 101

J.C. Nichols Prize for Visionaries in Urban Development, 62

JOBS Act (Jumpstart Our Business Startups Act), 166, 167, 168

"Jobs For A Future' campaign, 5

John Lang Training (UK), 110

Jones, Kevin, 163

J.P. Morgan: estimating impact investing market by 2020, 161, 165, 174–175; GIIN (Global Impact Investing Network) role of, 216; as IGNIA investor, 139; as one of LeapFrog's initial backers, 147; Social Finance Department opened by, 171; study on impact investors by GIIN (2014) and, 142, 145, 152; survey on impact investors (2010) by, 149; trillion-dollar projection on impact investing by, 146

J.P. Morgan Chase, 64, 130

Juma Ventures: Individual Development Account program of, 2–3; life-changing employment and educational opportunities

Juma Ventures
(*continued*)
offered by, 2;
mission to
empower others,
2–3; as a model of
entrepreneurial
non-profits, 2–5, 7
Juvenile offender
programs: Illinois
Pay for Success
initiative on, 118;
Rikers Island
Social Impact
Bond (New York),
115–116. *See also*
Gang members

K
Kamila, Mark, 66
Kamin, Blair, 62–63
Kellogg School of
Management
(Northwestern
University), 133
Kellogg Foundation,
59, 127, 136
Kellogg, William
Keith, 126–127
Kennedy, Joseph P.,
Sr., 132
Kent State University,
101
Kenya, 150
Khadija (Bangladesh
student), 205, 207
Khyber
Pakhtunkhwa, 203
Kings College
London, 198

KIPP charter schools,
151–152, 175
Kramer, Mark, 66
Kunesh, Jason, 52, 53
Kuri, Lillian, 104
Kyoto Protocol, 164

L
L3Cs (low-profit,
limited liability
companies):
capability to
engage diverse
stakeholders by,
61–62; compared
to other entities,
32*t*–33*t*;
Counseling Data
L3C case study in
collective impact,
64–66; description
and types of, 16,
29–30, 59–60;
foundation PRI
use of, 60–62;
providing
opportunities for
social
entrepreneurs, 49;
signaling
advantages
offered by, 30; The
Sustainability
Exchange
established by
Mayor Daley,
63–64, 66. *See also*
Limited liability
company (LLC)
Larson, Heidi, 201

Launching
mission-driven
venture, 35–38
Lauren, Lauren Bush,
135–136
Lawrence Hall Youth
Services, 118
Leadership in Energy
and
Environmental
Design (LEED)
gold doors
[Evergreen
Cooperatives], 102
Leadership model of
Mondragón
strategy, 92
Lean startups:
business model's
elements and
hypotheses used
for, 20, 21*t*; "hit the
ground running"
approach taken by,
20, 22; minimum
viable product
(MVP) assessment
process by, 20;
mitigating risk
through, 19–20;
steps for
maximizing
prospects of
financial success
and social impact,
22–26
LeapFrog
Investments,
147–148
"Learning agenda," 27
Lego, 226

Levitt, Steven D., 223
"Limited
    applicability"
    constituency
    statutes, 42
Limited liability
    company (LLC):
    characteristics of,
    32*t*–33*t*; for-profit
    mission-driven
    venture organized
    as, 29. *See also*
    L3Cs (low-profit,
    limited liability
    companies)
Lion's Head Global
    Partners (UK), 150,
    171
Livingstone, Linda, 14
Loan Loss Reserves
    (LLRs), 131
Local Initiatives
    Support
    Corporation
    (LISC), 125
Logic model, 27–28
London School of
    Hygiene and
    Tropical Medicine,
    201
Louisiana's "limited
    applicability"
    constituency
    statute, 42

M
MacPherson, Nancy,
    198–199
Madigan, Lisa, 64
Maisel, Charles,
    224–225
Market questions, 31

Marks & Spencer, 15
Martin, Maximilian,
    165
Maryville Academy,
    118
Massachusetts
    Juvenile Justice
    Pay for Success
    initiative: events
    leading up to the,
    113–114; Social
    Impact Bond for
    the, 114–115
Massachusetts Office
    for Administration
    and Finance, 113
MathMovesU
    initiative
    (Raytheon), 11
Mayor Richard M.
    Daley Legacy
    Award for Global
    Leadership in
    Creating
    Sustainable Cities,
    62
McKinsey, 164
MDRC: description of,
    115; New York
    City's Social
    Impact Bond role
    of, 115–116
Medicaid, 189
Men on the Side of the
    Road, 225
Merchandise Mart
    (Chicago), 132
Mercy Ships, 205–206
Mergers: Alabama's
    standard formula
    for constituency

statutes on, 41–42;
    constituency
    statutes on, 41;
    Iowa's "limited
    applicability"
    constituency
    statute on, 42
Metrics. *See* Social
    impact metrics
Metrics Conference
    (2009), 216
Michigan Community
    Health Project, 127
Microcredit programs:
    example of the
    positive impact of,
    67; Grameen
    America's
    expansion of the,
    78, 85; as
    ingenious solution
    for breaking cycle
    of poverty, 72–73;
    Muhammad
    Yunus' journey in
    founding the first,
    67–73; S-curve
    growth of, 176; as
    social business,
    74–75. *See also*
    Grameen Bank
    (Bangladesh)
Microinsurance funds
    (LeapFrog
    Investments),
    147–148
Microsoft, 157
MicroVentures
    crowdfunding
    platform, 166

Millennial generation, 142, 177

Millennium Park (Chicago), 62–63

MIND, 110

Minimum viable product (MVP), 20

Minneapolis race riot (1967), 8

"The missing middle," 210–211

Mission-driven entrepreneurs: collaboration as key to success by, 233; giving life to his vision, 36–38; how benefit corporations and L3Cs provide opportunities for, 49; moving from ideation to realization, 30, 31–35; preparing for launch, 35–38; reality check conducted by the, 22–23; testing the feasibility of the venture by, 23–26

Mission-driven venture development: business model's elements and hypotheses, 20, 21*t*; entity design choices to make during the, 28–30; "hit the ground running" approach during the, 20, 22; issues to consider when beginning your, 19–22; lean startup approach to mitigate risk, 19–20; logic model used to track input, output, and outcome indicators, 27–28; minimum viable product (MVP) assessment process during the, 20; preparing for launch, 35–38; questions to ask for moving from ideation to realization, 30, 31–35; reality check during the, 22–23; testing the feasibility of the mission-driven venture during, 23–26

Mission-driven ventures: breaking the cycle of poverty using, 1–2; collaboration as key to successful, 233; examples of how social change is driven by, 9–13; golden circles of why, how, and what of, 208; government outsourcing to, 227–228; historic origin of, 7–8; Homeboy Industries example of a, 5–6, 7; hope for those living in extreme poverty through, 222–227; increasing demands for accountability of, 230; increasing stakes for, 231–233; Juma Ventures example of a, 2–5, 7; mitigating risk of, 19–20; questions on size and scale of, 38–39; stakeholders looking for substance over form, 228–230; this book's agenda to promote, 17–18; "Triple Bottom Line" of, 5, 226; WorkSquare, LLC example of a, 6–7, 15. *See also* Social enterprises

Mission Markets, 160

Mission Measurement, 186

Mission statement, 26

Missouri's "limited applicability" constituency statute, 42

MIT Sloan Management Review, 9

Mithapur (Gnjarat, India), 9

MIX Market reporting platform, 221

Mondragón Cooperative Corporation: background of historic origins of, 91–92; Caja Laboral Popular bank financing the, 95–96; Don José Marís's leadership of, 95; entrepreneurial policies on capital followed by, 96; equitable wages paid by the, 96, 97; federation organization of the, 97; influence on other co-ops' success by, 99–100, 103; "patronage dividend" strategy of the, 95; "Statement on the Co-Operative Identity" adopted by the, 93–95

Mondragón (Spain), 91–92

Morgan Stanley Investing with Impact platform, 172

Mountain BizWorks, 124

"Move Your Money" project, 128

Mozambique malaria Social Impact Bond, 118

Mozilla Corporation, 10

Mtanga Farms, 150

Mullenweg, Matt, 53

Murphy, Eileen, 133–135

Mycoskie, Blake, 11

N

Nababa, Mamman, 202

NASA (National Aeronautics and Space Administration), 16

NASDAQ, 157, 159, 160

Nasir, Sheikh Nasir Muhammed, 202

National Center for Charitable Statistics, 87, 143

National Center for Children in Poverty, 1

National Impact Initiative (U.S.), 169

National Philanthropic Trust, 126

National Task Force for Polio Eradication, 203

Neighborhood Housing Services (Chicago, Inc. Housing Action Illinois), 64–66

New Jersey's "broad applicability;" constituency statutes, 42–43

New Markets Tax Credit (2000), 129–130

New York: on benefit corporation's third-party standard, 47; Center for Employment work in, 117; New York City's Social Impact Bond, 115–116; Pay for Success programs in, 117–118

New York City: Center for Employment work in, 117; Rikers Island Social Impact Bond in, 115–116

The New York Times, 96, 121, 136

Newmark, Craig, 43, 44

Newmark, eBay v. (Delaware), 43–46

Nigeria: polio victims (2013) in, 199; shared-outcomes network to eradicate polio in, 199–204

Nike, 84

Nobel Peace Prize, 68

Nonprofit corporations: customer-focused ventures by, 226–227; description of, 32t–33t; Juma Ventures as a model of entrepreneurial, 2–5; taxonomy of qualitative outcomes for, 214–215

Nonprofit Finance Fund, 129, 130, 144

Nonprofit Overhead Cost Project, 144

Norris, William C., 8

North American Securities Administrators Association, 168

North Dakota Bankers Association, 122

Northwestern University, 14, 133

Northwestern University's Safe Haven study (1999), 193–194

Nusserwanji, Jamsetji, 9, 10

Nyabenda, Goretti, 67, 70

NYC Center for Economic Opportunity (CEO), 16–17

NYSE, 159

O

Obama Administration: economic stimulus plan (2009) of the, 130; National Impact Initiative of the, 169; Pay-for-Success model introduced by the, 112; pledge to mission-driven ventures by the, 227–228; Startup America Initiative of the, 168; White House Office of Social Innovation and Civic Participation of the, 15. _See also_ Government; United States

Obama, Barack, 112, 168

Obama for America campaign (2012), 52

Ohio: Ohio Cooperative Solar (OCS) [Evergreen Cooperatives],

102–103; Pay for Success programs in, 117–118

Omidyar Network, 139, 165, 176

Omidyar, Pierre, 139, 148

OMNI Youth Services, 118

One Hope United, 118

Onwurah, Chi, 224

Open Books, 53

Open Table, 133

Organic cotton industry, 51

Organization for Economic Co-Operation and Development (OECD), 220

Ormiston Families, 110

Ormiston Trust, 107

Osborne Association, 116

Outcome indicators, 27–28

Outcome Indicators Project, 214–215, 218

Output indicators, 27–28

Owers, Anne, 106

Oxford University, 14

P

Pacific Gas & Electric, 128

Pages, Phillipe, 81

Pakistan: challenges during the

campaign to eradicate polio in, 201–204; murder of nine polio workers (2013) in, 201; Taliban factions attacking vaccinators in, 202

Partnerships, 29

Patagonia, Inc.: becoming California's first benefit corporation (2012), 50; "clean climbing" and alpinism heart of the, 50–51; "Common Threads Initiative" of, 51; Yvon Chouinard's values-centered leadership of, 50–52

Patrick, Deval L., 113

Pay for Success Investment Fund, 112

Pay-for-Success model: description of, 17; increasing use and examples of the, 117–118; Massachusetts Juvenile Justice Pay for Success initiative, 113–115; Obama Administration's introduction of, 112

Pension funds: ERISA permitting venture capital investing by, 166; TIAA-CREF, 147, 155

Pepperdine University, 14

Pershing Square Foundation, 117

Personnel questions, 34

PEST analysis, 35

Peterborough (England), 105–106. See also Her Majesty's Prison Peterborough (England)

Picciotto, Robert, 198

Pierce, Denis, 65

Pierce Family Charitable Foundation, 65

"Poison pill" plan (Delaware's eBay v. Newmark), 43–46

Polio eradication campaign case study, 199–204

Polman, Paul, 40

Porter, Michael E.: "The Five Competitive Forces that Shape Strategy" by, 24–25; "shared value" notion popularized by, 13

Positioning, 24

Poverty: Gallup report on global, 222; Grameen America's microloans to women living in, 85; how mission-driven ventures are providing hope for those living in, 222–227; microcredit programs for breaking the cycle of, 67–68, 72–78; rates of U.S., 1; widespread state of global, 13; World Bank's definition of "extreme," 222

Prahalad, C. K., 6

Presidential Medal of Freedom, 68

President's Domestic Policy Council, 15

Principles for Responsible Initiative, 170–171

PRIs (program-related investments): description and function of, 55; examples of successful, 58–59; first reporting and assessment process (2007) of,

PRIs (program-related investments) (*continued*) 171; history of foundations engaged in, 136–137; IRS examples on sanctioned, 58; IRS' "expenditure responsibility" requirement of, 56–58; L3C used as vehicle for, 60–62; three definitional tests of, 55–56. *See also* Impact investing

Prison recidivism interventions: New York City's Center for Employment opportunities for, 117; New York City's Rikers Island program for youth offenders, 115–116; Peterborough Prison pilot recidivism program, 106–107; Peterborough Prisoners' high re-offending rates, 105–106; Social Impact Bond used to fund, 107–112; "Transforming Rehabilitation"

strategy pursued for, 110
Pritzker, J. B., 132
Pritzker, Penny, 132–133
Private foundations: Bill & Melina Gates Foundation, 59, 134, 151–152, 171, 175, 198, 200, 204; California HealthCare Foundation (CHCF), 124; Calvert Community Investment Note, 127, 137; Calvert Foundation, 127, 139, 150; Case Foundation, 227; Citi Foundation, 78; Cleveland Foundation, 101, 104; Ford Foundation, 137; Hitachi Foundation, 6; Hope Foundation, 161, 173; IRS reporting on assets held by U.S., 143; L3C used as vehicle for PRIs of, 60–62; Omidyar Network, 139, 165, 176; Pershing Square Foundation, 117; Pierce Family Charitable

Foundation, 65; PRIs (program-related investments) made by, 55–59, 136–137, 171; required by U.S. law to distribute annual charity, 55; Rockefeller Foundation, 107, 140, 141, 158, 174, 187, 198–199, 215, 216; A Safe Haven Foundation, 178, 179–182*fig*, 184, 192; shared-outcomes networks formed by, 194, 198–208; as source of community capital, 126–127; Tony Elumelu Foundation, 165; William and Flora Hewlett Foundation, 158; W.K. Kellogg Foundation, 59, 127, 136
ProCredit, 155
Procter & Gamble's Pampers brand, 226
(PRODUCT)[RED], 84
Profits: Delaware's *eBay v. Newmark* case on community service culture

versus, 43–46; doctrine of shareholder primacy on financial returns of, 40, 43–46, 48; global movement toward social good combined with, 13–17; questions to ask about, 34; reframed as an outcome and not a purpose, 9; social good versus corporate good or, 12–13; stakeholder constituency statutes impacting decisions on, 41–43; steps for maximizing prospects of social impact and, 22–26; three ways in which an initial investment results in, 159. *See also* Financial issues; Social impact

Property questions, 34

Public Good Software, Inc., 52–53

Public policy. *See* Impact investing public policy

PULSE, 219

R

Rafiq Autovan Manufacturing Industries Limited, 88

Ramirez, Cruz, 3

RAPt's drug treatment program (UK), 106

"Rate the Raters" report (Sustainability), 48

Ratner, Dan, 52, 53

Raytheon's MathMovesU initiative, 11

RBS Social Enterprise 100 Index, 172

Real Food Challenge, 102

Reality check: conducted by the prospective mission-driven entrepreneur, 22–23; questions to be answered as part of the, 23

REDF (Roberts Enterprise Development Fund), 186–188

Revolution Foods, 135

Riboud, Frank, 79

Richley, Bonnie, 100

Riegle Community Development and Regulatory Improvement Act (U.S.), 123

Rikers Island Social Impact Bond (New York), 115–116

Risk management: Bank of America Merrill Lynch and Bridges Ventures LLP report (2014) on, 153–154; comparing Acumen's and BlueOrchard's approach to, 154–155; impact investment, 152–156; mitigating mission-driven venture, 19–20; pairing impact first investors with financial first investors for, 154–155

Roadmap for Impact (Root Capital), 183–184

Roberts Enterprise Development Fund (REDF), 186–188

Roberts, George R., 187

Roca, Inc., 114–115

Rochdale Society of Equitable Pioneers (England, 1844), 92–93

Rochdale Society Principles, 93

Rockefeller Foundation: B Lab funding by, 158; financial advisors survey (2012) sponsored by

Rockefeller Foundation (*continued*) Deutsche Bank and, 174; GIIN (Global Impact Investing Network) role of, 140, 141, 216; as impact investing pioneer, 187; shared-outcomes networks of, 198–199; UK Peterborough Prison pilot funding from, 107; universal taxonomy of social impact metrics supported by, 215–216

Rockefeller Impact Investing Collaborative, 215

Rodin, Judith, 198–199

Rodríquez Arregui, Álvaro, 149–150, 152, 156

Roosevelt, Franklin D., 137

Root Capital: description and clients of, 183–184; GPS-like approach of Social and Environmental Scorecard of, 189–190, 190, 211–212, 217; growth of, 139;

IRIS output metrics used by, 217–218; Mexican vanilla farmer cooperative leading to the creation of, 210–212; social metrics explored by, 184, 187, 211–212

Root Cause, 163–164, 186

Rotary International, 200

Rowland, Brian, 181, 192–193, 194

Rowland, Neli Vazquez, 181, 192–193, 194

RSF Social Finance, 124–125

Rubinger, Michael, 125

Rwanda, 150

S

S&P 500 Index, 8, 161

"Sacrifice zones" tragedy of cities, 1

A Safe Haven Foundation (Chicago): Charmaine Bowman's success at, 178, 181, 182, 191, 193; establishment of the, 181; examining how to measure social impact of,

179–180, 184, 194; impact value chain to measure success of, 181–182*fig*; Northwestern University's study (1999) on, 193–194; origins and development of, 192–193; recidivism rate of, 181–182; recognized as a "Champion of Change," 192

Salesforce, 219

San Francisco Business Times Bay Area's most admired non-profit chief executive, 2

Sarkar, Christian, 9

SAT exam, 3

Scholarship Management Program (Grameen Shikkha), 89

Schwartz, David, 101–102

SCOP (Société coopérative et participative) [France], 99

SEA (Social Enterprise Alliance): description and global membership of, 13; Social Enterprise Coalition sister organization of the, 17; Social Enterprise World Forum by the, 14

SeaMonkey web browser, 10

SEC (Securities & Exchange Commission), 166–167, 168

Second Chance Act (U.S.), 112

Segmentation of customers, 23–24

"Sensitivity analyses," 26

September 11 attacks, 177

SGA Youth & Family Services, 118

Shaffer, Don, 124–125

Shared-outcomes networks: campaign to eradicate polio cases study on, 199–204; charity:water case study on, 204–208; social impact metrics for creating, 194, 198–208

"Shared value" notion, 13

Shareholder primacy doctrine: benefit corporation legal protections related to, 48–49;

Delaware's *eBay v. Newmark* case (2010) on, 43–46; description and implications of, 40

Sharma, Aarti, 9

Shokti Doi ("Yogurt for Power") [Grameen Danone], 79–81

Shriver, Bobby, 84

Sinek, Simon, 208

Sisodia, Raj, 8

Sittercity, 52

Size and scale, 38–39

Skoll Centre for Social Entrepreneurship (Oxford University), 14

Skoll Foundation, 164

Small and growing business (SGBs), 211

Small Business Investment Company (SBIC) Impact Fund, 228

Smith, Adam, 12

Snapdragon, 52

SOCAP (Social Capital Markets) conference, 163, 164, 165, 171

Social and Environmental Scorecard (Root Capital), 189–190, 211–212, 217

Social Benefit Bonds (Australia), 17

Social business movement: continued growth of the, 78; Grameen Bank's commitment to, 74–75

Social capital, 230–231. *See also* Capital

Social change: Bosch Group's work for, 10; collaboration as key to successful, 233; crediting the causes of positive, 182–186; examples of how businesses drive, 9–13; Millennials embracing power of capital to drive, 177; Mozilla Corporation's work for, 10; planning the strategies for achieving, 26; Raytheon's work for, 11; TATA Group's work for, 9–10; TOMS Shoes' work for, 11, 12; tracking input, output, and outcome indicators of, 27–28; Verdigris Group's work for, 11; version of

Social change
(*continued*)
counterfactual
element of
measuring, 184.
See also Social
impact
Social co-operatives
(Italy), 97–98
Social Enterprise
Coalition, 17
Social Enterprise
Ecosystem and
Economic
Development
Commission, 16
Social Enterprise
World Forum, 14
Social enterprises:
benefit
corporations, 16,
29, 32*t*–33*t*;
collaboration as
key to successful,
233; competing
with for-profit
commercial
businesses,
228–230; as
for-profit
mission-driven
ventures, 29;
increasing stakes
for, 231–233; L3Cs
(low-profit,
limited liability
companies), 16,
29–30, 32*t*–33*t*,
59–66; limited
liability company
(LLC), 29, 32*t*–33*t*;

sustainable
business
corporation, 29,
32*t*–33*t*;
tax-exempt
nonprofit
corporation,
32*t*–33*t*, 214–215,
226–227;
traditional
corporations,
32*t*–33*t*. *See also*
Mission-driven
ventures
Social entrepreneurs.
See Mission-driven
entrepreneurs
Social Entrepreneurs
Fund (Bridges
Ventures), 155
Social Finance, Inc.
(U.S.), 118
Social Finance, Ltd.
(UK), 110
Social good:
capitalism
reinvented as a
force for, 15–17;
corporate good
versus, 12–13;
Counseling Data
L3C case study in
collective, 64–66;
Grameen
Danone's
contributions to
Bangladesh,
79–81; how
creditable social
metrics can create
more, 214–215

Social impact: B Corp
certification of, 6,
15, 53–54, 158, 160;
challenges in
measuring social
mission and,
178–191; definition
of, 180; Delaware's
eBay v. Newmark
case on profits
versus culture of,
43–46; global
movement toward
combining profit
with, 13–17;
planning the
strategies for
achieving, 26;
quantifying
impact investing,
157–159; steps for
maximizing
prospects of
financial success
and, 22–26;
tracking input,
output, and
outcome
indicators of,
27–28. *See also*
Impact investing;
Profits; Social
change
Social Impact Bonds:
alternatives used
by funders,
119–120; assessing
feasibility of,
118–119;
description of, 17;
empowering the

social sector through use of, 120; Her Majesty's Prison Peterborough turnaround using, 105–112; Massachusetts Juvenile Justice Pay for Success initiative using, 113–115; New York City's Rikers Island, 115–116

Social impact metrics: BUILD case study on scaling success using, 194–198; The Cara Program's approach to, 188–189; challenges related to, 178–179; creating shared-outcomes networks function of, 194, 198–208; crediting the causes of positive social change component of, 182–186; external accountability function of, 194, 208–209; G8 Summit (2013) discussion on importance of, 220–221; of GADC loans to displaced

Ugandan farmers, 182–184; how changes in mission-driven ventures impact, 185; impact satellites used for, 189; impact value chain used as, 180–181*fig*; imperative of precise, 185–186; increasing demands for more sophisticated, 228; Root Cause's strategy for, 186; A Safe Haven Foundation's approach to, 178, 179–182*fig*, 184, 194; type, scale, and depth of, 189–190; version of counterfactual element of, 184

Social impact metrics frameworks: B Analytics, 219; BACO (Best Alternative Charitable Option), 190–191; *Code of Good Impact Practice* (2013) [UK], 220; consequences of a disjointed, 212–213; ETO (Efforts to Outcomes) for

tracking, 196–197; *Funder Principles* (2013) [UK], 220; G8 Summit (2013) discussion on pursuing universal, 220–221; GIIRS (Global Impact Investing Rating System), 141–142, 159, 216, 218; *Guidelines on Measuring Subjective Well-Being* (2013), 220; how more social good is facilitated through creditable, 214–215; impact investing industry push for universal, 215–216; Inspiring Impact study (2012) on problem of inadequate, 213; IRIS (Impact reporting and Investing Standards), 141, 216–218, 221; lack of gold standard, 186; Mission Measurement's strategy for, 186; Outcome Indicators Project online tool, 214–215, 218; Root Capital's Social

Social impact metrics frameworks (*continued*) and Environmental Scorecard used for, 189–190, 211–212, 217; social return on investment (SROI), 27, 187–189; *Universal Standards for Social Performance Management* (2010), 219–220, 221

Social Innovation Fund (SIF), 15–16, 164

Social Investment Bond, 118

Social Performance Task Force (SPTF), 221

Social Purpose Corporation, 29

Social return on investment (SROI) framework: The Cara Program application of the, 188–189; Roberts Enterprise Development Fund (REDF) development of the, 187–188; tracking input, output, and outcome

indicators using the, 27

Social Stock Exchange (SSE): expansion of the, 160–161; Mission Markets as the first step toward, 160

Social Value Act (2012) [UK], 169, 170

Social Venture Connexion (SVX), 160

Social venture franchising, 86–87

SOCODEN (Société coopérative de dévelopement et d'entraide) [France], 99

Sole proprietorships, 29

Sorenson, James Lee, 117

South Carolina's Pay for Success programs, 117–118

South Shore Community Bank (Chicago), 123–124, 130–131

Specialized social enterprises, 30

Spectrum Group, 177

Spencer, Marc, 2, 5, 6

Spotify, 208

Springer, Jonathan D., 45–46

St. Giles Trust (UK), 106, 107, 110

Stakeholders: B Lab's approach to ensuring accountability to, 53–54; "business judgment rule" on consideration of interests of all, 40; constituency statutes on interests of non-shareholder and shareholder, 41–43; doctrine of shareholder primacy that impacts, 40, 43–46, 48; L3C capability to engage diverse, 61–62; looking for substance over form, 228–230; need for change in corporate law to promote interests of, 45–46

Standard & Poor's 500, 8, 161

Stanford Center on Philanthropy and Civil society, 158

Stanford Social Innovation Review, 66, 150, 152, 158, 164, 165, 176

Stanford University, 14

Starbucks, 84

Startup America Initiative, 168

"Statement on the Co-Operative Identity," 93–95
STEM education (Raytheon's MathMovesU initiative), 11
Straw, Jack, 107
Stuttgart Technical University, 10
Sub-Saharan Africa: Gallup report on extreme poverty in, 222; Nigeria, 199–204; reasons for hope by those living in poverty in, 222–223; Uganda, 118, 150, 182–184, 206–207. *See also* Africa Health Fund (Aureos Capital)
Summers, Larry, 117
Suppliers: power of, 25; questions to ask about, 35
Susan G. Komen for the Cure, 84
The Sustainability Exchange, 63–64, 66
Sustainability issues: B Lab's social and environmental accountability standards, 15, 53–54; business community's commitment to, 225–227; Mayor Richard M. Daley's contributions to, 62–64; Patagonia, Inc. commitment to, 50–52; Principles for Responsible Initiative on supporting, 170–171; Sustainability's "Rate the Raters" report on, 48
Sustainability's "Rate the Raters" report, 48
Sustainable Business Corporations, 29, 32*t*–33*t*
SWOT analysis, 35

T

Tanzanian agriculture investment (2011), 150
Task Force on Social Innovation, Entrepreneurship, and Enterprise (Illinois), 16
Tata Chemicals, 9
TATA Group, 9–10
Tata, Ratan, 9
Tata Salt, 9
Tata Sons Ltd., 9
Tax-exempt nonprofit corporations: customer-focused ventures by, 226–227; description of, 32*t*–33*t*; Juma Ventures as a model of entrepreneurial, 2–5; taxonomy of qualitative outcomes for, 214–215
Teen pregnancy intervention, 118
Templeton, Chuck, 133
Temporary Assistance for Needy Families, 189
Tesla, 135
Theory of change, 27
Think Orbitz, 52
ThinkCERCA, 134–135
Thinking Like a Freak (Levitt and Dubner), 223
Third-party standard, 47–48
Thomas, Andrea, 226
Thorpe, Devin, 167
Threat of substitutes, 25
TIAA-CREF, 147, 155
TOMS Shoes, 11, 12, 162
Tony Elumelu Foundation, 165
"Too Big to Fail" banks, 128
Tracking indicators, 27–28

Traditional corporation, 32*t*–33*t*
Trillium Asset Management, 159
"Triple Bottom Line," 5, 226
Twitter, 167

U
UBS, 172
UCAN, 53, 118
Uganda: charity:water work building wells in, 206–207; GADC's loans to displaced farmers in Gulu district of, 182–184; impact investing in, 150; Social Impact Bond for sleeping sickness, 118
UN Food and Agriculture Organization, 13
Underwriters Laboratories (UL), 48
UNESCO, 13
UNICEF, 200, 222–223, 226
Unilever, 40
Unique, 81
United Kingdom: Big Lottery Fund of, 107; Big Society Capital of, 168–169; CDC Group of the, 138; *Code of Good Impact Practice* (2013) of,

220; Community Interest Company (CIC) of the, 30; Department for International Development of, 169; first G8 Social Impact Investing Forum (2013) held in the, 169; *Funder Principles* (2013) of, 220; Her Majesty's Prison Peterborough turnaround in the, 105–112; Inspiring Impact study (2012) on problems with social impact metrics in the, 213; Ministry of Justice of, 107, 110; Organization for Economic Co-Operation and Development (OECD), 220; Social Impact Bonds of the, 17, 106–112; Social Value Act (2012) of, 169, 170; "Transforming Rehabilitation" strategy pursued by, 110. *See also* European Union social co-operatives
United Nations, 170

United States: ongoing debate over high CEO pay in the, 96–97; rates of poverty in the, 1; SEA membership by mission-driven ventures in the, 13–14; shrinking dollars and increased need for government assistance (2025) in the, 143; transfer of wealth from Baby Boomers to Millennials in the, 142, 177. *See also* Obama Administration; *specific states*; U.S. legislation
United States Agency for International Development (USAID), 216
United Way of Miami, 6
Universal social impact metrics: B Analytics, 219; *Code of Good Impact Practice* (2013) [UK], 220; consequences of a disjointed and need for, 212–213; *Funder Principles* (2013) [UK], 220; G8 Summit (2013) discussion on,

220–221; GIIRS (Global Impact Investing Rating System), 141–142, 159, 216, 218; *Guidelines on Measuring Subjective Well-Being* (2013), 220; how more social good would be facilitated through, 214–215; impact investing industry push for, 215–216; Inspiring Impact study (2012) on problem of inadequate, 213; IRIS (Impact reporting and Investing Standards), 141, 216–218, 221; Outcome Indicators Project online tool for, 214–215, 218; *Universal Standards for Social Performance Management* (2010), 219–220, 221

University Hospitals (Cleveland), 102

University of Arizona, 63

University of California, Berkeley, 14

University of Chicago, 133, 148

University of Maryland, 101

University of Michigan, 6

University of Utah, 117

Unreasonable Institute, 164

Urban Health Plan, 129, 130

Urban Institute, 214–215, 218

Urban League, 8

Urban Partnership Bank, 130

U.S. Agency for International Development, 169, 227

U.S. Census Bureau report on poverty (2012), 1

U.S. Centers for Disease Control and Prevention, 200

U.S. Conference of Mayors (2013), 63

U.S. Department of Commerce, 16

U.S. Department of Defense (DoD), 170

U.S. Department of Education, 16

U.S. Department of Housing and Urban Development, 64, 65

U.S. Department of Justice, 64, 112

U.S. Department of Labor, 97, 112, 114, 117, 182

U.S. Environmental Protection Agency (EPA), 164

U.S. Green Building Council, 62

U.S. House of Representatives, 16

U.S. Internal Revenue Service (IRS): on assets held by U.S. foundations, 143; "expenditure responsibility" requirement of the, 56–58; 501(c)(3) nonprofit status under the, 7, 103, 139, 144

U.S. legislation: Affordable Care Act, 124; American Reinvestment and Recovery Act (2009), 130; Community Reinvestment Act (CRA), 122–123; Employee Retirement Income Security Act (ERISA), 166; JOBS Act (Jumpstart Our Business Startups Act), 166,

U.S. legislation
(*continued*)
167, 168; New
Markets Tax Credit
(2000), 129–130;
Riegle Community
Development and
Regulatory
Improvement Act,
123; Second
Chance Act, 112.
See also Impact
investing public
policy; United
States
U.S. National
Advisory Board to
the G8 Social
Impact Investment
Taskforce, 221
U.S. Overseas Private
Investment
Corporation
(OPIC), 136, 175
U.S. Small Business
Administration,
168
U.S. Treasury, 123, 130
USAID, 228
The Use of Money
(Wesley), 138
USGBC's Greenbuild
conference, 62

V
Value proposition:
positioning your
venture by
providing a, 24;
"shared value"
notion of, 13

Vanderbilt University,
68
Vanguard Group, 126
Vanilla farmer
cooperative
(Mexico), 210–211
Venture capitalists:
community capital
from, 126, 128;
description and
function of,
150–151; ERISA
permitting
pension funds to
engage as, 166;
Good Capital, 163
Veolia, 81
Verdigris Group, 11
Verdrigo, Hector, 5–6
Vision (entrepreneur),
36–38
Volvic, 80

W
Wal-Mart, Inc., 226
The Wall Street Journal,
19
Wealth of Nations
(Smith), 12
Wells Fargo, 64
Wesley, John, 137–138
White House Office of
Social Innovation
and Civic
Participation, 15,
168
William and Flora
Hewlett
Foundation, 158
Wilobo, Erin, 182–183,
184, 213, 217

Wilobo, Richard,
182–183, 184, 191,
213, 217
W.K. Kellogg
Foundation, 59,
127, 136
Wolk, Andrew,
163–164
Women: Grameen
America's
microloans to, 85;
Grameen Bank
microcredit loans
made to
Bangladesh,
67–68, 88–89
WordPress, 53
Worker-owned
co-operatives:
Evergreen
Cooperatives
(Cleveland),
100–104; French
SCOP (Société
coopérative et
participative), 99;
Italy's "social,"
97–98;
Mondragón,
91–97, 99–100;
"Statement on
the Co-Operative
Identity" on,
93–95; why
they succeed,
99–100. *See also*
Employees
Workforce Innovation
Fun (U.S.), 112
Workplace
democracy: of

Mondragón co-ops, 95–97; "Statement on the Co-Operative Identity" on, 93–94; worker-owned co-ops succeed due to, 100

WorkSquare, LLC, 6–7, 15

World Bank: "extreme poverty" definition by, 222; Green Bonds issued by the, 136; International Finance Corporation of the, 138, 155; reporting on global poverty levels, 13

World Health Organization, 200, 204

Wyoming's constituency statute, 41

Y

Yale University, 14

YMCA, 107, 110

Yoplait "Save Lids to Save Lives" campaign, 83–84

Young, Whitney, 8

Youth Outresearch Services, 118

Yunus, Muhammad: on benefits of "social business," 74–75; celebrity endorsement of Danone by, 81; early life, education, and career of, 68; global recognition of his work, 68; Grameen Danone founded by Frank Riboud and, 79–81, 176; his journey in founding microcredit program, 67–73; his realization about the failure of the banking system, 71–72; his visit to Jobra, 70–71; on the value of social business, 74–75; Yunus Social Business Global Initiatives of, 90. *See also* Grameen Bank (Bangladesh)

Yunus Social Business Global Initiatives, 90

Z

ZipCar, 135